MIND BEYOND DEATH

MIND BEYOND DEATH

by Dzogchen Ponlop

SNOW LION PUBLICATIONS
ITHACA, NEW YORK

Snow Lion Publications
P.O. Box 6483
Ithaca, NY 14851 USA
(607) 273-8519
www.snowlionpub.com

ISBN-10: 1-55939-301-7
ISBN-13: 978-1-55939-301-0

Designed and typeset by Gopa & Ted2, Inc.

The Library of Congress catalogued the previous edition
of this book as follows:

Dzogchen Ponlop, Rinpoche, 1965-
  Mind beyond death / by Dzogchen Ponlop.
    p. cm.
  Includes bibliographical references and index.
  ISBN-13: 978-1-55939-276-1 (alk. paper)
  ISBN-10: 1-55939-276-2 (alk. paper)
    1. Intermediate state—Buddhism. 2. Death—Religious aspects—
Buddhism. 3. Spiritual life—Buddhism. 4. Buddhism—China—
Tibet—Doctrines. I. Title.
BQ4490.D96 2007
294.3'423—dc22   200603968

Printed in Canada

This book is dedicated to my beloved father,
the late Dhamchoe Yongdu,
and my kind mother, Lekshey Drolma,
for giving birth to endless precious opportunities
to develop wisdom and compassion.

Table of Contents

List of Illustrations

Foreword

KHENPO TSÜLTRIM GYAMTSO RINPOCHE

༄༅། །འར་མེད་པས་བར་དོ་མེད་པའི་ཆོགས་བཅད། །

THERE IS NOTHING IN BETWEEN, SO THE BARDO DOES NOT EXIST—A VERSE

སྐྱེ་དང་འཆི་བ་ངོ་བོ་མེད་པའི་ཕྱིར། །
དེ་གཉིས་བར་ཡང་སྐྱེ་མེད་སྤྲོས་བྲལ་ཙམ། །
བདག་དང་གཞན་ལ་ངོ་བོ་མེད་པའི་ཕྱིར། །
དེ་གཉིས་བར་ཡང་སྐྱེ་མེད་སྤྲོས་བྲལ་ཙམ། །

Birth and death have no essence,
So in between those two is merely the unborn, free from fabrication.
Self and other have no essence,
So in between those two is merely the unborn, free from fabrication.

ཞེས་མཁན་པོ་ཚུལ་ཁྲིམས་རྒྱ་མཚོ་རིན་པོ་ཆེས་འབྲུག་ཀརྨ་སྒྲུབ་སྡེ་དགོན་པར་ཐོལ་བྱུང་དུ་
སྨྲས་སོ། །

Spoken extemporaneously by Khenpo Tsültrim Gyamtso Rinpoche,
Karma Drubdey Gonpa, Bhutan, October 9, 2006.

Translated by Ari Goldfield.

སློན་འགྲོའི་ལུ་ཚིག

ཚེ་འདིར་དབང་ཁྲིད་གདམས་པས་རྗེས་འཛིན་ཞིང་།།
ཕྱི་མར་ཐར་པའི་ལམ་དུ་འཁྲིད་མཛད་པ།།
བར་དོར་འཇིགས་པའི་འཕྱང་ལས་སྐྱོབ་པ་པོ།།
མཚུངས་མེད་བླ་མ་མཆོག་གིས་བྱིན་གྱིས་རློབས།།

དེ་ལ་འདིར་སྐྱུར་འཇིག་རྟེན་ཁལ་པ་མང་པོ་ཞིག་གིས་བར་དོ་ཞེས་པ་
ནི། འཇིག་རྟེན་ཚེ་འདིའི་སྐྱང་བ་འགགས་པའི་རྗེས་སུ། ཞག་བདུན་བདུན་བཞི་བཅུ་ཞེ་
དགུའི་རིང་ལ་འཇིགས་ཤིང་ཡང་ངའི་སྐྱང་བ་སྤྲ་ཚོགས་པ་ཞིག་འཆར་རྒྱུ་ཡོད་པ་ཞིག་ལ་
ངོས་འཛིན། མོ་ཕྱོགས་སུ། བོད་ཡིག་ཏུ། ཚེས་མཛིན་པ་མཛོད་ཀྱི་འཇིག་རྟེན་བསྟན་
པའི་སྐབས་སུ་རང་གཞུང་ལས་བར་དོ་ཞེས་པའི་ཚིག་ཉིད་དངོས་སུ་མེད་མོད། རྒྱ་
བར། འདིར་གང་འཆེ་དང་སྐྱེ་བ་ཡི། སྲིད་པའི་བར་དུ་འབྱུང་བའོ། །ཞེས་འཆེ་བའི་སྲིད་
པ་དང་། སྐྱེ་བའི་སྲིད་པ་དང་། བར་མའི་སྲིད་པ་སྟེ་སྲིད་པ་གསུམ་གྱི་ཐ་སྙད་མཛད། དེ་
དག་ལས་བར་གྱི་སྲིད་པའི་ཡིད་ལུས་ཀྱི་རྣམ་པ་དང་། ཁྱད་ཆོས། ཚེ་ཚད་སོགས་ཀྱི་རྣམ་
བཞག་ཀུང་མཛོན་ཚམ་མཆེས། རྒྱ་ཡིག་ཏུ། བྱེ་བྲག་བཤད་མཛོད་ཆེན་མོར་བར་དོའི་སྐོར་
སྤྱི་དང་། བྱེ་བྲག་དགོང་ཞག་ཞེ་དགུའི་སྐོར་གྱི་རབ་བྱེད་ཅིག་ཀུང་ཡོད་པར

གྲགས། སྤྲགས་ཕྱོགས་སུ། བར་དོ་སྟོར་གྱི་ཁྲིད་ཡིག་དང་དོ་སྟོང་རྒྱས་འབྲིང་བསྡུས་
གསུམ་སྟ་ཚོགས་པ་ཞིག་ས་དགེ་བཀའ་རྙིང་གི་གསུང་རབ་རྣམས་སུ་བཞུགས། དེ་དག་ཏུ་
བར་དོ་སོ་སོའི་མིང་གི་འདོགས་ཚུལ་དང་། དབྱེ་བསྡུའི་རྣམ་བཞག་འདུ་ལ་ཁྱད་ཚོས་མང་
བ་ཞིག་སྣང་། གྲུབ་ཐོབ་ཀརྨ་གླིང་པའི་ཟབ་ཚོས་ཞི་ཁྲོ་དགོངས་པ་རང་གྲོལ་ལས་བར་དོ་
ཐོས་གྲོལ་ཆེན་མོའི་གཞུང་དུ། སྲི་གནས་བར་དོ་དང་། རྨི་ལམ་བར་དོ། བསམ་གཏན་
བར་དོ། འཆི་ཁ་བར་དོ། ཆོས་ཉིད་བར་དོ། སྲིད་པ་བར་དོ་སྟེ། བར་དོ་དྲུག་གི་གདམས་
ཁྲིད་ཟབ་ཅིང་རྒྱས་པ་ཞིག་དང་། ཆེ་ལེ་སྣ་ཚོགས་རང་གྲོལ་གྱིས་བར་དོ་སྟྲི་དོན་དུ་གསར་
རྙིང་ཕྱིན་མོང་ཡུགས་སུ། རང་བཞིན་སྐྱེ་གནས་ཀྱི་བར་དོ་དང་། འཆི་ཁ་སྐྲག་བསྲལ་གྱི་
བར་དོ་དང་། ཆོས་ཉིད་འོད་གསལ་གྱི་བར་དོ་དང་། སྲིད་པ་ལས་ཀྱི་བར་དོ་སྟེ་བཞི་རུ་
བསྡུས་ཏེ། གོ་བདེ་ལ་གནད་ཡིག་པར་གསུངས།

    བར་དོ་ཐོས་གྲོལ་ཆེན་མོའི་གཞུང་ནི། རྒྱུ་ཡིག་ཏུ་བསྒྱུར་ཡོད་པ་མ་ཟད། དབྱིན་ཡིག་
ཐོག་འགྱུར་སྟུ་ཕྱི་མི་འདུ་བ་ལྟ་དང་། ཐྲ་རན་སིའི་སྐད་ཡིག་ཏུ་ཡང་བསྒྱུར་ཡོད་པར་གྲགས།
ཆེ་ལེ་སྣ་ཚོགས་རང་གྲོལ་གྱི་བར་དོ་སྟྲི་དོན་དེ་འང་དབྱིན་ཡིག་ཏུ་བསྒྱུར་འདུག

    དེ་དག་ཆར། ༈སྐྱབས་མཚོག་རྫོགས་ཆེན་དཔོན་སློབ་རིན་པོ་ཆེ་གང་གི་ཞལ་སྣ་
ནས། དབྱིན་ཡིག་ཐོག་ལྤགས་རྩོམ་གནང་བའི་འཆི་བ་ལས་བརྒལ་བའི་སེམས་ཞེས་བྱ་བ་
བར་དོའི་ཁྲིད་ཡིག་འདི་ནི། བདག་དང་བདག་འདྲ་བའི་སེམས་ཅན་ལས་དང་། འདིར་སྣང་
བདེན་འཛིན་གྱི་ཨ་འཐས་ཆེ་བ། ཉིན་པར་ཚོས་བཀུད་ཀྱི་ཁྱིལ་བོར་གྱུར་པ། མཚན་མོར་
གཏི་མུག་གི་རོ་ཉལ་བྲིང་པ། སྲིད་སྲུག་གཏུམ་རན་གྱིས་མི་ཚེ་གཏན་མཁན་རྣམས། འདི་
ཕྱི་བར་དོ་ཀུན་ཏུ། འཁྲུལ་མེད་རྗེས་སུ་འཛིན་ཕྱིར། ཐོག་མར་སྐྱེ་གནས་བར་དོའི་ཁྲིད་ཀྱི་
རིམ་པས་རྗེས་འདྲག་རྣམས་འདིར་སྨྲང་ལ་ཞེན་པ་བཟློག་པ་དང་། དཔལ་འབྱོར་ལ་སྲིད་པོ་

ལེན་པར་བསྐུལ། ཞི་གནས་ཀྱི་ལམ་ལ་བསླབ་ནས་རྩེ་ལམ་བར་དོའི་ཁྲིད་ཀྱི་རིམ་པས་
རྗེས་འཇུག་རྣམས་སླུ་ལུས་དང་རྩེ་ལམ་གྱི་རྒྱལ་འབྱོར་ལ་བློ་སྦྱོང་། རྩེ་ལམ་དོས་ཉེན་ཅིང་
སླལ་བསྐྱར་བྱེད་ནུས་པར་བསྐུལ། བསམ་གཏན་བར་དོའི་ཁྲིད་ཀྱི་རིམ་པས་རྗེས་འཇུག་
རྣམས་ལ་ཕུག་རྟོགས་ལུགས་ཀྱི་ལྷག་མཐོང་ལ་བརྟེན་ནས་སེམས་ཀྱི་ངོ་བོ་ཐད་ཀར་དོ་
སྒྱུད་པའི་ཐབས་རྣམས་གསལ་བར་གསུངས་ནས་སྒོམ་དུ་འཇུག་ཅིང་། འཆི་ཁ་བར་དོའི་
ཁྲིད་ཀྱི་རིམ་པས་རྗེས་འཇུག་རྣམས་ཀྱིས་འབྱུང་བའི་ཐིམ་རིམ་དང་། སྣང་མཆེད་ཐོབ་
གསུམ་གྱི་སྣང་བ་དང་། འཕོ་བའི་ཁྲིད་ཀྱིས་མཚམས་སྦྱར་ཏེ། འཆི་ཁར་གྲོལ་ཐུབ་པའམ།
ཏོ་ཤེས་ཀྱི་གདེང་ཐོབ་ཏུ་འཇུག ཆོས་ཉིད་བར་དོའི་ཁྲིད་ཀྱི་རིམ་པས་རྗེས་འཇུག་རྣམས་ལ་
སེམས་ཆོས་སྐུའི་ངོ་གསལ་དང་ལོངས་སྐུ་འོད་གསལ་གཉིས་སུ་ངོ་སྤྲད། ལོངས་སྐུ་འོད་
གསལ་དེའང་རྒྱལ་བ་ཞི་ཁྲོའི་ལྷ་ཚོགས་ཀྱི་སྐུ་འོད་ཟེར་གསུམ་གྱི་ཚུལ་ལས་ཤར་བས་
བདེན་མེད་སྒྱུ་མ་ལྟ་བུར་བློ་སྦྱོང་། སྣང་ཆུལ་དེ་དག་ཐམས་ཅད་རང་སྣང་ཡིན་པར་ཏོ་སྒྱུད་
དེ། བར་དོ་ལོངས་སྐུར་གྲོལ་བའམ། བར་དོའི་འཇིགས་པའི་འཕྱུང་ལས་སྒྲོལ་བའི་དཔའ་
བོའི་སྐྱེ་ལམ་ལྷ་བུའི་གདམས་ཁྲིད་གནང་བོ། །ཁྲིད་པ་བར་དོའི་ཁྲིད་ཀྱི་རིམ་པས་རྗེས་
འཇུག་རྣམས་ལ་སྐྱར་འཆི་ཁའི་བར་དོར་རང་ངོ་མ་ཤེས་པས། སྐྱར་སྲང་གསུམ་ལུག་སྤྱོག་
ཏུ་འཁར། ཆོས་ཉིད་ཀྱི་རྒྱལ་ལས་ཁར་བའི་སྐྱུ་འོད་ཟེར་གསུམ་རང་ངོ་མ་ཤེས་པར། སྒྱ་
ཡིས་འཇིགས། ཟེར་གྱིས་དངངས། སྐུ་ཡི་སྲང་བས་སྐྲག་པ་ལ་བརྟེན་ནས་བར་དོའི་
འཁྲུལ་སྲང་སྣ་ཚོགས་སུ་འཁར་བ་ན། དེ་དག་གི་སྲང་ཆུལ་རྣམས་རེ་རེ་བཞིན་རང་སྲང་
ཡིན་པར་ཏོ་སྒྱུད། རབ་རང་བཞིན་སྤྲུལ་སྐུའི་ཞིང་ཁམས་རྣམས་དང་། འབྲིང་དག་པ་
མཁའ་སྤྱོད་ཀྱི་གནས་དང་། ཐ་མ་འཇིག་རྟེན་གྱི་ལུས་རྟེན་བཟང་པོ་ལེན་ནུས་པ་བསྐྱེད་
རྟོགས་ཀྱི་གནད་ལ་འརེས་ཤེས་སྐྱེད་དུ་འཇུག་པ་སོགས་ཀྱིས་ཚེ་འདིར་དག་པའི་ཆོས་ཀྱི་

འབྱོར་བས་མཛེན་པར་ཕྱུག་ཅིང་། ཕྱི་མར་དགེ་བའི་ལམ་རྒྱགས་ཡོངས་སུ་ཕོངས་པ་མེད་
པར་འབྱིར་རྒྱུ་ཡོད་པར་གནས་བའི་ཐབས་རབ་མོ་ཁྱད་པ་ཅན་ཐམས་ཅད་བཀའ་དྲིན་དུ་
སྤྱལ་གནང་མཛད་ཡོད་དོ།།

དེ་ལྟ་བུའི་བར་དོའི་ཁྲིད་ཡིག་འདི་ཉིད་ཀྱི་ཆེ་བའི་ཡོན་ཏན་ནི། བློ་གྲོས་ཀྱི་མིག་སྟོང་
བ་རྣམས་ལ་ལམ་སྟ་ཁྲིད་མཁན་གྱི་དམིག་ཐུ་ལྟ་བུ་དང་། ལམ་གོལ་དུ་འཁྱུན་པའི་སྐྱེ་བོ་
རྣམས་ལ་ལམ་དངོས་སྟོན་མཁན་གྱི་ས་མཁན་ལྟ་བུ། དད་ལྡན་གྱི་འཕོར་སྤྱོབ་སློས་བཅས་
རྣམས་ལ་བར་དོའི་འཇིགས་པ་ལས་སྐྱོལ་བའི་དེད་དཔོན་ལྟ་བུ། འཁད་ཉུན་སློམ་སྐྱབ་ཀྱི་
བྱ་བ་ལྱུར་ལེན་བྱེད་པའི་གང་ཟག་རྣམས་ལ་ཤེས་བྱའི་སློ་བརྒྱ་འབྱེད་པའི་རིན་ཆེན་མཛོད་
ལྡེ་ལྟ་བུ། ཐོས་ལྡན་གྱི་སྐྱེ་བོ་རྣམས་ལ་ཤེས་རབ་ཀྱི་ཀུ་མུད་རྒྱས་པར་བྱེད་པའི་ཟླ་བའི་
དཀྱིལ་འཁོར་ལྟ་བུ། སྐྱབ་ལ་གཅིག་ཏུ་གཟིགས་བའི་རྣལ་འབྱོར་བ་རྣམས་ལ་བར་དོ་རང་དོ་
འཕྲོད། སྐྱ་གསུམ་ལམ་དུ་བྱེད། རང་སྣང་དོད་གསལ་གྱི་སྣང་བ་འཆར་བར་བྱེད་པའི་ཉི་
མའི་དཀྱིལ་འཁོར་ལྟ་བུ། མོ་རྒྱུད་ཀུན་གྱི་དགོངས་པའི་བཅུད་ཕྱུང་བ། ལག་ལེན་ཀུན་
གྱི་སྙིང་པོའི་དོན་འདུལ་བ། གདམས་ངག་ཀུན་གྱི་མན་ངག་ཆ་ཆོང་བ། ཕ་ཆ་སྒྲུབ་ཀུན་གྱི་
ཞལ་རྒྱུན་རི་ལྟ་བུ། མཁས་འཇམས་རྒྱས་སྤྱོས་ཀྱི་དགག་སྒྲུབ་མ་གནང་། གཉེན་ཟེར་རྗེས་
བློས་ཀྱི་ལད་མོ་མ་མཛད་པར། ཨྰ་སྒྱུབས་མཆོག་རང་ཉིད་ཀྱི་དགོངས་ཉམས་རྗེ་བཞིན་པར་
སྟོན་པའི་གདམས་ཁྲིད་དོ་མཆར་སྤྲུ་དུ་བྱུང་བ་ཞིག་ལགས་སོ།།

དེ་ལྟ་བུའི་བཀའ་རྫོམ་ཤིན་ཏུ་ཁྱད་པར་འཕགས་པ་འདི་ཉིད། སྐྱེ་འགྲོ་མང་པོའི་
འདྲེན་བྱེད་ཀྱི་ཡུལ་དུ་སྐྱེལ་བའི་སློ་ནས་མཐོང་ཐོས་དྲན་རེག་གི་འབྲེལ་བས་འཕུལ་ཡུན་
ཕན་བདེའི་དཔལ་ལ་འགོད་པར་དམིགས་ཏེ་པར་དུ་བསྐྲུན་པའི་ཐན་ཡོན་ནི། ས་གཞི་ཆེན་
པོའི་རྡུལ་གྲངས་ཀྱིས་མི་ལང་ཞིང་། རྒྱ་མཚོ་ཆེན་པོའི་རྒྱུ་ཕྱལ་གྱིས་འཇལ་མི་ནུས་པ་ལྟར་

ཆད་གཙང་དུ་མེད་པ་ལྟ་ཅི། དཔ་ལྟ་རང་རེ་རྣམས་ཀྱི་མིག་གི་བདུད་རྩིར་ལོངས་སུ་སྤྱོད་དུ་

ཡོད་པ་འདི་ཡང་ཆེ་གད་དུས་བཅུའི་ཟ་མ་ལན་གཅིག་ལྟ་བུ། སྤྲིན་བསགས་བསོད་ནམས་

མང་པོས་བསྐྲུན་པའི་སྐལ་བཟང་གི་དགའ་སྟོན་ཞམས་སུ་སྤྱོང་བ་ཡིན་པ་གོར་མ་ཆག

དེ་ལྟ་བུའི་བར་དོའི་ཁྲིད་ཡིག་འདི་ནི། བཀའ་མདོ་རྒྱུད་ཐམས་ཅད་ཀྱི་སྙིང་པོ་

གཅིག་ཏུ་དྲིལ་བ། སྒྲུབ་བརྒྱུད་ཤིང་རྟ་ཆེ་བརྒྱུད་ཀྱི་གདམས་ཟབ་ཡོངས་སུ་ཆུང་བ། རྒྱ་

བོད་མཁས་གྲུབ་ཀུན་གྱི་དགོངས་དོན་རྟེན་པར་བཀྲོལ་བས། ཆོས་ཐམས་ཅད་འདིར་སྟོན་

འདིས་སྟོན་འདི་ཕྱིར་སྟོན་པའི་ལུག་གི་སྲི་ཞིག་ཡིན་པར་སེམས་ཏེ། དེའང་། ཆེ་ལེ་སྲ་

ཆོགས་རང་གྲོལ་གྱི་བར་དོའི་སྲི་དོན་ལས། བརྒྱུད་འབྲི་བཞི་སྟོང་གི་ཆོས་ཐམས་ཅད་རྟོགས་

པས་རྟོགས་པ་ཆེན་པོ། ཐམས་ཅད་སྐྱ་གསུམ་ལས་འདའ་བ་མེད་པས་ཕྱག་རྒྱ་ཆེན་

པོ། བློས་བྱས་ཐམས་ཅད་ལས་འདས་པས་ན་ཤེས་རབ་པར་ཕྱིན། མཐའ་ཐམས་ཅད་དང་

བྲལ་བས་དབུ་མ། ལམ་གྱི་མཆོག་འབྲས་བུ་མཆོག་དུ་བྱེད་ཕྱིར་ལམ་འབྲས། ཉོན་མོངས་

རང་སར་ཞི་བས་ཞི་བྱེད། གཉིས་སྣང་གི་ཞེན་འཛིན་ཆུད་ནས་གཅོད་པས་གཅོད་

ཡུལ། སངས་རྒྱས་ཀྱི་གོ་འཕང་ལ་དངོས་སུ་སྤྱོར་བས་སྤྱོར་དྲུག མ་རིག་འཁྲུལ་བའི་བློ་

ཏོག་སྤྱོང་བས་བློ་སྤྱོང་སོགས་མདོར་ན་ཆོས་ཟབ་དགུའི་རྣམ་གྲངས་མཐའ་ཡས་པའི་དོན་

དོན་གྱི་སྙིང་པོ་ནི་འདི་ཁོ་ན་ལས་གཞན་མེད། ཅེས་གདམས་པ་ཁྱད་པར་ཅན་གྱི་བཀའ་

ལུང་གནང་བ་དེ་ཉིད་ཀྱིས་རྟེན་འབྲེལ་གྱི་མཐའ་བཀྲུན་ཏེ་མཇུག་གྲུབ་པར་བྱས་པ་ལགས་

སོ།།

ཨ་སྐུ་བས་མཆོག་རྟོགས་ཆེན་དཔོན་སློབ་རིན་པོ་ཆེའི་བཀའ་ལུང་གི་ཚོད་པར་སྤྱི་བོའི་གཙུག་ཏུ་

བགོད་དེ། གུས་འབངས་ཐ་ཤལ་བ་ཐུབ་བསྟན་ཉི་མས་དད་པའི་མེ་ཏོག་གི་སྙིམ་པ་སྙིང་ནས་བགོད་

ནས་ཕུལ་བ་ལགས།

Foreword

VENERABLE ALAK ZENKAR RINPOCHE

In this life, you guide us with empowerments and key instructions.
In the next life, you lead us down the path of liberation.
In the bardo between those two, you free us from the chasms of fear.
Unequalled guru, bestow your blessing upon me.

THE *bardo*, or intermediary state, has become a popular catchphrase in Buddhist circles. The appearances of this life, we are told, fade away, and for forty-nine days we experience awesome and terrifying visions in a disembodied state. That is what the bardo has signified to most people. Let us explore, however, the way in which the concept of the bardo has evolved from the perspective of Buddhist literature.

Sutra-based Indian treatises that were translated into Tibetan, such as Vasubhandu's *Treasury of Abhidharma*, make reference to the bardo, yet without employing the term per se:

> *There is a level of existence*
> *Experienced in between death and birth.*

The text goes on to discuss three levels of existence: the existence of death, the existence of birth, and the existence of what lies in between those two. It also briefly discusses the mental body of the intermediary state, its distinctive traits, and its lifespan.

An Indian sutric text translated into Chinese, the *Great Treasury of Expositions*, discusses the bardo in a general way and also devotes an entire chapter to the unfolding of the forty-nine day journey.

The Tantra-based collection of bardo teachings in Tibetan literature is richer still, with all four of Tibet's main Buddhist lineages—Sakya, Geluk,

Kagyu, and Nyingma—contributing exegeses and quintessential instructions of varying lengths. These writings discuss the names of the different types of bardo and the classifications of each. Their styles of presentation are for the most part similar, yet they also highlight the uniqueness of each tradition's inherited legacy.

Karma Lingpa, a great master of the Nyingma lineage, revealed a cycle of profound texts, *The Self-Liberated Wisdom of the Peaceful and the Wrathful Deities*, that were said to have been entrusted to him by the Indian mahaguru Padmasambhava. One of the most famed writings from that group of texts is *The Great Liberation through Hearing in the Bardo*, commonly known as *The Tibetan Book of the Dead*, a deep and extensive exposition on the six bardos: birth, dreams, meditation, dying, dharmata (or true reality), and becoming.

Another teacher renowned for his instructions on the bardo was Tsele Natsok Rangdrol, who explained that, in terms of what is held in common by the earlier and later schools, the above six bardos can be condensed into four: the natural bardo of birth, the painful bardo of dying, the luminous bardo of dharmata, and the karmic bardo of becoming. This fourfold presentation, he says, cuts to the heart of the matter in a way that is easy to understand.

Although Tsele Natsok Rangdrol's main writing on the bardo has been translated into English, it is the *Liberation through Hearing* that has enjoyed the widest dissemination throughout our multilingual world. It has been translated into Chinese, into English at least five times, and into French.

It is timely, therefore, that The Dzogchen Ponlop Rinpoche, a Tibetan lineage master learned in the ways of the West and in the English language, has bestowed on us a direct and fresh explanation of the bardo principles that transcends the distance of translation. In writing *Mind Beyond Death*, Rinpoche has taken into his compassionate care beings like myself: people with bad karma who steadfastly cling to the confused appearances of this life; who are slaves to the eight worldly concerns in the day and turn into corpses of ignorant sleep at night; who waste our lives away with misdeeds and meaningless prattle. Rinpoche's words light the way for us, offering us guidance in this life, the next life, and the bardos in between.

In exploring the bardos, Rinpoche begins with an explanation of the bardo of birth in which he encourages readers to reverse their attachment to the appearances of this life and extract the most meaningful essence from their precious human existence. For this bardo, Rinpoche provides instructions for developing a calm and stable mind through the practice of shamatha meditation.

Next is the bardo of dreams, in connection with which Rinpoche instructs readers on the trainings in the illusory body and dream yoga practices, which make it possible to recognize one's dreams, transform dream appearances, and emanate new ones. Rinpoche also explains the view of luminosity yoga, through which one recognizes the state of deep sleep as being luminous awareness. For the bardo of meditation, Rinpoche guides us through the meditation of vipashyana, according to Mahamudra and Dzogchen, and clearly explains its methods for directly recognizing the nature of mind.

Rinpoche's discussion on the bardo of dying details the stages of the dissolution of the elements of the coarse body, as well as the dissolution of the subtle consciousness, which occurs with the threefold visionary process of appearance, increase, and attainment. Concluding with instruction on the transference of consciousness, he enables devoted aspirants to attain liberation at the time of death—or, failing that, to gain a strong glimpse of recognition of the mind's true nature.

In his synopsis of the bardo of dharmata, Rinpoche gives a detailed explanation of the two stages of the manifestation of mind's luminosity: the dharmakaya, or motherlike, luminosity, and the sambhogakaya luminosity. The latter arises as the display of vivid lights, sounds, and visions of the hundred peaceful and wrathful deities. He encourages us at this time to cultivate an awareness of the unreal, illusionlike nature of these visions. By gaining confidence in all appearances being our own mind's display, it is possible for us, in the bardo of true reality, to attain sambhogakaya freedom. Rinpoche's instructions for this stage are like the fearless warrior-guide who delivers us through the ravines of the fearful bardo.

Finally, Rinpoche guides us through the bardo of becoming. Rinpoche explains how, if one fails to recognize one's own true nature during the bardos of dying or the luminous bardo of dharmata, then the threefold visionary process of appearance, increase and attainment occurs in reverse order. One's earlier lack of recognition gives birth to tremendous fear. As this fear intensifies, further manifold confused appearances of the bardo arise. Each confused appearance, Rinpoche points out, is none other than the reflexive appearance of one's own pristine awareness. Nevertheless, there are options available to us still: the supreme practitioner will be capable of taking birth in the naturally present pure realms of the nirmanakaya, the emanation body. The middling practitioner will take birth in a pure realm, such as Amitabha's. And the common practitioner will take a favorable birth in the mundane world. Here Rinpoche explains the key points of the creation and completion stages. In doing so he instills certainty in the interested reader, enabling one to be rich in the genuine dharma during this life and to carry this wealth of virtue, without any sense of poverty, to one's next life. Since Rinpoche's instructions reveal the profound methods for taking advantage of all the above-mentioned avenues of liberation and benefit, his kindness is inconceivably great.

This guide to the bardos is invaluable. For those whose eyes of intelligence are dull, it takes the reader by the hand and walks with them. For those who have taken a wrong turn in their journey, it is a cartographer who corrects their direction. For faithful ones who aspire to fulfill its instructions, it is a steadfast captain, skillfully delivering them from the bardo's terrors. For diligent students engaged in hearing, explanation, and meditation, it is a master key to a mine of treasures, opening a hundred doorways to knowledge. For the learned, it is a full moon whose unveiled radiance opens the night-blooming flowers of insight. For yogis and yoginis who fully immerse themselves in practice, it is a sun whose brilliant rays light up the window of the bardo's opportunities to recognize the true nature, live the three kayas, and experience all perceptions as luminosity.

By seizing the heart of all sutras' and tantras' intentions, condensing the pith of all practical applications, excluding nothing from his profound, quintessential instructions, and preserving the stream of the lineage's oral transmissions, Rinpoche, shunning the polemics of logicians and the hearsay repetitions of impersonators, has, in reliance on his own personal and experiential wisdom, placed in our hands a miraculous gift of a teaching.

It is my heartfelt wish that many beings will derive immense benefit—both short and long term—from this book, through seeing it, hearing its words, remembering its contents, or even placing their hands on it once. The merits of publishing such an exalted discourse cannot be outnumbered by the particles of dust in the earth; they cannot be overwhelmed by the water of all oceans combined. To have such a wondrous apparition merely flash before our eyes is itself the fruit of a great many virtuous labors of the past.

Not only does this book contain all of the key and profound instructions of the eight great practice lineages of Tibet; it also expounds with great freshness and intimacy the heart intention of all the accomplished masters of India. I see this work of The Dzogchen Ponlop Rinpoche, therefore, as an all-encompassing jewel.

For auspiciousness, I would like to conclude with a special quotation from Tsele Natsok Rangdrol's writings on the bardo which, I believe, describes very accurately the qualities of the book you now hold:

Since in it all the Buddha's 84,000 teachings are perfectly complete, it is the Great Perfection *(Dzogchen)*. Since is reveals how nothing goes beyond the three kayas, it is the Great Seal *(Mahamudra)*. Since it transcends all concepts, it is the Perfection of Knowledge *(Prajnaparamita)*. Since it is free from all extremes, it is the Middle Way *(Madhyamaka)*. Since it brings about the supreme results of all paths, it is the Path and Result *(Lam Dre)*. Since it pacifies the mental afflictions right where they are, it is Pacification *(Shijey)*. Since it thoroughly cuts through dualistic fixation, it is Cutting Through *(Chö)*. Since it directly unites one with the state of buddhahood, it is the Six Unities *(Jor Druk)*. Since it transforms the confused ignorance of thoughts, it is Thought Transformation *(Lojong)*. In sum, there is no other teaching apart from this very instruction that holds the essence of all the profound dharmas there are.

Placing the writings of the supreme refuge, The Dzogchen Ponlop Rinpoche, on the crown of my head, I, Tudeng Nima, the worst among his devoted followers, offer these words, flowers of faith tossed into the sky, from the center of my heart.

Editors' Note

Mind Beyond Death is based on teachings presented at the 2002 Treasury of Knowledge Retreat in San Antonio, Texas, where The Dzogchen Ponlop Rinpoche presented fourteen lectures on the topic of the six bardos, or intermediate states of existence. While many participants had had some previous exposure to the bardo teachings, the combination of the retreat atmosphere, the potent subject matter and the direct and personal style of Rinpoche's transmission proved deeply affecting for students. Over the course of the next few years, requests for transcripts and videos of the teachings continued to arrive. Several study groups were formed, provoking questions that went beyond the scope of the original presentation. Eventually, Rinpoche agreed to suggestions that this series of lectures be edited for publication, and that he would include additional instructions and explanations.

The present expanded text preserves the original teaching while drawing on further oral and written commentary provided by Rinpoche for this book. His presentation of the bardos is based primarily on the following Tibetan texts: Padmasambhava's *Instructions on the Six Bardos* from the Shitro Cycle of Teachings as revealed by Karma Lingpa; Tsele Natsok Rangdrol's *Mirror of Mindfulness*; and Jamgon Kongtrul the Great's *Treasury of Knowledge*. It is based as well on the oral instructions Rinpoche has received from his own teachers. *Mind Beyond Death* therefore follows the basic structure of these classic and authoritative texts. Each bardo is defined, its way of being experienced by ordinary and enlightened beings is described, and the meditation practices for transforming its confused aspect into a state of clarity in which wisdom may be realized are set out.

In order to make these teachings as accessible as possible, a number of supplementary materials are furnished in the appendices. Technical terms are explained in a glossary; and Tibetan language equivalents are provided where possible. There are two charts; one outlines the extensive description in the text of the gradual process of death ("The Stages of Dissolution"); the other provides further details relating to the order of appearance and symbolism of the deities that appear in the after-death state ("The Hundred Peaceful and Wrathful Deities"). An index by subject is also provided. These offerings are augmented by the inclusion of Rinpoche's succinct historical perspective on the development of the foundational practices known as *ngondro*; a selection of yogic songs of realization, or *dohas,* which simultaneously teach dharma and manifest the enlightened state; a translation of the "Sutra on Wisdom for the Time of Death," in which the Buddha offers advice to bodhisattvas on the verge of dying; and two poems of Rinpoche's own composition. Finally, a list of the Nalandabodhi Centers established by Rinpoche is provided for those wishing to receive further information about study programs or meditation instruction.

This book is intended for those who are familiar with Buddhist philosophy and practice as well as for those newer to such thought and language. While Rinpoche's presentation is grounded in a precise scholarly framework, it is not essentially a technical or academic treatment. At heart, it is a story we are hearing from a lineage of awakened masters. The instructions presented here, however, are not theistic or even religious in nature. They are clearly a science of mind involving, and even requiring, the application of critical intelligence to our experience. It is said that through studying and practicing these teachings, it is possible to penetrate the confusion of death. At that time, we transcend the rift between life and death that makes the two separate and antithetical experiences, and discover our ultimate condition of indestructible wakefulness.

Introduction
Gambling with the Lord of Death

THIS BOOK is the retelling of a story first heard centuries ago by a small group of students of the great Indian master Padmasambhava. This extraordinary master, whose life was filled with many adventures and accomplishments, achieved the greatest accomplishment of all—the realization of the stainless and indestructible nature of his own mind that instantly dispels all illusions, even the fearful illusion of death. It is said that Padmasambhava departed this world in a mass of rainbow light, leaving behind many precious instructions and descriptions of his journey of transformation for students of the future. Though nothing in this story has changed, whoever hears it and takes it to heart might be changed by it. Like classic stories of all times, it takes you on a journey; only in this case you are the main character and the outcome is in your hands.

The story we are looking at here, then, is our own. It is the story of our bodies and minds, our birth and death, and the undeniable truths about our existence as human beings. While we know the facts of life and the inevitability of death, it is a reality we rarely face. When we do, our impulse is to turn away. Though we do not wish to confront death or the fear it inspires, running away from this inconvenient truth will not help us. Reality will catch up to us in the end. If we have ignored death all our lives, then it will come as a big surprise. There will be no time on death's bed to learn how to handle the situation, no time to develop the wisdom and compassion that could guide us skillfully through death's terrain. We will have to confront whatever we encounter there as best we can—and that is a genuine gamble.

Why would we take such a risk? We have a choice: to prepare ourselves to face the most uncomfortable moment of our lives, or to meet that moment unprepared. If we choose to look into the face of death directly, then we can be certain of transforming that meeting into a profound experience that will bring untold benefit to our spiritual journey. If we choose denial, then, when we meet the Lord of Death, we will be like an innocent youth walking into a late-night gambling den with a pocket full of cash. What are the odds that we will be richer and happier in the morning?

Whether or not we are prepared, we will all meet the Lord of Death. Who is this great Lord and what is his power over us? This legendary figure that inspires so much fear is merely the personification of impermanence and cause and effect, or karma. In Buddhist literature, this "Lord" is invincible. No one can beat him at his game—except a true holder of wisdom. It is wisdom that slays the slayer, that cleans the table and walks away with the prize.

From ancient times to the present, many cultures have developed a literature—both oral and written—rich in the lore of death and dying. Many of these world wisdom traditions have addressed the question of how the experience of "dying" can be made a meaningful and powerful point at which to connect with one's own deeper or higher nature. In recent years, "death and dying" has become a hot topic, and "death" itself has become a buzzword. But while some people seem to want to talk about it, no one really wants to face death, or to be in an environment where death is actually happening. Woody Allen once said, "I'm not afraid of dying; I just don't want to be there when it happens." This is a reflection of the minds of many people in our twenty-first century world. In reality, we try to avoid death altogether. We are afraid to hear about it or look at it, let alone experience it, because we have created a negative and fearful cultural image of death. We believe that death is the end of all that we are, the loss of everything we hold most dear. Yet our fear prevents us from knowing our own story, which is ultimately a tale of renewal and liberation.

According to Buddhist teachings, the reality is that death and birth take place continually. This understanding is also found in Christian teachings, where St. Paul said, "I die every day." The point is to learn that dying is part of the process of living; it takes place in every moment—not just at the end of life. How do we learn to recognize this sense of moment-to-moment death in our lives?

To go beyond our abstract notions about death, we have to look deeply into our own minds and hearts. This journey requires that we contemplate what death means to us individually—not from the medical or technical points of view—such as the cessation of respiration or the beating of the heart, and not from the perspective of our religious or cultural traditions. Instead, we need to ask ourselves, "What does death mean to me, personally, from my own experience of life? What is my most basic, visceral feeling about what death is?" This is an important question, because how we define death largely determines how we will experience our own. It also becomes our guide for how to die well.

According to the spiritual insight of Buddhism, in order to die well, one must live well. Dying well can only be accomplished when we know how to live well. Could it be that because we don't know how to live fully, or live well, we are afraid to die? In order to transform our fear of death and overcome it, we must come into contact with death instead of denying it. We must connect with death through genuine reflection. We must contemplate its image with a calm and clear mind, not just with the image of death that our thoughts have created on the basis of superstition and rumor. We must actually see and feel that state nakedly. The way to meet death fully is to die every day, to every moment, to everything; to our thoughts, to our agony, to our emotions, to our loving relationships— even to our joy. We cannot meet death if we don't die every day!

From the Buddhist perspective, death does not just mean coming to an end. It also means coming to a beginning. Death is a process of change. Ending itself is neither positive nor negative; it is just reality. Death was part of the deal when we accepted the idea of birth. Our entrance into this world came with a contract to leave it. So, whether you sigh with relief at the end of a torturous moment, or desperately wish some Hollywood movie-like instant could last forever, every moment comes to an end. Every story has an end, regardless of whether that end is happy or sad. Nevertheless, when a moment or a lifetime ends, we cannot argue with it. There is no room for negotiation. Recognizing this reality is the way we come into contact with death in everyday life.

Ultimately, what we call "life" is just an illusion of continuity—a succession of moments, a stream of thoughts, emotions and memories, which we feel is our possession. And therefore we, too, spring into existence, as the possessors of that continuity. However, upon examination, we discover that that continuity is dreamlike, illusory. It is not a continuous or substantial reality. It consists of single moments, which arise, dissolve and arise again, like waves on an ocean. Therefore, this "I" arises and dissolves in each moment as well. It does not continue from one moment to the next. The "I" of one moment dissolves, and is gone. The "I" of the next moment arises afresh. These two "I"s cannot be said to be the same or different, yet they are identified by conceptual mind as a single, continuous self: "Yes, this is me . . . ."

Within this flux, we can clearly see the process of death; the dissolving of fleeting thoughts, the fading of vibrant emotions, the quick alternation of our perceptions—a sound, a touch is there and then gone. But at the very instant we experience the end of a moment, we experience the process of birth; a new world is born as fresh thoughts and colorful emotions arise in response to shifting perceptions. Therefore, the end of a moment is also a renewal, as it is only through death that a new thing can come into being.

Dreading death, we do not see the obvious; that which has the power to renew itself is eternal, while that which is truly continuous has no creative power. Without the play of birth and death, the world would be stagnant, like a scene in an art house movie shot with a still camera. The world that is caught in its lens is held fixed and motionless. Nothing changes for a long, long time. Without the continual play of death and rebirth, our lives would be just as fixed and senseless—only the consequences would be torturous. Nothing would change at all. In contrast, how wonderful and refreshing it is to have these momentary changes, to be blessed by impermanence!

If we were continuous, impervious to change and death, then seeking something beyond or outside ourselves would be fruitless. Whatever we might call it—the real, the creative, the divine mystery, the sacred world or the grace of god—we could never find it. We would find only further projections of our own mind. It is only by dying every day that we can be truly in contact with life. If we think we can find a meaningful connection between life and death—while still clinging to our belief in the continuity of our own existence—then we are living in a fictional world of our own creation.

When this illusion of continuity comes to an end, however briefly, we have an opportunity to glimpse the deeper reality that underlies it. This is the true and abiding nature of the mind, which is inseparable from the mind and realization of Padmasambhava. It is the primordial awareness, the luminous wisdom, from which all phenomena spontaneously arise. This wisdom is unknowable in the ordinary sense because it is beyond concept. Therefore it is also beyond time. It is called "birthless and death-less." If we can connect with that experience, past and future are tran-scended, and we naturally wake up to a vast and brilliant world.

When we truly know that with every ending, there is also renewal, we begin to relax. Our minds become open to the process of change. We feel we can actually touch reality and are no longer afraid of death. We can learn to live well and fully now, with the understanding that death is not something apart from life. From the Buddhist point of view, we have a choice; to direct our story of living and dying now, or to wait, closing our eyes to the message of impermanence, until death itself opens them. Since we value happy endings, why choose to gamble with the Lord of Death?

Ancient Buddhist wisdom has much to offer to our modern world com-munity on the topic of "death and dying," and in this book I will explore how we can understand and apply these timeless teachings in our every-day lives. It is my hope that this book will bring clarity and insight to these issues from the spiritual perspective of the Vajrayana Buddhist tra-dition. May the profound wisdom and genuine compassion embodied in these teachings swiftly dispel all illusions of beings and relieve their great-est fears. May the true nature of mind, the buddha within, guide us all on the path of living and dying well.

Dzogchen Ponlop Rinpoche
Nalanda West
Seattle, Washington
October 7, 2006

MIND BEYOND DEATH

The Moment of Truth

1

WHENEVER WE EMBARK on a long journey, there is a sense of death and rebirth. The experiences we go through have a transitional quality. The moment we step outside our house and close the door, we begin to leave our life behind. We say goodbye to family and friends and to the familiar rooms and routines that we inhabit. We might feel regret mixed with excitement as we climb into the taxi that will take us to the airport. As our vision of home recedes, we are both sadly parted and joyfully released from all that defines us. The further from home we go, the more focused we become on our next destination. We think less of home and more about where we are going. We begin to look at a new map; we start to think about where we will land, about the new people, new customs and new environment—the new sets of experiences to come.

Until we reach our destination, we are in transit—in between two points. One world has dissolved, like last night's dream, and the next has not yet arisen. In this space, there is a sense of total freedom: we are free from the business of being our ordinary selves; we are not tied to the day-to-day world and its demands in quite the same way. There is a sense of freshness and appreciation of the present moment. At the same time, we may have moments of feeling fearful and groundless because we have entered unknown territory. We do not know with certainty what will arise in the next moment or where it will take us. The moment we relax, however, our insecurity dissolves, and the environment becomes friendly and supportive. We are at ease in our world once again and can move forward naturally and with confidence.

Still, journeys do not always go according to plan. If we are traveling by air, the flight might be delayed or cancelled. If we are on a train, weather conditions might slow us down. If we are on the road, in one moment, a tire could blow in heavy traffic, diverting us off the main highway to a small-town garage. It is sensible, therefore, to plan carefully for what may arise. We should be sure to bring with us whatever we might need. We should know our route, the location of amenities and services along the way, and the local customs. Then we can simply relax and be wherever we are, which is the experience of being in the present moment.

Leaving this life is similar in many ways to going on a long trip. In this case, the trip we are making is a journey of mind. We are leaving behind this body, our loved ones, our possessions, and all our experiences of this life, and moving on to the next. We are in transit, in between two points. We have left home but have not yet reached our next destination. We are neither in the past nor in the future. We are sandwiched between yesterday and tomorrow. Where we are now is the present, which is the only place we can be.

This experience of the present moment is known as *bardo* in Tibetan Buddhism. Bardo in a literal sense means "interval"; it can also be translated as an "intermediate" or "in-between" state. Thus, we can say that whenever we are in between two moments, we are in a bardo state. The past moment has ceased; the future moment has not yet arisen. There is a gap, a sense of nowness, of pure openness, before the appearance of the next thing, whether that is our next thought or our next lifetime. It is the same when we take any trip. We are in transition—even when leaving work to go home or leaving home to move to another state. If we pay attention to these transitions, if we can remain conscious of our environment at these times, then we are much more likely to be aware of our environment during the bardos that go beyond this life—that encompass our passage through the bardos of dying and death. We will be more in control of our journey and able to meet new or challenging experiences with a clear and steady mind.

When we can be fully present with them, the experiences we meet throughout the bardos of death become simple and natural. We can actually afford to relax and let go of hope and fear. We can be inquisitive about our new experiences. We can also learn something about ourselves—that, ultimately, who we are in the most genuine sense transcends our limited notion of self. At this transitional point, we have an opportunity to go beyond that perception and transform the appearance of death into an experience of awakening by recognizing the true nature of mind.

Thus, just as we would prepare for any trip—packing clothes and so forth—it is highly advisable to make good preparations for our next major journey—our passage from this life to the next. Those preparations are the topic of this book.

The Bardo Teachings

According to the teachings of Tibetan Buddhism, the essence of the spiritual journey can be said to begin and end with the present moment. Its extensive philosophical and meditative traditions all point to this state of simplicity. Among the most renowned and provocative of these systems are the tantric teachings on the six bardos, or intermediate states, of existence. In particular, these teachings describe six distinct sets of experiences: three that are related to this life and three that are related to experiences of death, after death, and our entrance into the next life. When the six bardos are viewed in full, we see that they encompass the entire spectrum of our experience as conscious beings, both in life and in death.

The teachings on the six bardos point out the fundamental continuity of mind through all states of existence. From this perspective, what we call "life" and "death" are simply concepts—relative designations that are attributed to a continuous state of being, an indestructible awareness that is birthless and deathless. While impermanence—the constant ebb and flow of appearance and dissolution—characterizes all phenomena that we can see, hear, taste, touch, or mentally conceive, this pure, primordial mind endures all transitions and transcends all boundaries created by dualistic thought. Although we may cling to this life and fear its end, beyond death there is mind; and where there is mind, there is uninterrupted display: spacious, radiant, and continually manifesting.

However, whether this understanding remains merely a comforting idea or becomes a key to accessing deeper levels of knowledge and ultimate freedom depends on us. Relatively speaking, we are *not* free, so long as we do not recognize the true nature of our mind. That nature is empty, luminous wisdom; it is primordially pure awareness; it is the state of wakefulness that transcends duality.

Although we are never separate from this nature, we do not see it. Instead, we see who we *think* we are, who we believe ourselves to be. We see a self that is fabricated by thought and thus we see a fabricated world, similar to the state of dream. However, through the practice of methods that cultivate mindfulness and awareness, we develop insight, or *prajna*, that directly sees this nature of mind. In the instant that this nature is fully recognized, our journey through the bardo states comes to an end. The opportunity to connect with such a full recognition is said to be greatly enhanced at the time of death and in the intermediate states after death, so long as we have prepared ourselves to meet it.

What Is Bardo?

The cycle of the six bardos describes our journey through various states of conscious experience in both life and death. In order to fully understand and appreciate the instructions on these bardos presented in the following chapters, it will be useful to first examine what bardo is on the most fundamental level. The instructions themselves cannot be of genuine help if we do not know in any meaningful way what is being pointed to. To begin with, we must see that bardo has more than one meaning. One is easy to understand and recognize, and that is the conceptual, or relative, bardo. The other is more subtle and more difficult to grasp, and that is the nonconceptual, or absolute, bardo. The nonconceptual bardo is regarded as the very essence or true nature of the bardo experience.

The understanding of bardo develops in stages, in the same way that all knowledge is accumulated. This realization can occur any time your mind is relaxed and open. It may be that you realize the nature of bardo when you are watching TV or eating a meal, and not while you are poring over words in a book. However it occurs, the journey you undergo to arrive at this understanding is a path that leads you to a direct experience of your own mind. It leads to an experience of pure awareness that is beyond thought. As you will hear over and over again, that pure mind is with you right now—it is closer to you than your own shadow.

Once we have some understanding of what bardo is, we will benefit from the rich variety of these instructions. When we begin to apply the instructions to our mind, what we are doing is preparing ourselves well for a   long   journey. We are preparing ourselves to meet, recognize and master our own mind under a number of diverse and at times challenging situations. All Buddhist mind training is precisely for this purpose, whether or not we are familiar with the word "bardo."

CONCEPTUAL AND ESSENCE BARDOS

From one perspective, bardo is an experience of a certain duration of time, marked by a clear beginning, a sense of continuity and distinct end. The duration of that interval may be as short as a finger snap, or it may be much longer, such as the duration of time between birth and death, or between birth and the achievement of enlightenment. Therefore, bardo refers to a moment of experience—no matter how long that moment is.

Here we can note that the duration of any moment is not the actual experience itself. Our sense of time comes afterwards, outside of it. For example, when we have had a headache, we might say, "I got a headache this morning and I had it until around 4 o'clock this afternoon." When we attribute a measurable amount of time to our headache, that designation is conceptual. From an experiential point of view—what it felt like—its actual duration is not definite in any sense. That is why Buddhist teachings often describe time and space as relative phenomena, a view that corresponds to Western notions of relativity, such as the space-time observations of Albert Einstein. For example, a particular event may seem to pass in an instant for one person, while the same experience may seem to last an eon for someone else. So when we look at bardo from the perspective of a fixed amount of time, we are seeing the relative or conceptual aspect of bardo. When we say "from birth until death," for example, we are talking about a long chain of moments that are connected by conceptual mind and then viewed as a whole.

When we look at bardo from the perspective of essence, we are seeing the absolute, or nonconceptual, aspect of bardo. The essence of bardo is discovered in the experience of nowness, in the gap between the cessation of one moment and the arising of the next. That essence is nothing other than the self-aware wisdom that is the fundamental nature of our own mind. In the Mahamudra teachings, this nature of mind is called "ordinary mind," and in the Dzogchen teachings, it is called *rigpa*, which means "bare awareness," or "naked awareness." This wisdom does not exist in substantial form. It exists as pure awareness, as the light of mind. When we do not recognize this nature, we perceive the world in a way that gives rise to confusion and suffering. When we do recognize it, we perceive the world clearly, in a way that gives rise to liberation.

THE FORK IN THE ROAD

The experience of the gap between the cessation of one moment and the arising of the next is nothing less than the "moment of truth" that will determine our direction and shape our future experience. In Tibetan, we say that in each moment we are at a fork in the road. If we recognize the nature of our mind, then, through our clear vision, what arises before us are the appearances of absolute truth, of actual reality. If we fail to recognize the nature of our mind and take the other fork in the road, then through our obscured vision, what arises before us are the delusive appearances of relative truth. Therefore, bardo is a pivotal moment, a crucial and decisive point in our journey.

Whichever fork or direction we take, it is important to realize that *all* appearances are, ultimately speaking, aspects of the nature of our own mind. They do not exist in a manner that is independent of our minds. It is taught that anyone who recognizes this does not have to continue on through the cycle of the six bardos. All bardos are naturally self-liberated. Anyone who fails to recognize this must continue on this journey. However, it is also taught that every living being possesses this naked awareness. It is naturally present within the mindstreams of all beings.

In order to experience the nature of mind, you do not need to fulfill any prerequisites. You do not need any special training. You do not need to be initiated into any form of religion. You do not need to be a scholar, a great meditator, a great logician or philosopher. The pure awareness that is the essence of the present moment of our consciousness is free from all such labels and concepts—whether philosophical or religious. There is no question of whether or not we possess this awareness. The question is simply, do we recognize it? While we all have the opportunity to do so, we consistently miss the moment. However, there are certain times when it is easier to see. The opportunity seems to be greatest when mind becomes intensified.

Such heightened states of mind occur under a variety of circumstances, both painful and pleasurable. We might be experiencing anger, jealousy or irritation; we might also be feeling happiness, joy or bliss. Either way, our experience can intensify to the point where we recognize the naked awareness that is the essence of all such experiences. It does not matter what our circumstances or conditions are. If we can simply watch our minds and observe the arising of our thoughts and emotions, then recognition of the nature of mind will arise naturally. If you seem to miss it right now, then just keep looking. One day that looking will strike that vital point. However, if you do not make an effort, then there is not much hope that you will recognize the nature of mind.

TRAPPED IN TIME

If we look carefully at our experience of daily life, we will see that we are rarely in the present moment. Instead, we are living in the past or in the future. Our experience remains primarily on the conceptual level because we are always lost in our thoughts, one moment thinking of how life was, and next about how it will be.

We spend a great deal of time and energy on the future—to fulfill our hopes and dreams for a time that is yet to come. All of this hard work is for the benefit of the person we *will* be when that time comes. It is not for us now, the "I" or "me" of the present. The future is out there ahead of us but never comes into this world so that we can enjoy the results of our hard work. Since that is the case, why are we working so hard, like crazy machines? It is like cooking meal after meal but never eating a single dish. It is as though our hunger and thirst are so great that we are driven by fear to stockpile food and drink. We put bottles of soda in the refrigerator and cans of food on our shelves, but we never eat or drink because these supplies are for our future hunger, our future thirst. This is what is happening in our ordinary life, where we are always working for the future. How can we overcome the pain of our hunger and thirst and the fear it causes? There is no way that we can truly overcome them so long as we are always missing the present moment.

Another habitual tendency we have is to live in a fantasy world of the past, in which we are incessantly recalling bygone events. We are either enjoying reliving certain past occurrences or becoming depressed about them. However, the past is not here; the person we were, our friends and enemies, as well as the actual events themselves, are long gone. When we try to relive a former experience, we are not actually reliving the same event. Each time we recall it, it is a slightly different experience. Why? Each experience differs because the environment of our mind is always different.

Our experience is affected by the thought that we had immediately before, as well as by the thought that is going to arise next. Thus, our recollection of the past is necessarily distorted. We cannot undergo the same experience again, whether we consider it to have been wonderful or horrible.

For these reasons we say that the truth is found only in a moment of present experience, which is always fleeting. So why do we call memories "the past"? Each thought occurs in the present. What we are experiencing now is new. It is not what we have experienced before but what we are creating now in the present moment. Simply reliving the past in a neurotic or obsessive way is not going to help us with anything. On the other hand, if we direct our experience properly, reflecting on past events with mindfulness and awareness, then we may gain some insight into our actions. If such reflections help to free us from our habitual patterns, then there is some benefit to those memories.

In general, however, if we do not have a proper means of working with our minds, then these recurring recollections of the past and projections of the future are not very fruitful. We are never here, in the present moment. We never actually see reality or recognize the true nature of bardo.

NEITHER HERE NOR THERE

If we are neither in the past nor in the future, then where are we? We are here, now. We have emerged from the past and we have not yet projected the future. When we can relate directly to the present moment in this way, it is a very subtle, profound and powerful experience. From this point of view, death is taking place in every moment. Every moment ceases, and that is the death of that moment. Another moment arises, and that is the birth of the next moment.

If we truly penetrate this experience, there is a sense of nonconceptuality—of clear awareness without thought. Whenever mind's steady stream of thought ceases, there is a sense of openness, of being nowhere. I am not talking about being "nowhere" in the mundane sense. In conventional speech, when we say someone is nowhere, they are still somewhere. In this context, nowhere is actually nowhere. In this experience of the present, of nowness, there is already a sense of non-solidity, of dissolution. From a tantric perspective, that is how we understand the bardo. We feel that we are neither here nor there, neither in the past nor in the future.

At this point, we begin to encounter the sense of dissolution that occurs constantly in our present life but is almost never noticed. When thought dissolves, we dissolve with it. Whoever we think we are dissolves into awareness that is free of the concept of self. In that very moment, we can directly experience the non-solidity of phenomena, the reality of emptiness, or *shunyata*. At the same time, there is so much energy present—so much so that it forms into another moment. The energy brings a sense of clarity that is so sharp, it is like a clear mirror in which mind can at last recognize itself. In this mirror of mind, we see the radiant yet transparent nature of our own awareness.

Whether we focus our minds on the perceptions of form, sound, smell and so forth, or on conceptual thoughts, or place our minds in a meditative state through the practices of *shamatha* and *vipashyana*, in every case there is this sense of nowness. When we look at it on the subtle level, it is the same experience. We have the experience of being nowhere. There is a sense of groundlessness, of having no solid ground on which to stand; yet there we are. Being in that space is a somewhat mysterious experience. It is also the experience of bardo.

Day-to-day Business

Since the bardo is this present moment, it is not unreachable. We might think, "Oh, the bardo teachings and practices are too difficult to understand; they are too complicated and enigmatic." However, when we have familiarized ourselves with them, we find that these teachings are neither inaccessible nor esoteric. In fact, they relate to our ordinary, day-to-day experience of working with our minds. We do not need to feel discouraged and think that the bardo teachings are too difficult to contend with. At the same time, the bardo teachings may be seen as depressing or as dwelling on topics that are frightening. Most often, people think the teachings are all about death and dying and the suffering of those states. However, the teachings are not only about suffering and death. As already mentioned, they are essentially about this moment, this present experience. Thus, the bardo teachings are absolutely practical and reachable—something that we can all grasp.

These teachings are also refreshing in the sense that, when we practice them, it is like taking a break from our regular job. Our regular job, in this case, is to be in the past or future. In the same way that we would walk out of the office and go for a coffee break, we can turn away from thoughts of past and future and move into the space of the present moment. In this way, the bardo teachings are a relaxing and uplifting practice.

OVERWHELMING EMOTIONS

In the bardo states of death and after-death, we are very susceptible to intense emotional states, to overwhelming moments of panic and fear. So learning how to work effectively with our emotions *now* is regarded as crucial training for these later bardo experiences. If we have studied and contemplated teachings on the emotions and have learned and practiced the methods of meditation, then, when emotions arise in our day-to-day life, we are prepared to work with them. We become more mindful and more skillful, and they become more workable. They do not cease right away, but when they do arise we recognize them. We think, "Oh, now I am starting to get angry," or "Now I am feeling really jealous." We can see the emotion coming and we can control it and, gradually, transcend it. However, if we are not at all familiar with our emotions, then when they come, we do not even notice that they are coming. Not only do we fail to recognize their arising, we don't even realize that they have come and gone. Under such circumstances, it is very hard to even begin working with our emotions because we are so habituated to simply reacting to their energy.

For example, when the doctor strikes your knee in a certain spot with a small hammer, your leg automatically kicks out. In a similar way, we tend to react automatically in response to the arising of an emotion. Based on our habituation, we can react in one of two ways, one negative and one positive. If we are habituated to negative states of mind, to reacting to situations with no awareness and no mindfulness, then no matter how much we want to bring positive energy into our state of mind—to ease our depression, anger, fear and so forth—it is very difficult and challenging. When anger comes, we will continue to react rashly. Our anger may burst out and we may begin to shout at someone, bang doors or smash objects. Regardless of the emotion, we know what happens when we react in such a way. One emotion leads to another and we experience further and further suffering. We may have trouble sleeping; our resentment and jealousy turn to rage, and rage brings hatred. It becomes more and more natural for us to react negatively. It may feel good to "finish our business" by yelling at someone or beating them up, but it does not end our suffering. The problem is that this kind of reaction brings about more suffering.

On the other hand, if we become habituated to positive thoughts, actions and states of mind by cultivating mindfulness, awareness, loving-kindness and compassion, it is much easier to generate a positive mind in the midst of a crisis. Then when a powerful emotion like anger arises, awareness arises naturally with it. We can take time to reflect, "Now I've become angry. What do I have to do?" When we react in this way, we can calm our mind and reflect on the positive qualities of the person toward whom we feel anger. We aspire to develop greater compassion for others, as well as ourselves, through all means available to us on our path.

When viewed in light of the teachings on the six bardos, all our practices in this lifetime are a form of habituating our minds to positive states and preparing ourselves for the extreme emotions and provocative situations that we will experience at death and in the after-death states.

Preparing for these experiences begins with simply being who we are and where we are in this very moment. If we want to be successful in terms of experiencing our death and journey after death, then we have to master the experience of nowness. Whatever we are going through, that is who we are in that moment. When we speak about nowness, we are not talking about anything external, so we should not look for it outside. We should look directly at the space of our immediate experience, which is always right in front of us—the space that is neither yours nor mine, neither theirs nor ours. That "in-between" space is the bardo.

By taking these teachings to heart and practicing them, it will be very easy to react in a positive way to the vivid projections of our mind that appear in these bardos. The teachings say that even if we do not realize the nature of mind and the reality of all phenomena in this lifetime, it will be possible to recognize it at the time of death, because at death mind manifests in such an intense and powerful way. Even if we fail to realize the nature of mind at the moment of death, it is said that we will have further opportunities in the two bardos that arise after death. Further, even if we are unsuccessful during that time, we will at least be able to maintain a calm and peaceful state of mind and accomplish a favorable rebirth as a result of our habituation to mindfulness and awareness practices.

Learning how to work with these teachings can also be of benefit to others. If we have a friend who is dying, or if someone we know is having an emotional meltdown, we can be a calming force for that person to some degree, provided that our own mind is reasonably calm. If we can manage to remain grounded, to not act or speak rashly when somebody is angry and shouting at us or banging on our door, then we can have a positive influence on that person. That in itself is a great benefit derived from our practice.

Message from the Lineage

It is important to see that the bardo teachings are a complete cycle of instructions. This means that if we were to practice only the instructions on the bardo, these instructions by themselves would be sufficient for us to achieve enlightenment in this lifetime. It is crucial that we develop confidence in these instructions, that we trust in their message and that we trust our own hearts so that we can take these instructions into our lives effectively.

A frequent problem is that we think, "Although the teachings are perfect, I am not practicing them properly." We may have thoughts like these because we feel that we are not doing them the way someone else does. Because we are not practicing the way "he" does or "she" does or "they" do, we think, "I am not doing it right." Then, gradually, we stop practicing. That is a big problem for us. However, we should be clear that the way each and every person practices any instruction is individual. The way we hear, the way we understand, and the way we express that understanding in action are all individual. When you put what you hear and study into practice, it will be—and has to be—your own. The way that you practice is not better than another person's way, nor is it worse. It is exactly the way that it should be for you, and the way that someone else does it is exactly the way that it should be for them. It is important for us not to lose heart in our way of practicing and to have confidence that we are putting these instructions into effective use in our lives.

If what was required was to match exactly the way that a practice was previously done, then we would have to conclude that, of all the previous gurus of the Buddhist lineage, none of them practiced properly. The great Tibetan yogi Milarepa built a nine-story tower for his guru, Marpa; but Marpa did not build such a tower for his own guru, Naropa. Was one of them wrong? If so, which one? Similarly, Marpa, who lived in Tibet, traveled to India three times to study with Naropa. This wonderful Indian master was very kind, and he treated his Tibetan disciple in a very caring and generous manner. Naropa, however, had been tormented by his own Indian guru, Tilopa; nevertheless, he did not do the same thing to Marpa. Marpa did not have to go through all the same trials and tribulations.

These gurus were not all the same and they did not practice in the same way. So to some degree, the idea of uniform, institutionalized practice is very new in Buddhism. While it is important for a group to do the same practice together, this does not mean that each individual has to do everything in exactly the same way. One person may practice for three hours a day, while you can practice for only one hour a day. That is good enough for you. What really matters is how you do it—not how long you do it.

When we look back into the history of the Buddhist lineage, all of the teachers of the past give us this message. They all practiced individually, yet they all achieved the same enlightenment. Why can't we achieve the same goal by doing it our own way in this century? We can take great delight in the individuality of our own practice, doing it as often and as effectively as possible. That is the key to recognizing the nature of mind and mastering the teachings of the bardo.

It is important to realize that there is nobody else who can wake us up and save us from samsara. There is no such thing in Buddhism. That may be Buddhism's biggest drawback, and at the same time its greatest advantage. This view shows us that there is nobody else in control of our lives, our experiences, our freedom or our bondage. Who *is* responsible? Who is in control? It is *us*. We are in control. We can bind ourselves further in samsara or we can free ourselves from it right now. It is all up to us. *We* are the ones who have to keep looking at our thoughts, looking for the nature of our mind. There is no guru, deity, buddha or bodhisattva out there to look for it for us. Although they would happily do this, it would not help us; it would only help them. We have to do it for ourselves. That is the key point.

Classifications of the Bardos

Within this cycle of instructions, there are various systems of classification of the bardo teachings. The system presented here is the complete classification, consisting of six bardos. The first bardo is called "the natural bardo of this life." The second is called the "bardo of dream." The third is called the "bardo of meditation." These first three are mainly related to the appearances and practices of this life. The fourth bardo is called the "painful bardo of dying." The fifth is called the "luminous bardo of dharmata."[1] The sixth is called the "karmic bardo of becoming." These last three relate to the appearances and practices for the after-death states.

Briefly, the natural bardo of this life is the interval between the moment of our birth and the moment that we meet with the condition that will cause our death. It contains all our experiences of joy and suffering and is the basis of our practice of the spiritual path. The bardo of dream relates to the interval between falling asleep and waking: the appearances of the waking state dissolve, there is a gap in which the illusory dream appearances arise, and then the appearances of the waking state become perceptible again. The bardo of meditation refers to the interval in which our minds are resting in a state of meditative absorption, or *samadhi*. At this time, our minds are not subject to the full power of confusion of the normal day-to-day state.

The painful bardo of dying is the interval between the moment we meet with the condition that will cause our death and the actual moment of our death. During this period, all the elements of our coarse and subtle bodies and consciousness dissolve gradually into space, and the clear light of death manifests. The luminous bardo of dharmata is the interval that begins immediately following the moment of death and ends when we enter the bardo of becoming. At this time the empty yet luminous appearances of the primordial and utterly pure nature of mind arise vividly. The bardo of becoming is the interval that begins after the luminous bardo of dharmata and ends when we enter the womb of our future parents.[2] Having not recognized the nature of our minds, and thus having failed to achieve liberation, we "wake up" from a state of unconsciousness and wander for forty-nine days, undergoing a variety of intense experiences while our longing for a home and parents grows stronger and stronger. At the culmination of this bardo, the appearances of the natural bardo of this life arise again, as we enter the next lifetime. Thus, the cycle continues, and we experience further suffering, along with further opportunities to develop our wisdom and compassion.

The bardo teachings may also be condensed into four divisions: the natural bardo of this life; the painful bardo of dying; the luminous bardo of dharmata; and the karmic bardo of becoming. In this case, the bardo of dream and the bardo of meditation are included within the natural bardo of this life. When you see instructions on the bardo that are classified in this slightly condensed way, you may find that the terminology varies somewhat. Regardless of how the bardo teachings are classified, a discussion of these six basic points of bardo will be included. While the approach of this book is based on the classification of six levels of bardo, we should remember that this is not the only way to understand and classify the bardos. All approaches lead to the same goal: to understand the reality of the bardos and to transcend our pain and confusion.

Sources of the Bardo Teachings

The bardo teachings are found in all levels of Buddhism. Although the Buddha gave many teachings on this subject in the sutras, the bardo instructions originate principally from the tantras, or the Vajrayana teachings. They were brought to Tibet by the great Indian mahasiddha Padmasambhava in the eighth century.[3] He is sometimes called the "second Buddha," and is also known by the names Padmakara (the "lotus-born") and Guru Rinpoche. He transmitted this cycle of teachings in very precise and clear language to a number of fortunate disciples, in particular to King Trisong Detsen, Dakini Yeshe Tsogyal and Chokro Lui Gyaltsen, all members of the group of "twenty-five disciples" regarded as the primary heirs to Padmasambhava's lineage of teachings. Padmasambhava then buried these teachings at Taklha Gampo for the benefit of future generations.

Padmasambhava's teachings were later revealed by Karma Lingpa, one of the great masters known as "treasure revealers," or *tertons,* and the lineage of their practice and realization was continued. Many other tertons also revealed additional teachings by Padmasambhava on the same subject. These teachings are thus part of the direct lineage, the lineage that belongs to the teachings of discovery, or *terma.* There are many different types of termas. Some are discovered in the sky, some in the water, some in the earth or in rocks. Others come as visionary experiences, which are called "mind *terma.*"

It is important to be aware of the breadth of the bardo teachings. We do not need to narrow them down to only one perspective or to a particular text such as *The Tibetan Book of the Dead.* The bardo teachings are more extensive than that, and they comprise a variety of teachings in Vajrayana Buddhism, most notably those of Padmasambhava. Consequently, we see slight differences or variations in the presentation of these teachings, differences that reflect both the individual experiences and expressions of various beings. While the order of certain bardo experiences may be presented differently, for example, these experiences definitely do occur within our lives.

The presentation of the bardo in this book is based primarily on the teachings of Padmasambhava in *Instructions on the Six Bardos* from the Shitro Cycle of Teachings revealed by Karma Lingpa as well as the oral teachings that I have received personally from my own masters; other sources are the Tibetan text of *Mirror of Mindfulness,* by Tsele Natsok Rangdrol, and *The Treasury of Knowledge* by Jamgon Kongtrul the Great.

All of our preparations—our efforts to develop our conceptual understanding of bardo, as well as our attention to developing confidence in the teachings and trust in our own capacities—are important steps to take before going into the details of each of the six classes of the bardo. If we know what the bardo is, as well as its classifications and purpose, then we will be able to appreciate the wisdom of each phase of this instruction. When a realized master such as Padmasambhava gives such teachings, he is teaching from his own experience of enlightened wisdom. He knows the full reality of the bardo and what living beings endure in each of these states. Therefore, as we go through each stage of explanation, try to take as much as you can into your own practice. You never know when these instructions are going to come in handy.

The Six Root Verses of the Six Bardos

The following translation of the root verses of the six bardos is an excerpt from Padmasambhava's *Instructions on the Six Bardos of the Peaceful and Wrathful Deities* revealed by the terton Karma Lingpa at the mountain of Gampo Dar. These verses can be recited in your practice, or can be used as synopses or short reminders for you to reflect on the six bardos.[4]

E MA
At this time, when the bardo of this life appears to you,
Abandon laziness since there is no time to waste.
Establish yourself in the meaning of hearing, contemplating and
    meditating without distraction.
Taking the path of appearance-mind, actualize the three kayas.

E MA
At this time, when the bardo of dream appears to you,
Abandon the heedlessness of the delusory sleep of a corpse.
Enter into the nature of mindfulness and nonwandering.
Recognizing dreams, practice transformation and luminosity.

E MA
At this time, when the bardo of meditation appears to you,
Abandon the accumulations of distractions and confusion.
Rest in the nature of nonwandering and nonfixation free from
    extremes.
Achieve stability in the development and fulfillment stages.

E MA
At this time, when the bardo of death appears to you,
Abandon attraction, attachment and fixation to all.
Enter into the nature of the clear oral instructions without
    distraction.
Transfer into the unborn space of self-arising awareness.

E MA
At this time, when the bardo of dharmata appears to you,
Abandon all shock, terror and fear.
Enter into the recognition that whatever arises is pristine
    awareness.
Recognize the appearances of the bardo in this manner.

E MA
At this time, when the bardo of becoming appears to you,
Hold the one-pointed mind of intention.
To continuously perform excellent activity
Closing the entrance to the womb, remember to reverse
    samsara and nirvana.
This is the time to be steadfast and to hold sacred outlook.
Abandoning jealousy, meditate on the guru and consort in union.

Pure Delusion
The Natural Bardo of This Life

2

THE TEACHINGS on the natural bardo of this life are concerned with how to make our life meaningful and transform its circumstances into the path of awakening. This life lasts for only so long—then the unborn mind, not recognizing itself, must continue its journey. Whatever mental stability and insights we develop in this life will unfailingly guide and support us through the bardos of death. Likewise, those habitual negative tendencies that we have *not* overcome will condition our experiences at that time and become reliable supports for the continuation of our suffering.

From the Buddhist point of view, whenever any being takes birth, what is taking birth is the *mind*—our individual consciousness. The relationship of our mind to our body is that of a traveler to a temporary abode. We are like a guest who stops for a while in an apartment or a hotel. Our stay is indefinite, but we can reside there only for as long as our lease allows. We do not know the length of our lease because we signed it in our past life. Sooner or later, as soon as our contract is up, we will either leave voluntarily or else the merciless landlords will kick us out. Some landlords are kind and will let us stay a few extra days; but we have to be ready to leave at any time and continue our journey. Leaving does not necessarily mean that we will be going to a bad place. It might be that we will be moving from a hotel to a palace—or to the street. It is totally up to us—to our own actions and effort.

The first verse of the Root Verses of the Six Bardos says:

E MA
At this time, when the bardo of this life appears to you,
Abandon laziness since there is no time to waste.

Establish yourself in the meaning of hearing, contemplating and
meditating without distraction.
Taking the path of appearance-mind, actualize the three kayas.

The first of the six bardos is the natural bardo of this life; it is also
known variously as the bardo between birth and death, the natural interval, or the bardo of birth and dwelling. When we cross the threshold into
this bardo, it means that we have ceased our existence in the last bardo,
the bardo of becoming. The natural bardo of this life starts at birth, when
we leave our mother's womb and enter this life. It continues until the time
we meet the condition that will cause our death—that is, the condition
that becomes the fundamental cause for leaving this body. This bardo
encompasses all of the appearances that we go through from birth,
through childhood and adulthood, until we face a terminal condition.

The Dance of Appearances

What the world looks like to us in any given moment—a pleasure palace
or a battleground—depends on how we relate to the appearances we meet
with in our life. "Appearance" is a key term in Buddhist philosophy, and
it is helpful to have a general understanding of the ways it is used. On one
level, appearances are simply whatever we experience through the faculty
of mind. This includes whatever we can see, hear, smell, taste or touch.
Those objects become the appearances of the five sense consciousnesses.
In addition, "appearances" includes what we think and how we feel about
those objects. Therefore, our thoughts and emotions become the appearances of mind—specifically, the aspect of mind that is our mental consciousness.

When we look at the notion of appearances from the perspective of
our spiritual journey through the six bardos, we look at two things: the
relationship of mind to appearance, and the nature of mind itself. When
we begin to explore this subject, it becomes quite vast. We are also introduced to the idea of pure and impure appearances, as well as to appearance-emptiness. Altogether, an understanding of appearances leads us to
a deeper understanding of how and why we experience the world the way
we do. We pursue this knowledge because it leads in the direction of freedom. There is no need, ultimately, to continue to suffer. Beyond even the

cessation of suffering, there is an opportunity to become more awake, wise and compassionate, to fulfill the great potential described as the state of enlightenment.

Once we have the idea of working with the appearances of life as the basis of our path in this bardo, then we look more closely at appearances themselves. Whether we are looking at sights or sounds, feelings or thoughts, we will see that appearances are momentary and changeable. They are produced by multiple causes and influenced by a numberless variety of conditions, which themselves are fleeting, produced and influenced by yet other causes and conditions. Moreover, the myriad appearances that make up our world arise unceasingly.

This is the dance of appearances. Mind is dancing with phenomena in the field of the senses. How we respond to and engage with these physical, psychological and emotional phenomena that comprise the objects in our environment in one moment conditions our experience, for better or worse, in the next moment, and the next. All of this is the momentum of karma, or, more precisely, our individual and collective karmic patterns. Karma is the linked chain of cause and effect: the seed that produces the flower that produces the seed, and so on. There are two sides of appearance: the subject side that is the perceiving aspect, and the object side that is the perceived aspect.

The notion of appearance is relevant to our experiences in all six bardos. In the death and after-death stages, the appearances of mind continue to arise and dissolve, and their expression is linked closely to our insight into their actual nature. It is in the natural bardo of this life—while we have the benefit of a precious human birth and the physical support of a body—that we have the best opportunity to work with our minds and bring the appearances of this life onto the path of enlightenment. Whether those appearances are positive or negative, we need to take full advantage of our situation to further develop our mindfulness, awareness and stability of mind.

To the degree that we can accomplish this, we will possess the equanimity and strength of mind that allow us to reflect with awareness on whatever appearances arise for us without reacting to them in our repetitive, habitual way. Our thoughts and emotions will not instantly propel us into negative states of mind and actions. Developing this quality of calmness, this ability to pacify disturbed or agitated mind states, is not only immediately beneficial in the bardo of this life—it is also extremely beneficial during the bardos after death.

PURE AND IMPURE APPEARANCES

Appearances are said to be of two types: pure appearances and impure appearances. "Pure appearance" refers to the perception of realized beings who have fully recognized the nature of mind as clear, luminous emptiness. When such beings look at the world, they do not see solidly existing phenomena that are separate from the nature of mind. They see and appreciate the dance of appearances as the luminous display of pure awareness. Therefore, they do not fixate on appearances or cling to them as real, and their interactions with them are free from any trace of attachment.

"Impure appearance" refers to the perception of ordinary beings who mistakenly see relative appearances as existing in a manner that is distinctly separate from mind. Therefore, due to their habitual tendencies, their experience of appearances is confused and their interactions with dualistic phenomena are bound up with fixation and clinging. Thus, there are two types of experience of the bardo of this life: one for those who directly perceive the true nature of mind and reality, and one for those who mistakenly perceive a solidly existing, "external" world.

When we are mistaken about the nature of reality, it is difficult to discover how to see beyond our normal dualistic perspective. Our everyday experiences reinforce our conventional perception. Fundamentally, we feel that we exist as a single, continuous and permanent self, and we naturally develop great attachment to that idea. That is called the development of ego and ego-clinging. In addition, we develop a secondary level of clinging when we begin to attribute further qualities to this self. We are not just "me" but we are also the "me" who is smart or handsome or funny. Or we may use other labels like rich or poor, artistic or athletic. Then we need to remind ourselves that we are a Buddhist, or a Republican, or a NASA scientist. The story only gets more interesting and more solid. We identify ourselves using social, philosophical, spiritual, scientific and political labels, and each of those has further elaborations.

There is an endless process of imputation. We label ourselves and then we label the whole world around us. On that basis, our attachment to self deepens and our relationship to others becomes very interesting. We make friends and enemies. We develop values and belief systems, and fall into camps. We may feel the need to improve this self, based on all the competition. We need to find a better job and become more successful. When we have achieved that, we want to be more powerful, famous, and, of course, richer. When we have a billion dollars, then we will soon need a trillion. It is endless.

Underlying all of our experience in the bardo of this life is a fundamental level of ignorance that simply does not see the way things are. The ignorant aspect of the basic mind incorrectly perceives the self and outer phenomena to be real—to inherently exist when they do not. This is also called "false imagination." Due to this, the appearances of samsara arise and we engage in the action of duality between subject and object. Some things are adopted or accepted, and we experience attachment towards them; other things are abandoned or rejected, and we experience aversion towards them.

This is the nature of samsaric existence, which is simply a way of saying that the sensory world around us, as well as our emotional world and our intellectual world, are all seen, experienced, and thought of in a superficial way. We do not see their deeper truth, their profound nature, which is emptiness. We do not recognize the true nature of all appearances—all phenomena—to be empty of inherent existence on the ultimate level, while continuing to appear on the relative level. We do not recognize the union, or inseparability, of appearance and emptiness.

As a result of these misconceptions about appearances, we give rise and are subject to intense states of suffering, called *kleshas*. "Klesha" is translated as "afflicted mind," or "disturbing mind," and in general this term refers to our ordinary, confused experience of the emotions. However, "klesha" includes not only the emotions, but also the basic cause of suffering, which is ignorance. In Buddhist literature, there are three root kleshas: passion, aggression and ignorance. They are regarded as the "three poisons," or the three roots of afflicted mind. The kleshas also include the emotions of jealousy and pride, as well as any other emotion or combination thereof that we might experience. Such afflicted mental states are seen as destructive from the point of view of the spiritual journey. They obscure the natural clarity of mind and are the cause of many unskillful actions. Thus, when the emotions are unattended by mindfulness and awareness, they are regarded as kleshas—as impure or defiled mental states that always increase our suffering and bring more pain and devastation into our lives.

Essentially, however, there is no difference between pure and impure appearances, because the nature of all appearances is the same—clear, luminous emptiness. Labels do not affect the absolute nature of mind. From a relative perspective, though, the perception of difference is disastrous. It is the beginning of our loss of sanity. Because the appearances that arise before us are believed to be separate, we approach them from the perspective of gain and loss, or hope and fear. Our experience of the world becomes characterized by struggle and doubt. Finally, this state of persistent suffering becomes our normal condition. This is the state of affairs for ordinary beings in the natural bardo of this life. However, we have the opportunity to transform our confusion about appearances by bringing the experiencer—the mind—to the path of enlightenment. When we look directly at our confusion with mindfulness and awareness, we begin to see through that confusion to mind's primordially pure, awake nature.

Finally, it is said that those who have a strong connection from the past with the wisdom of the spiritual path will naturally connect with it after they are born and will develop that connection throughout their lives, fulfilling their potential for profound realization. There are many masters whose lives exemplify this profound connection, none more so than the great master Padmasambhava, transmitter of this cycle of bardo teachings. Still others who have a genuine connection to the practice of dharma may come to sudden glimpses of realization. They may spontaneously experience the world as appearance-emptiness—like the moon's reflection on water. At that moment, their ordinary perception of the world is transformed into pure appearance.

Embodied Mind

Right now, you may be at home, sitting comfortably in your apartment. If you live in San Francisco, perhaps you are looking out the window enjoying your view of Golden Gate Bridge. However, though your body is in a particular location, your mind might be somewhere else. You could be thinking of all the work piled up on your desk at your office, the new restaurant opening up just down the block, or going on pilgrimage in India. Suppose you had the thought, "I haven't seen my old friend from college in a long time. I wonder what she is doing?" While you are in the bardo of this life, that is just a mundane thought. When the thought dissolves, you are still sitting in the same chair. However, suppose you had that same thought and then found yourself actually sitting in your friend's living room?

And what if in the next moment you found yourself in whatever place came to mind with your next thought—your office, your local bistro or the banks of the Ganges River?

In the bardos after death, this kind of spontaneous movement is not pure fantasy or speculation. Sudden shifts of consciousness bring about corresponding shifts in the environment. When our mind jumps from one thought to the next, we go along with it. Why? At that time there is no physical body to anchor the mind. There is only the mind, only the consciousness, which is traveling and manifesting in a way that is difficult to control. Even in this life, if we have no method for working with our thoughts and emotions, then our mind runs wild. After death, it becomes even wilder.

It is important to remember that although our mind is presently connected to this body, it is only a temporary guest. While we have this bodily shelter, we feel somewhat grounded. Our body stabilizes our mind; it provides a fixed reference point. When our mind flies off, no matter how often or far it goes, it comes back to this body, just as a bird returns to a ship in the middle of an ocean. The bird may fly off for a while but it will always return; it has nowhere else to go. In all the other bardos, there is no anchor to hold our minds stable—apart from the equanimity of mind we have developed previously through meditation practice.

Such instability can be a fearful experience, which is compounded by the arising of our emotions. We are not only groundless, but also we react to our shifting environment with fluctuating emotions. Now we feel anger, now jealousy, now we are blissful. Our emotions manifest as vividly as our perceptions and thoughts. However, by developing the power of a stable mind, we naturally transcend all our fears. This is so because the after-death state is an experience of mind, and when we have full control of our mind, there is nothing more to fear. We know how our mind is going to react. We know how it is going to manifest under pressure. We know that we will remain calm, clear and focused.

Right now, we have the benefit of a human birth and a body that supports our mind. This birth becomes a "precious human birth" when we have the advantage of conditions that support the development of spiritual understanding and bring an increase of the qualities of love, compassion and altruism. Therefore it is important to take full advantage of our situation by developing further mindfulness, awareness and meditative stability. If we are calm and clear, then not only can we realize the nature of mind, but we can also clearly plan our days, our lives and our rebirths very precisely. Since we like to make plans, this is an opportunity to make a clear plan—a definitive rather than provisional plan. If we lack control of our mind, then all the plans that we make are provisional. We have no idea how they will work out. However, if we have control of our mind— our emotions and the whole environment of our mental states—then we can make a definitive plan, not only for the bardo of this life, but beyond. Whatever conditions we meet become harmonious and favorable. The experiences of all six bardos become powerful circumstances for us to further the realization of mind's nature.

The Three Stages of the Path

When we enter a genuine spiritual path, our purpose is to overcome our bewilderment and confusion and to discover who we really are. So long as we do not know ourselves fully, there is an underlying sense of suffering. Yet the desire to know oneself deeply and truly, regardless of where our path might lead, is itself an expression of that which we seek—the wisdom and compassion of mind's true nature.

From the perspective of the Buddhist teachings, the most effective means for following such a path is through the development of knowledge, or *prajna*. In a general sense, prajna is both intelligence, the sharpness of our awareness, and the knowledge or understanding that results when we cultivate our intelligence. Further, prajna is of two types: mundane and transcendental. Mundane prajna relates to our knowledge and understanding of the relative world. It may be scholarly knowledge or simply the sharp mind that sees precisely how things work. Transcendental prajna is "higher" knowledge. It is the penetrating insight that cuts through all confusion and sees directly mind's ultimate nature—its clear, lucid emptiness. In its perfected state, higher prajna is synonymous with wisdom. The teachings upon which this path is based constitute the skillful methods by which we cultivate the knowledge, or *prajna,* that will bring our search to fruition.[5]

On this path we make two discoveries: one is the discovery of the true nature of our mind, and the other is the discovery of that which obstructs us from seeing this true nature. That is the reality of the relative world. Every discovery is preceded by a preliminary finding: the discovery of the obstacles that have prevented us from seeing what has been there all along. Wisdom here is learning how we can overcome these obstacles and realize our innate potential, the basic state of our own mind and heart that is fundamentally pure and awake, that is already free from all defilements. That basic potential in Buddhism is called "buddha nature."

The Buddhist path, with its emphasis on knowledge and the fulfillment of our potential for enlightenment, can therefore be said to be both a science of mind and a philosophy of life. It is not a religion in the conventional sense. It does not attribute divinity or supreme power to any external being or force. Rather, it is a way of viewing our existence that brings meaning into our lives and benefit to the world as we become more and more capable of manifesting the compassionate activity that is inseparably linked to wisdom.

How do we make these discoveries and manifest our potential? We bring the appearances of the natural bardo of this life onto the path of enlightenment by engaging in the three-stage process of study, contemplation and meditation. These are the three stages of the spiritual path from which the three prajnas develop. From the process of hearing or studying the dharma, the *prajna of understanding* arises. From the process of contemplation or reflecting on the dharma, the *prajna of experience* arises. From the process of naturally abiding meditation, the *prajna of realization* arises. These three stages are taught in the songs, or yogic instructions, of the great yogi Milarepa. They describe the living process by which we absorb the essence of dharma and transform our experience.

There are a number of practices, both formal and informal, that support the development of the three prajnas and that work directly to penetrate our disturbing emotions and ego-clinging in the natural bardo of this life. The stage of study involves activities such as listening to teachings, attending classes and the reading and discussion of texts. In this stage, we initially develop a conceptual understanding of mind's ultimate nature, as well as its relative appearances—our confused thoughts and disturbing emotions. We hear how these appearances cloud the mind and conceal that nature from our direct perception. Furthermore, we study cause and effect to learn theoretically how these delusive appearances are produced and how they are pacified.

The stage of contemplation consists of training in analytical meditation, in which we begin to work directly with relative appearances. By applying our intellect to an examination of mind, we learn to see those appearances with greater precision and clarity. This is the point in our path where we begin to penetrate the solidity of our thoughts and emotions and glimpse the pure nature of mind.

Finally, in the stage of meditation, we let go of our conceptual examination and simply rest our mind in a state of one-pointed meditative concentration, or *samadhi*. At this time, we experience a cessation of our usual agitated state of mind and can rest peacefully in the present moment. This is the beginning of our journey of meditation, which leads finally to the culmination of transcendental knowledge—the complete realization of the nature of mind. This stage is accomplished in two phases. First one trains in the preliminary practices known as the "four foundations," and then one engages in the actual practice of calm abiding, or *shamatha*, meditation.

As we progress through the three stages, we gain an ever-deepening knowledge of the full reality of mind.

The Stage of Study

In the first stage of listening to and studying the dharma, we develop the prajna of understanding. Our objective is to develop a clear conceptual understanding of the entire spiritual journey—its basis, its paths and stages and its final result. We begin by studying the basic principles of dharma in general and by familiarizing ourselves with the bardo teachings in particular. While we usually think of these activities as very easy, as something we have been doing for years, as an aspect of our training, listening and studying are regarded as practice in the same way that meditation is practice.

Hearing in this context refers to both listening to oral teachings and studying written texts. Listening to the dharma is regarded as an art or skill that develops the prajna of understanding through the application of mindfulness. As a practice, it is important to begin this activity with a sense of pure intention—the heartfelt wish that all beings, yourself and others, will benefit from your study. That is how to begin. Next, it is essential to hear the teachings with a nonjudgmental mind. This means that you are truly trying to understand what you are hearing. Your mind is not filled with your own opinions and preconceptions. The final instruction for developing this prajna is to listen with a one-pointed mind, a state of attentiveness that is free from distraction. Beyond this, it is important to simply appreciate the opportunity you have in a genuine way, so that the teaching touches your heart.

The result of applying these instructions to the activity of study is that it becomes a discipline that is inseparable from meditation. Just as it does in meditation practice, your mind becomes calm and focused, which naturally produces a state of mental clarity. Consequently, your understanding becomes very clear. At this stage, your knowledge is still conceptual. When you hear or read the words of the dharma, you understand them with conceptual mind. But that conceptual mind has a quality of clarity; it is not just your confused thoughts. Therefore, that mind has a greater power of insight.

At this point, we have the ability to discern what is called "right understanding," or "right view," which broadly refers to seeing within our own experience the basic truths of suffering, impermanence and egolessness, as well as the significance of ethical conduct. We can see these truths in the display of thoughts and emotions that continually arise. Further, we can recognize thoughts, emotions and actions as being negative or positive. All of these things first become clear through developing a clear conceptual understanding through listening to and studying various teachings.

Developing the prajna of understanding is therefore the first step in learning to work with our mind and its obstacles, which in turn becomes the means for discovering the heart of our own buddhahood, or wakefulness.

Milarepa said that our knowledge at this point is like a patch sewn over a hole in our clothes. Even though the patch can cover the hole, it never becomes one with the fabric. It always remains a foreign substance, a patch that can fall off at any time. In the same way, at this stage, the knowledge that we have accumulated so far is not one with our mindstream. Whenever doubts arise, we can apply an intellectual patch, but that does not really solve our problems or heal our suffering. Consequently, although the prajna of understanding is very beneficial, it is not final or absolute.

The Stage of Contemplation

In the second stage, contemplation of the dharma, we develop the prajna of experience, the insight that arises when we reflect deeply on the knowledge we have acquired through our formal studies. That knowledge needs to be processed and internalized through the practice of contemplation. In this way, we become one with our intellectual understanding; we are no longer frozen in theory. Our knowledge becomes part of our being.

The method taught for this stage is called "analytical meditation." Although it is termed "meditation," it is regarded as contemplation because it is a method of training that actively engages the intellect and conceptual mind. This form of practice involves the methodical and precise analysis, in a formal meditation session, of a particular topic or issue you have studied, and which interests you. There are many suitable areas of investigation. However, although there is a certain structure or formality to such contemplations, the exercise is fundamentally very personal. When you contemplate the words of a teaching on suffering, for example, you might analyze the meaning of each word, as well as the meaning of an entire verse. But you carry out your analysis in your own words, on your own terms, from the point of view of how you know and relate to suffering.

In this way, your understanding is clarified and you arrive at a deeper meaning. The knowledge you began with expands and opens as you make an experiential connection to the teachings on suffering. Their meaning becomes a living experience and your knowledge of it goes beyond the purely conceptual.

This second stage is what we seem to be missing in the West. We have a great deal of study and also of meditation, but we have no contemplation in the middle. That is why we have so much trouble joining daily life with meditation. Contemplation is the bridge between our conceptual understanding and everyday experience and the nonconceptual experience of meditation. It is like the lab that goes along with our coursework in college. First we read our books and go to classes. Then we go into the laboratory, where we get hands-on experience by conducting experiments and observing and testing the results. In this way, our experience becomes fuller and more complete. The knowledge we develop is not limited just to our "head." We experience greater synchronization of body, speech and mind—physical being, emotions and cognition—working together harmoniously.

Milarepa said that the prajna of experience is like the mist that appears in the early morning. It looks so solid and so real, but later in the day, when the sun has risen, the mist simply disappears. Likewise, experiences of contemplation are temporary. They come and go like the morning mist. At this stage, we are developing genuine experience, but it has not yet developed into complete realization or the full state of wisdom.

Our experiences in contemplation may be very powerful and may seem to be experiences of realization; however, we should not mistake them for actual realization. For example, we may have experiences of emptiness, bliss or nonthought. When such an experience occurs, it may feel quite substantial and have a powerful impact on us. We may believe that we have achieved an enduring insight; but then it is completely gone—like mist that suddenly disappears from sight. This type of fluctuating experience is common while we are on the path and is a sign that it is mere experience rather than genuine realization. This indicates that it is necessary for us to go on to the next stage, which develops the prajna of meditation.

PRACTICES FOR THE STAGE OF CONTEMPLATION

Once we have developed our theoretical understanding of the path by listening to and studying the basic principles of the dharma, we can engage in the analytical meditation practices taught for the stage of contemplation. In order to identify those appearances that obstruct or obscure our recognition of the nature of mind, it is necessary to look at our lives. This requires something more than mere daydreaming. We need to engage in a process of focused reflection and analysis in order to develop an awareness of our habitual emotional and psychological patterns. While we are focusing our attention here on the details of this life, we are at the same time distinguishing those patterns of mind that will impact us most as we face our death and undergo the experiences leading to rebirth.

Mindful Life Reflection

Analytical meditation includes the formal methods of analysis conducted within meditation sessions as well as more informal reflections that are practiced when we are off the cushion, so to speak. Mindful life reflection is practice that can be done more informally, at the end of each day, before going to sleep. However, to be effective, it must be done with a clear intention and with mindfulness.

To begin this practice, we can start by reflecting on a single day. For example, in the evening, we review the day, recalling what we have done from morning until the present moment. We reflect on the thoughts we have had and on any incidents that took place in the course of everyday events and activities: "I got up early, did this and that, and then I drove to work. I remember I got really angry when someone cut me off at an intersection." We bring this type of incident to mind and then we reflect on it. We begin by looking at the major incidents and then, slowly, we begin to examine the minute details. We can start by reflecting on today and then we can include yesterday and then the day before. Again, it is important to go slowly, beginning with major incidents and then going into greater detail.

Another approach is to review a whole week. If we have had any major emotional turmoil during the week, then we reflect on those major incidents first. We spend time with these shorter timeframes and gradually come to reflect on our entire life up to the present. It is important to identify major life patterns—those behaviors that have been repeated again and again. We may see that our lives are like that of the main character in the movie *Groundhog Day*, who wakes up every morning to the same day and continues to repeat the same mistakes over and over. When we repeat our patterns like that, without any awareness, we may have a feeling of *déjà vu* and wonder, "Haven't I had this experience before?" Yes, we have, and here is the same klesha, the same negative pattern, attacking us yet again. We should look at our whole life experience in order to discover our major difficulty, our greatest suffering and our greatest fear. It is these life patterns that we should look for in our practice of reflection.

Usually, we prefer not to acknowledge these experiences. Whenever a klesha brings us great suffering, we try to sneak away from it. Ordinarily, we are afraid of our emotions. The more intense an emotion becomes, the more fear we feel. However, sneaking away does not help us; the klesha continues to come back. Therefore, it is better to bring these experiences into our analytical meditation and to try to identify which one repeats most often and which one gets most out of our control. Although every klesha arises in every person's mind, there are some we are able to control to a certain degree and others over which we have no control. We seem to just burst inside ourselves and give in to their power. The klesha over which we have the least control is the one we should identify and work with first; then we can apply whatever insights we gain to all of our other habitual tendencies. If all five major kleshas are equally strong for someone, that is good news. That person is very rich, since he or she has a wealth of emotional resources that can be used as a basis for contemplation and meditation. Another person may be a little poorer, having only one klesha.

Analytical Meditation on the Emotions

In order to gain further insight into the workings of our habitual patterns and disturbing emotion, we also bring the raw energy of our emotions— anger, jealousy, passion, attachment, and pride—directly into our formal sessions of analytical meditation.

To begin a session, the instruction is to sit in an erect and comfortable posture and settle your mind. Then you simply watch the coming and going of your thoughts. When an emotion appears, you observe the emotion without stopping it or indulging it. If, for example, it is attachment you are feeling, then bring to mind the person or object toward which the emotion is directed. With an alert and calm mind, allow yourself to feel the attachment rising. Without becoming distracted from the emotion, look at its qualities and feel its energy. Then simply let go of all thoughts of attachment and relax as the emotion dissolves. When you are able to remain present with your attachment and experience it fully, then you get to know it.

It is the same for the intensity of passion, aggression and all our emotions. We meet them once, then again and again, and each time they become a little more familiar to us and a little less disturbing. As a result, our minds become more stable, which helps us gain control of our mental states. Gradually, we can let go of some of our fear—as well as our clinging to our emotions as solidly existing. In the post-meditation state, we continue to practice these kinds of contemplations.

BEFRIENDING INTENSE EMOTIONS

If we do not become familiar with our emotions, then we will always fear them—even more so in the bardos after death. It is like the fear we have of a stranger. When we do not know somebody, we tend to maintain a certain distance from them. We might be willing to have a formal conversation with the stranger, but we do not want to get too deeply involved. We do the same thing with our emotions. We do not really "talk" with them because we do not really know them, and we prefer to maintain that distance in some cases.

For example, if we hear that someone who has just completed a prison sentence has moved into our neighborhood, and we suddenly bump into him on the street, then we are likely to panic. Sometimes we are able to avoid him, but other times we find ourselves in a situation where we cannot. Then we have to face our fear.

In these situations, we often react with prejudice. We think, "This guy is really bad. He scares me—I don't want to talk to him!" However, if we actually did sit down and talk with him, then our experience might be different. We might see this individual as a person going through emotional or mental difficulties and begin to feel that we could help him in some way. Moreover, whatever he shares with us also benefits us. From talking together we learn to recognize emotional perspectives different from our own and we realize how fortunate we are to not be caught up in disturbed mental states such as aggression. We appreciate our precious human birth more. In this sense, we need to learn how to work with "scary" people— anyone who frightens or intimidates us. When we get to know them, when we can talk to them, when we can subdue the suffering of their emotions, we can become friends; and nobody harms anyone. We have more influence and power when we use this approach: the power of love, compassion and clarity of mind.

We have a similar, strong prejudice against emotions, especially anger. Consequently, we tend to segregate emotions instead of integrating them into our experience. We try to ignore them or run away from them, or we just "blow up." Instead, we can make friends with our emotions as we contemplate them and gradually learn more about them. This process is like making a connection with somebody who is a stranger; it is a means of overcoming the separation we feel between "us" and "them." In this case, we are making a deeper connection with our emotions. If we rely on this approach when our emotions come up, we will not want to run and hide. Even as emotions arise, the mind that is becoming unstable will be stabilized through the power of hearing, contemplating and meditating. We will be able to say, "Oh, this is my friend, anger, and I know how to talk to this anger. I know how to subdue it. I know what will free this anger from its suffering."

In this way, we can calm our minds and pacify our emotions. Slowly but surely, we will realize the true nature of our emotions, even our most disturbing emotions, such as anger and jealousy. That nature is the true nature of mind itself: open, luminous wisdom, primordially pure awareness. When we know how to work with our emotions in the bardo of this life, they are no longer obstacles. They become vehicles for our awakening, both now and in the bardos of death.

The Stage of Meditation

In the third stage, meditation, we gradually develop the prajna of realization, the transcendental knowledge that sees directly the true nature of mind and all phenomena. This is the realization that gives birth to egoless compassion—the pure heart of love for all beings. This is also known as *absolute bodhichitta,* the union of compassion and emptiness, in which compassion manifests spontaneously, unconditionally and without bias.

In the Buddhist path, many methods of meditation are taught, but all are essentially included in its two most fundamental practices, *shamatha* and *vipashyana.* We train first in shamatha, which means "calm abiding." Shamatha meditation is a practice that supports the development of a stable, one-pointed concentration, which brings the mind to a state of peace and tranquility. Thus, it is also known as "resting meditation." Our habitual agitation is characterized by restlessness and dissatisfaction. The mindfulness and awareness developed in shamatha meditation illuminate and tame this agitation. Our obsessive concern with past and future are pacified, and we can rest wakefully and at peace in the present.

Once we can rest in a state of nondistraction, we begin training in the practice of vipashyana. Vipashyana means "clear seeing" or "superior seeing." Fundamentally, it consists of methods that bring about the recognition of the nature of mind, and is marked by a sense of openness and spaciousness. Mind's natural clarity becomes more brilliant, and we discover the state of self-existing liberation that is the actual remedy for our suffering and the suffering of others.

According to Milarepa, meditation is not meditating *on* anything; rather, it is simply a process of familiarization—familiarizing ourselves with the nature of our mind. The actual practice of meditation is to go beyond concept and simply rest in the state of nondual experience. The ability to rest in that way comes from contemplation, from analytical meditation, which gradually leads us to the stage of nonconceptual meditation. Thus, meditation is the actual cause that produces the genuine prajna of realization. Milarepa said that true realization is like a clear, open sky, or like vast space that is unchanging. Once you have reached the level of realization, that realization is always the same. It does not come and go like the morning mist.

It is helpful to note that Padmasambhava's comprehensive instructions for meditation differentiate practices that are associated with the natural bardo of this life from those that are linked to the bardo of meditation. What is the basis for this distinction? The bardo of meditation occurs within the natural bardo of this life, and all of our practices are therefore part of our experience of this bardo. However, according to the system of the six bardos, the actual experience of the bardo of meditation occurs when we are not only resting in a state of peace and tranquility, but also resting directly in a state of nonconceptual awareness. The bardo of meditation therefore is associated with the practice of vipashyana.

For the natural bardo of this life, we begin our training in meditation with the foundational practices called the *four common* and *four uncommon preliminaries*. This is the training that prepares us for the main practice of shamatha which follows. In addition, Padmasambhava's instructions include the practice of deity yoga, which is briefly mentioned here and which is presented in detail in the chapter on the bardo of becoming, the bardo with which it is most closely linked.

FOUNDATIONAL PRACTICES: TRAINING AND PURIFICATION

Meditation practice always begins with developing a good foundation. The foundational, or preliminary, practices of the Buddhist path, often referred to as *ngondro,* are the means of both training and purifying one's mindstream. These practices are also the means of bringing the heart of the meditation experience into one's own being. Therefore, they are considered to be profound and important, since without them the main practice will have little meaning, just as a building without a solid foundation will be unstable and of little value.

The *common preliminary* practices consist of the *four reminders.* These are the reflections on (1) precious human birth, (2) impermanence, (3) karma and (4) the shortcomings of samsara. These are reflections that turn our minds away from our attachment to samsaric existence, and towards the practice of dharma. Unless we generate a proper experience of the four reminders, it will be difficult for us to connect with any other experiences on the path.

The four reminders are followed by the *four uncommon preliminaries.* These are (1) refuge and bodhichitta, which purify the coarse level of negative karma of the body; (2) Vajrasattva mantra recitation, which purifies the karma of speech; (3) mandala practice, which is the basis of acquiring the two accumulations of merit and wisdom; and (4) guru yoga practice, which invokes the blessings of the lineage.

The first of the four uncommon preliminaries begins with *taking refuge and generating bodhichitta,* the enlightened attitude or "awakened heart" that genuinely desires to free all living beings from their suffering and lead them to the state of buddhahood. In the general Buddhist path, there is the threefold refuge of Buddha, Dharma and Sangha, known as the Three Jewels. In the Vajrayana path, one practices a sixfold refuge. One goes for refuge to the Three Jewels and the Three Roots: (1) the root of blessings, the guru mandala; (2) the root of accomplishments, the *yidam* or deity mandala; and (3) the root of activities, the *dakini* mandala, which includes *dakas, dakinis,* and *dharmapalas,* or protectors. When we take the sixfold refuge, we are actually entering into the path of the buddhadharma in general and Vajrayana in particular. The six roots are the primary figures displayed in paintings of the "refuge tree," which symbolically represents the qualities of enlightenment—the wisdom, loving-kindness, compassion and activity of teaching the dharma that will bring all beings to the state of liberation.

The second uncommon preliminary is the profound practice of *Vajrasattva*. In order for our path to proceed smoothly toward realization, it is essential to purify our negativities and obscurations, which are obstacles to our practice. Vajrasattva is the first and foremost of all practices for training and purifying one's mindstream. It is known as the king of purification practices. Purification is the process of both exposing the shortcomings or defilements of mind and uncovering its true nature—the clear, transparent and inherent wisdom of our mind.

The third uncommon preliminary is the *mandala offering*. After purifying our negativities, we have to let go of our ego-clinging—our basic attachment and clinging toward the whole universe and its contents, which exist all around us. Therefore, in this practice, we visualize the entire universe and fill it with offerings to the objects of refuge; thus, the mandala offering is the practice of letting go. Since our intention in making these offerings is the accomplishment of enlightenment for the benefit of limitless beings of different capacities, this is the practice that accomplishes the two accumulations: the accumulation of merit and the accumulation of wisdom. Without these accumulations it would be impossible for us to achieve any state of realization, any glimpse of the nature of mind.

The fourth uncommon preliminary is *guru yoga,* which is a method for increasing and enhancing our devotion and our respect. Why is this necessary? In the Vajrayana tradition, the key to our realization is found through the blessings of our gurus, our lineage forefathers and through primordial wisdom itself. This transmission is not possible without opening ourselves fully to our lineage gurus. Opening to the lineage blessings and transmissions is catalyzed by the practice of guru yoga.

These are the traditional foundational practices. Other purification practices include the recitation of liturgies such as the *Heart Sutra,* and the practices of Medicine Buddha.

SETTLING THE MIND: THE THREE POSTURES

Before we begin any meditation practice, it is necessary to familiarize ourselves with the *three postures:* the posture of body, the posture of speech and the posture of mind. These are the instructions of Padmasambhava for working with the three gates of body, speech and mind. Through these three postures, we naturally arrive at a state of resting or quiescence that is conducive to the development of meditation. First, we naturally rest our physical body; then, we naturally rest our speech; and finally, we naturally rest our mind. Within each of these three postures, there are three further aspects: outer, inner and secret. Body, speech and mind are referred to as "gates," as they are the means by which we enter into the meditative state and thereby develop knowledge or understanding of our true nature of mind.

Body Posture

The outer posture of body refers to letting go of all worldly activities of a physical nature. We abide in a state that is free from all mundane activities, such as attending to business or domestic activities. Resting freely while refraining from these external activities is the outer sense of resting.

The inner posture of body refers to resting by refraining from any religious or spiritual activities that involve physical movement, such as prostrations or counting mantras with a *mala*. When we leave all of these activities aside, we settle down, relax further and attain a sense of inner peace or quiescence on the physical level.

The secret posture of body refers to being free from any kind of movement at all. When we sit, regardless for how long—five seconds, five minutes, or one hour—we make an effort to sit completely still, although, practically speaking, we may move from time to time. That is the secret or absolute sense of physical quiescence—being free from any movement of the body.

For the actual practice of meditation, the instruction is to adopt a correct physical posture, such as the seven postures of Vairochana.[6] This instruction emphasizes straightening the body and maintaining an erect posture. This is very important, as our outer, physical posture has a direct and powerful impact on the state of our mind. It serves as a support for our inner subtle body, which consists of the *nadis,* or "channels," *pranas,* or "winds," and *bindus,* or "essences." These are the basic elements of the subtle vajra body. The nadis are the channels or pathways through which the pranas move, and the bindus are the essences of the physical body. The teachings say that if your body is straight, then the *nadis,* or channels—

and in particular, the central channel of your body—will also be straight. Therefore, the core of your body will be straight. If the core or central channel of your body is straight, then the *pranas*, or winds, will function properly or in a straight fashion. If the pranas are functioning properly, then the mind will also function properly. If the mind is functioning properly, then the meditation will also be functioning properly; it will be natural. There will not be any difficulty.

The Sanskrit word *prana*, when translated into Tibetan, is *lüng*. The English equivalent is "wind" or "air." This element is associated with sensation. It is said that the relationship between prana and mind is similar to that between a horse and a rider. Prana is like a horse and mind is like its rider; they travel together through the channels, which are like the roadways of the subtle body. If the horse goes crazy, then the rider has a wild time of it and may even fall off. If the horse remains calm and moves forward in a straight direction, then the rider will also naturally be calm and move forward in a steady and straight direction. In the same way, when the prana is straight, then the mind is also naturally straight. Therefore, maintaining an upright physical posture is a means of facilitating the proper flow of winds through the channels, making it possible for mind to come to rest.

Speech Posture

The outer sense of the speech posture is to be free from all worldly conversation and idle chatter, which tends to increase our confusion. The inner sense of the speech posture is to be free from all religious dialogues or discussions, such as debates. The secret sense is to be free from the recitations of mantras and *sadhana* practices. In short, being free from all such verbal activities is the way to rest naturally in the posture of speech.

Mind Posture

The mind posture in the outer sense is to be free from negative thoughts. When we are trying to calm down and relax our mind, we first need to free ourselves from negative thoughts and emotions, the source of our ordinary confusion. The aim is to remain in a lucid and clear state without engaging in any such mental movements.

The mind posture in its inner sense is to be free as well from any positive thoughts. Even the thought that says "I should do something to benefit all sentient beings. I want to free them all from samsara" is still a thought. We should generate bodhichitta at the beginning of our session, but not while we are meditating. The practice of visualizing deities is also an engagement in positive thoughts. When it comes to meditation, we should be free from all such thoughts.

The posture of mind in its secret sense is to be free from any aspect of thought, regardless of what it is. No matter how appealing or how positive it may appear to be, no matter how profound an insight into the meditation of Mahamudra or the view of Dzogchen, if it is a thought, then we definitely need to try to be free of it. Resting freely in a state free of thought is the secret posture of mind.

When we are free from these three types of movements of mind—outer, inner and secret—we experience the perfect posture of mind, which becomes the perfect ground for developing meditative concentration, or *samadhi,* and meditative experience. In the beginning, establishing the ground is very necessary: the physical ground, the ground of speech and the ground of mind. After that, we begin our meditation.

The Actual Practice:
Padmasambhava's Instructions for Shamatha

Having completed the preliminary practices and settled our body, speech and mind, we next engage in the actual practice of meditation. For the natural bardo of this life, Padmasambhava instructs us to focus primarily on the samadhi of shamatha, the development of a one-pointed and peaceful meditative state. According to the instructions, before we actually engage in meditation, we should first generate the motivation of bodhichitta by thinking, "I am doing this practice not solely for my own benefit but also for the benefit of all sentient beings." While it is important to focus on overcoming our own shortcomings and kleshas, we also expand our aspiration to include others.

After we have aroused bodhichitta, it is also important to develop confidence in our practice right at the beginning. In that very first moment, we awaken our confidence by saying, "I am sitting here in order to realize the nature of mind in this very session." This confidence transcends our regular mode of thinking, the voice in us that says, "I want to achieve enlightenment someday in the future."

In the case of enlightenment, we always think in terms of the future, never the present. We think, "Someday I will become Buddha," but that day is not today. This shows how we lack confidence. We never think that our enlightenment could happen in the session we are doing right now. But how do we know that? It is important to think more positively, which helps us gradually to develop real confidence. So, instead of envisioning some prospect of future liberation, we think, "I want to achieve enlightenment through the realization of the nature of mind in this very session. I want to overcome my disturbing emotions *now*."

SHAMATHA WITH EXTERNAL OBJECT

The first method taught by Padmasambhava for the main practice of meditation in this bardo is *shamatha with external object*. In this method, an external object is used as a focal support for bringing your mind to rest. The focal support may be an ordinary object, such as a pebble or flower, or an object with some spiritual significance, such as a picture or statue of the Buddha. The object should be placed in your line of vision so that your gaze is out yet slightly downward along your nose. Then, with open eyes, direct your attention one-pointedly to the focal object. The process of focusing your eye consciousness on a particular object is, at the same time, the process of withdrawing that consciousness from engagement with other visual objects. In this way, you mix your mind with the visual perception of the object and bring your mind to rest.

When we place our minds with open eyes on an external support like this, we can experience greater mental clarity than we might using other methods of shamatha. For example, when we practice shamatha that focuses on the breath, our mind can become vague or "wooly" at some point. When we focus on an external object, however, the clarity of our mind is more apparent and distinct; it becomes sparkling and vivid. At the same time, it is important not to overemphasize our visual focus. Our gaze should be focused yet relaxed. We look at the focal object in the same way that we usually look at any object. The technique should not cause stress. If it becomes stressful, it is not going to be beneficial. The object on which we focus is just a reference point, and the whole point is simply to not lose that focus.

When you finish a session of shamatha, it is important not to arise too quickly from the meditative state into postmeditation. Postmeditation is simply the period of time that follows your meditation practice. You should allow for some period of transition before moving into other activities. We have a tendency to think, "OK, I'm done. What's next? What's on my list?" We jump into the next thing right away. Instead, you should move gradually into your next project, maintaining some mindfulness and awareness. That is the key to bringing meditative stability and awareness into our postmeditation experiences.

Shamatha with White Bindu Visualization

Padmasambhava also provides instructions for other methods of shamatha. One of these is to visualize a small white *bindu*, or sphere of light, at your forehead between the eyebrows. This bindu is bright and shining, luminous yet empty. It is not a solid physical object; rather, it is pure, transparent light like a shimmering rainbow. Adopting the same physical posture and eye gaze as when practicing shamatha with an external object, visualize this pure, clear light between your eyebrows, and rest your mind freely on that, letting go of all discursive thought. The bindu simply serves as a reference point so that your mind does not wander. The key point of this practice is to allow your mind to be completely relaxed and natural—or as natural as possible—while maintaining an undistracted focus on the object.

Shamatha with Red Bindu Visualization

Another method is to visualize your body as a transparent, hollow form, as clear and empty as a crystal ball. This is similar to the way the pure, lucid forms of deities are visualized. Inside of this particularly pure form of your body, you visualize a red bindu at your heart center. The term "heart center" refers not to the actual heart itself but to the area in which the heart sits—the upper-middle region of the body. Visualize there a red bindu about the size of a candle flame. It is also visualized in the form of a flame of light, luminous and transparent. Although it is red, it is tinged with blue, like the hot outer core of a candle flame. The color blue helps to convey the sense of its transparency and emptiness. The bindu is positioned in the very middle of the heart center, touching neither the front nor back of your body. Focus your mind on that red-blue, flamelike bindu, resting naturally without distraction. If thoughts arise, simply bring your mind back to that focus. Again, do not create tension or stress in your practice by applying too much effort. Remain relaxed and natural.

These teachings set out three basic methods for shamatha meditation with object that you can try in your sitting sessions. Moreover, if you are practicing the tantric visualizations that are integral to the sadhanas of yidam deities, such as Chenrezig, Amitabha, Vajrasattva or Vajrayogini, then you are also practicing shamatha with object, and the instructions are the same. Later in the Vajrayana practices, methods involving subtle body visualizations become particularly important.

Shamatha without Object

We can also practice shamatha meditation without a focal object. Padmasambhava gives instructions for two such methods. Both are done while sitting in the seven postures of Vairochana.

In the first method, you look straight into space with your eyes wide open and your gaze turned slightly upward. Without bringing anything before your mind as an object, you simply rest within that experience of space in a very relaxed and easygoing manner. On the one hand, there is a sense of focusing on the space before you, but on the other, there is no particular spot on which you are focusing. Your gaze is like space itself—wide and spacious. At this point, since there is no focal object, it is very easy to lose your mindfulness and become distracted by whatever is happening in the space. Mind can become very wild and agitated or very dull, torpid and listless. It can go either way. You can begin to feel heavy or kind of spaced-out. When any of these states occur, it is helpful to intensify your mind and increase your concentration. Make a fresh start and concentrate again on establishing your focus. After that, simply rest and let go.

In the second method of shamatha without object, you lower your gaze a bit so that you are looking slightly downward, rather than upward, into space. Again, there is no particular object upon which you are focusing; for example, you are not looking at the floor, but only into space. You are simply experiencing space from another angle—from the perspective of your downward eye gaze. At the same time, you should relax your mind.

The main difference between the two methods is how you work with your eyes. In the first method, there is more emphasis on the aspect of focusing, while in the second method, there is slightly more emphasis on relaxing your mind. Without bringing anything into your mind as an object of focus, simply experience space and bring it to your attention.

Nonmeditation

These two methods of shamatha meditation without object have a quality of *nonmeditation*, which is the actual meditation in both Mahamudra and Dzogchen. When we are practicing, if we are holding tightly to some focal object and we have the thought, "I am meditating," then we are not meditating at all. Instead, we are having a perception of an object and the thought of meditation. Our minds are not free because we are holding on to something. We are not abiding in a state of calmness and clarity. There is a sense of subtle distraction when we are thinking, "I am meditating…I am meditating." This is why it is said in these instructions that the actual meditation is nonmeditation.

When we are sitting, it is essential to be free from the thought of meditation. We have to be free even from thoughts about how well our meditation is going or about the methods we are using. We often think, "How am I doing?" or "Is this the right posture? Is this the wrong focus?" All of these are discursive thoughts. They are not meditation. Being free from such thoughts and simply resting in space is the beginning of nonmeditation.

Many Short Sessions

In the natural bardo of this life, it is important to establish a rhythm for your practice and to maintain some regularity. The most effective practice is daily practice. Practicing only occasionally is still helpful, although not as effective. When you practice every day—whether for ten minutes or an hour—there is a sense of continuity or uninterrupted flow to the process of familiarizing yourself with your mind and working with your mind to develop a more positive environment. Through consistent practice, you become less subject to negative emotions and can exert more conscious choice with regard to your actions. You do not immediately react to situations but can view them with a stable, clear mind. The power of such mindfulness and awareness has a strong effect on your experience of the bardos of dying and after death. In this way, consistent practice is a key to working with the last three bardos: the painful bardo of dying, the luminous bardo of dharmata and the karmic bardo of becoming.

Padmasambhava's instructions tell us to keep our shamatha sessions short but to repeat them again and again. This means that within one session you may do many short sessions. A "session" is the period in which you are practicing a specific technique and closely following the instructions for that method. To take a break between sessions simply means that you let go of the technique and rest your mind for a short while. For example, you may rest your mind on your breath or simply rest your mind freely. It does not matter if thoughts arise; simply try to relax. Then return to the technique. This process may be repeated several times within a session. Taking a break does *not* mean that you get up every five minutes, and then sit again.

It is said that by keeping the sessions short, your meditation is freed from the two primary obstacles of meditation: wildness and dullness. If your sessions are long, without any break, then you are more susceptible to distraction. At one point, you may become agitated and restless, and at another point, you may feel sleepy or your mental state may become very vague and unclear. In either case, you may feel very irritated with your practice and lose your motivation. To leave your practice while feeling this kind of irritation or dullness is considered to be a negative way to end a session. It will hinder you from returning to sit again. Instead, it is important to do short sessions, full of enthusiasm and energy. This will facilitate your practice and help move you toward an authentic experience of nonconceptual meditation.

There are many methods taught that lead toward the realization of the nature of mind. The practice of shamatha is generally practiced first and for some time before one takes on another method as a main practice. Once you have developed a clear and stable shamatha, then you may choose to focus on another method, such as deity yoga, to further develop and quicken your realization.

DEITY YOGA

Deity yoga meditation is a way of transforming our usual clinging to ourselves as ordinary, confused beings into confidence, or pride, in our own basic nature as fully awakened and existing in the form of the ultimate buddha, or ultimate deity. According to Padmasambhava, for the natural bardo of this life, the deity yoga practices of the Vajrayana tradition are among the most important methods we have for transforming our emotions and realizing the nature of mind. Through this training, we realize the profound view of the union of appearance-emptiness, which counteracts our clinging to true existence, or taking things to be solid and real. We train ourselves to experience these vivid appearances of mind as sharply and precisely as we can, and to realize them as manifestations or the play of the ever-present clarity of mind.

Deity yoga meditation includes visualization practices such as Amitabha and Vajrasattva. When we practice these visualizations, we are working directly with the process of bringing the appearances of this life onto the path of enlightenment. We are transforming impure, mundane appearances into pure appearances.

This training is extremely important because whatever appearances we experience here in this life or in the life after death arise solely from our minds. There is nothing that exists in a substantial and real way outside the mind. The way that we define any object, as well as our experience of it, is simply our mind's projection. Whether fearful or blissful, our experiences arise from our mind. Whatever after-death experiences we may have, they are also simply projections of our mind. If we can transcend our confusion through understanding the nature and qualities of mind, then our experience of all appearances becomes very workable.

Deity yoga practices are particularly associated with our experiences during the bardo of becoming, the sixth bardo. If we have trained in deity yoga practice during this life, then, at the time of our impending rebirth into another samsaric existence, we will be able to arise in the form of a deity and establish our environment as a sacred mandala. If we can do this with full confidence, then we will attain liberation; if we do not attain liberation, then we will at least be ensured of an auspicious rebirth.[7]

Deity yoga also represents a Vajrayana approach to shamatha and vipashyana. The Vajrayana method consists of training in two aspects known as the "creation" and "completion stage" practices. The creation stage, in which we generate a clear visualization of a particular deity, is the shamatha aspect. The completion stage, in which that visualization is dissolved, is the vipashyana aspect. Shamatha and vipashyana practices are taught as well in the traditions of Mahamudra and Dzogchen.

Here we can see that shamatha and vipashyana are not merely beginner's practices; they are the most advanced practices for working with the appearances of this life. By using them in their myriad forms, we bring whatever we experience—from our sense perceptions to our thoughts and emotions—to the path. While at first it is necessary to exert some effort to develop our faculty of mindfulness, later we will discover that our mindfulness automatically returns to us. It becomes progressively more continuous. That mindfulness will persist even through the bardo of dying and in the bardos after death. At those times, we will also have a clear, precise and stable awareness of our present experience. When the opportunity for enlightenment arises, we will be prepared to take advantage of it; at the very least, we will have some degree of control over our bardo journey and our next rebirth.

Setting a Specific Intention for Our Practice

We should think about how we can make the best use of our practice so that we get the most out of it in the short time we have in this life. We do not have the leisure of wasting our time here by delaying the benefits of our practice. We have to use these situations as effectively as we can.

Before you begin any practice, first think very carefully about your motivation. When we are engaged in the threefold process of study, contemplation and meditation, we should be very specific, very clear about why we are doing it. We should remind ourselves, "I am doing this to transcend my negative emotions and my ego-clinging." This is a general example of a specific intention. However, to be more precise, we need to consider the unique make-up of our own individual kleshas. Once we have identified our strongest emotion, then we can focus on the practices that will alleviate it. We begin with whichever emotion is strongest for us and then we move on to the next strongest, followed by the next, and so on.

It is important for us to prioritize our practice in this way. We have to keep our intention very clear in all three phases—in our study, in our contemplation and in our meditation. During shamatha or other practices, when thoughts come up, we recall that our purpose is to overcome our disturbing emotions and kleshas. We have to have a sense of willpower or determination in our minds. In order for the remedy to work, we must tell ourselves, "Yes, I am going to transcend this anger. I am going to work with it." Otherwise, if we do not have a clear idea, if we simply sit there with an indefinite or vague intention, then the effect also will be vague. We may have sat for one hour and although that time will not have been wasted, because it was not directed in an intentional way, the experience will not be so sharp, to the point or effective.

It is important for us to confront our disturbing emotions and ego-clinging as directly as we can. Our practice has to be more sharply focused than, for example, a general awareness practice. It is said that when our practice is directed with specific intention, the effect is certain; and when it is not, the effect is correspondingly vague. It is similar to the difference between a direct and indirect antidote. An example of an indirect antidote would be informing a hungry person where a grocery store is located; a direct antidote would be like offering that person a bowl of soup on the spot. The suffering of their hunger is immediately alleviated. When we do not focus sharply, our practice becomes an antidote that indirectly helps, whereas when we focus very clearly it becomes an antidote that produces a direct effect.

Working directly and effectively with our disturbing emotions and deeply rooted ego-clinging is like shooting an arrow. Before we shoot an arrow, we first need to identify our intended target. Only then will the arrow be able to strike it. We identify our target through contemplation and through analytical meditation. When we are looking for our target, we do not simply analyze external appearances—forms, sounds, smells, tastes and tactile objects. Instead, we analyze our mind first. We look at our mind and identify our dominant emotion as accurately as possible— that is our target. Our arrows are the antidotes to our ego-clinging and disturbing emotion: our practices of hearing, contemplating and meditating.

At the end of each practice session, we dedicate the merit. As altruistic practitioners, we say, "May I and all sentient beings who have trouble with this particular klesha be able to overcome it and thereby free ourselves from this fear and suffering." Furthermore, we should also dedicate all of our postmeditation practices for that same purpose.

Although maintaining a daily practice may help us to develop a good tendency or habit, our practice can become mechanical and mindless without proper and mindful motivation. We get up in the morning, do our sitting practice, go to work, return home and sit again. On the other hand, when we are clear about the methods, when our motivation is genuine and fresh, and when we have reaffirmed our purpose, then our practice becomes like the well-shot arrow that effectively hits the mark.

For Only So Long

The bardo of this life does not last forever. We know that, like a guest in a hotel, our mind is only temporarily sheltered in this body. As we face the challenges of this life and the impending challenges of the bardos to come, how does engaging in the three-stage process of study, contemplation and meditation help us? By applying ourselves to these three, we acquire the skills to stabilize our mind and we develop actual insight into how our mind functions. First we gain an understanding of the nature of mind; then, we experience that nature; and finally, we arrive at the ultimate benefit, which is fully realizing that nature.

When we practice these stages of the path, it is like accumulating the exact things we will need to take with us on our trip. When we are ready to pack our suitcase, we will have what we need without looking further. We will not have to go out at the last minute and buy a map or a guidebook. We will not have to worry about whether we are forgetting something crucial.

We have knowledge and experience that has blossomed into realization; therefore we can handle any situation. We have confidence in ourselves, in the teachings, and the guidance of our lineage teachers. At this point, we can let go of all our doubt and hesitation. We can simply relax and be who we are, wherever we are, with the message of Padmasambhava firmly in our hearts.

A detailed discussion of the confusion of the natural bardo of this life would be unlimited and endless. It would necessarily include not only a description of our confusion as individuals, but also a description of the general confusion of all six realms of samsaric existence.[8] In short, however, this presentation has focused on the most significant elements of this bardo: the definition, or how it is characterized; the experience, or how both realized and ordinary beings perceive and interact with the appearances of this life; and the main instructions for practice, or the three trainings of study, contemplation and meditation as the means for transforming the experiences of this bardo into means for enlightenment. More particularly, Padmasambhava teaches that the main practices for this bardo consist of the four foundational practices and shamatha meditation.

In addition to formal meditation, it is important to maintain a sense of mindfulness in the postmeditation state. In some ways, it is easy for us to relate with postmeditation since we are always out there in the world, busily engaging in a variety of activities involving body and speech. When we apply a little mindfulness to these activities, they become practice. If we can add a little awareness, too, then our practice becomes even stronger. We can see that mindfulness and awareness are indispensable in this life. If in this bardo we dwell in mindfulness and awareness, then this birth and the experiences of this life become very useful and positive conditions. Formal sitting meditation helps us to cultivate these qualities in daily life, which in turn helps our meditation to be stable and continuous. If we are capable of being mindful, alert and aware in the postmeditation state, then that will add fuel to the fire of our meditation. These two—meditation and postmeditation—go hand in hand; they are mutually reinforcing.

If we fail to make good use of this lifetime, then we have missed a priceless opportunity. It will be very difficult to acquire such an opportunity again. The teachings of all schools of Buddhism state that once we have attained this precious human birth, if we can use it properly, then it becomes a very powerful basis for achieving something greater, enlightenment—the state of utter purity and full awakening that signals the end to our interminable cycling through the bardos of samsaric existence.

Waking the Dreamer
The Bardo of Dream

3

WITHIN THE NATURAL BARDO of this life, we experience a rhythm of waking and sleeping. Each day, our mind slips from the state of waking consciousness into the state of sleep, and from sleep into dream. While we are in this intermediate state, we are either completely unconscious or only dimly aware of floating through visionary worlds where we have little or no control. Then the process reverses and our waking consciousness reemerges and connects us back to the "real" world. We are alternately delighted, mystified and terrified by these experiences.

The transitions from waking to dreaming and back are not always so clear and definite. We may have had dreams where we recognize that we are dreaming and wake up; but then we realize that our waking up was also a dream. We were not really awake; we were just dreaming that we were awake. Right now, we believe we are awake, but we are not thinking, "Yes, I am awake." We are rarely conscious of it. When we look carefully at our experience, we can see that we often function as though we were half-asleep; we simply react to whatever is in front of us, just as we do in dreams.

From the absolute, or enlightened, point of view, our experience of this life is definitely not the awakened state. It is a dream—a longer dream—that we call samsara. What we usually refer to as a dream is actually a "double illusion" or a "double dream," and our everyday, waking life is the primary illusion. The teachings of Padmasambhava provide us with instructions for working with the intermediate state of dream, which is the second bardo; these practices teach us how to recognize and transform our dream state into the experience of genuine wakefulness.

The second root verse says:

E MA
At this time, when the bardo of dream appears to you,
Abandon the heedlessness of the delusory sleep of a corpse.
Enter into the nature of mindfulness and nonwandering.
Recognizing dreams, practice transformation and luminosity.

The bardo of dream is the time in between the dissolving of the appearances of one's present waking state and the arising of the appearances of the next occurrence of the waking state. In other words, we fall asleep today and, in a sense, we "leave this world" and enter the bardo of dream. Tomorrow, when we wake up, the appearances of the world manifest for us once again. Between falling asleep and reawakening, we experience the state in which dreams occur. Sometimes, we can also enter this state when we are daydreaming.

Appearance-Emptiness

Padmasambhava teaches three primary methods for working with the confusion of the bardo of dream and bringing that experience onto the path of enlightenment. They are the trainings in illusory body, dream yoga, and luminosity yoga. These practices cultivate the recognition of mind's true nature through the recognition of the appearances of both daytime and nighttime as being inseparable appearance-emptiness, and through the recognition of the state of deep sleep as being luminous awareness.

In order to train most effectively in these practices, it is essential to understand the concepts of both "appearance" and "emptiness." One cannot be fully appreciated without the other. Conventionally speaking, we think that something either exists or does not exist. If it is something that exists, then we can see it or hear it and so forth. It is an appearance, something that can be perceived and conceptually grasped. If something does not exist, then there is nothing to perceive, to know or to conceptualize. There is merely an absence of being, an emptiness that is like a vacuum. Accordingly, what exists from this point of view is opposite to whatever does not exist. Therefore, in our ordinary experience, "appearance" and "emptiness" are mutually exclusive. According to the Buddhist view, however, the actual condition of phenomena is the inseparability of appearance and emptiness, and this inseparability is the working basis for the dream yoga practices. If the reality of mind and phenomena is different from this, then how can we know it?

In order to understand the Buddhist view of appearance-emptiness, we must look at appearances from the perspectives of both relative truth and absolute truth. Relatively speaking, everything in our world and experience appears and exists. Absolutely speaking, those same entities are not what they seem to be. The solidity of these objects begins to fall apart when we examine them more closely, whether we use the logical reasoning of analytical meditation or the empirical methods of science as the basis of our investigation. That is, our perception of them is transformed through a stage-by-stage process that breaks down the object into different, smaller and smaller parts, and then into nothing at all.

Conventionally speaking, we accept that matter exists on a subtle level as countless infinitesimal particles, or atoms, which then become the building blocks of larger forms on a coarser level. However, when we analyze these atoms using various kinds of reasoning, we cannot find any solid matter, any physical substance that truly exists. Instead, we find that these subtle particles are further divisible and are not, therefore, the "last remaining thing." Regardless of how deep and refined our analysis is, we will not be able to find any kind of basic building block of which coarser objects are composed.

When we analyze thoroughly and do not find anything that truly exists on the subtlest of levels, then we question what the basis is for the tangible forms that we see and use every day. All forms can be broken down to an atomic level, from the largest manifestations of nature, such as oceans and mountains, to the objects that comprise the minutiae of our daily existence. If, for example, we look for the true existence of our cell phone, then we apply the same analysis. First, we identify the object—the cell phone—and then we reduce it into its smaller and smaller components—the casing, the key pad, and so forth. Then these parts are reduced to their component parts, which increasingly lose their original identity. When, through the analytic process, we are left with only fragments of plastic, we do not call these fragments "a cell phone." When we have penetrated these fragments to the atomic level, we do not call these atoms "fragments of plastic." When we have determined that even these atoms can be further divided, we are getting to a very subtle level of matter and of mind. When these subtle traces of matter are analyzed, we discover that there is nothing left that is "a thing in itself," solidly and truly existing. There is just space, and energy, which is the same state as the analyzing mind. The question arises then: How does the cell phone exist? Furthermore, we might ask: Where now is the boundary between "my cell phone" and "my mind"?

The cell phone is still there, but it has become form-emptiness; it is there for you to see, feel, hear when it rings, speak into, and pay the bill for; yet, finally speaking, it is not there. It functions perfectly on the level of conventional reality without ever truly existing. And all phenomena, analyzed in this way, are found to be the same. In the Buddhist view, this is called "appearance-emptiness." All these forms we experience are like vividly appearing rainbows, transparent and unreal. They are like the reflection of the moon floating on the still surface of a pool of water. When you see such a reflection, the image is so distinct that you sometimes feel confused and think, "What is that? Is that the real moon?" The moon's reflection is *that* clear, that lucid, and that real. Yet there is no moon on the water; it never existed there. This lack of a solid object leads us to also understand that the consciousness or self that perceives this reflection is equally a mirage.

It is important to remember that the purpose of analysis is to determine if a particular object truly exists on the absolute level. That is what we are looking at in this process. We do not question whether it is there, before our eyes, on the relative level. In the very beginning, before our analysis, we have both an object and a subject: an object of perception and a perceiving consciousness. During the analysis, when we arrive at a more subtle level of the object's material existence, then the subject side—the perceiving consciousness—apprehends it.

When we reach the final stage of finding "nothing at all," then the perceiving consciousness is transformed. It is no longer a "perceiving" consciousness because the object of perception and the act of perception are discontinued. The true existence of the object is no longer there—what is there is a transparent appearance, and an equally transparent awareness. There is no solid existence anywhere. Without solid existence, there is no way to delineate or define identity. Therefore, the separation between self and other, subject and object, becomes illusory.

What occurs in that moment is the direct apprehension of the ultimate nature of mind, which is beyond the subject-object split. Fundamentally, there is just space and awareness. Relatively speaking, of course, the object and subject are still there. Analysis does not destroy the relative world, nor does emptiness.

When we practice meditation with that view and understanding, we recognize that there is an inherent clarity within our nonconceptual experience. When we speak of emptiness, we are speaking of a state of awareness that is beyond the duality of existence and nonexistence, or birth and death; it is beyond concepts of any kind. Far from being merely "an absence," this clarity is the true nature of our mind, which is luminous, brilliant, empty and in the essence of buddha *jnana,* or buddha wisdom. It is the union of space and awareness that is the source of all phenomena in samsara and nirvana. It is the state of enlightenment that unifies all polarities of the outer and inner worlds.

When you recognize the true nature of mind and all relative phenomena as appearance-emptiness, you are directly experiencing pure appearance, which is the perception of realized beings who have mastered the mind. On the other hand, when you do not recognize that, you are directly experiencing impure appearances, which is the perception of confused beings who perceive phenomena as permanent, distinctly separate from mind and as a basis for clinging. These misconceptions about the nature of appearances prevent us from seeing how we can transform the negative states that may arise in any of the six bardos, such as intense fear, anger or bewilderment, into positive, even joyful, states. Therefore, when we train in the practices of illusory body and dream yoga, we work specifically with relative appearances as a means to recognize the transcendent nature of mind.

Impure and Pure Dreams

ENTERING THE DREAM STATE

While we are falling asleep, we experience the dissolution of our five sensory perceptions into a deeper level of mind called the all-base consciousness, or *alaya-vijnana.* At the point at which the sense perceptions totally dissolve, there is a moment of going blank, which is like the experience of fainting. In effect, we become unconscious, which is very similar to the experience of death. Watching this process of dissolution is therefore a very helpful practice for working with the experience of death.

What is occurring during the process of dissolution is that our sense consciousnesses begin to withdraw from active engagement with external objects.[9] Accordingly, we begin to feel a sense of fuzziness or lack of clarity. However, at the same time, we are also having a nonconceptual experience of those perceptions.

There are times, for example as we drift off to sleep, that we will see something—the shape of a lamp, the color of curtains in the moonlight— without really registering it; as a result, there is no concept about it. Similarly, we may have a slight awareness of a sound, like the ticking of a clock, but it will remain a simple, nonconceptual experience of sound because our mind does not produce a label for it. We may feel the weight or texture of our blanket in the same way, without formulating any solid thoughts about it. In such moments, it is possible to look at the nonconceptual experience of perceptions.

CONTINUATION OF CONFUSION

In the process of falling asleep, after the dissolution of the senses, we move into a dream state, where another set of appearances arises due to our habitual tendencies. So long as we do not recognize that we are dreaming when these appearances arise, we take all of our experiences to be just as real and solid as in our waking experience. Therefore, for ordinary beings, our dreams are a continuation of our confusion.

All six objects of our consciousnesses are present in dreams. We see forms and hear sounds; we might experience smells, tastes, and tactile sensations. We think various thoughts—a function of our mental consciousness—and we respond to our dream experiences with all the hope and fear, passion and aggression, that we go through in our waking life. All objects and experiences are there, as vividly and solidly as in our day-time state. For example, in a dream, when you put your hand on a table, your hand stays there. It does not go through the table's surface. When you see a poisonous snake, you naturally react with fear and run away from it. In a dream, when you see a beautiful object, you desire it and would like to get closer to it. This holds true for so long as we do not recognize that we are dreaming.

Waking Up in the Dream

Once dreams are recognized as dreams, however, they can become antidotes for confusion. How is this possible? If dreams that are not recognized as dreams are confusion—and are therefore samsaric—then how can the recognition of those dreams become an agent for transforming our confusion? This is possible because when we "wake up" in the dream state and recognize the nature of the dream appearances to be appearance-emptiness, that dream is no longer deluded. It is no longer mixed with our habitual tendencies and mental afflictions that take things to be real. We can say, "I know I am dreaming. I know these appearances are illusions." Thus, when dreams are recognized as dreams, they are antidotes. When they are not recognized, they are simply confusion on top of confusion. The same goes for confusion in general. If we recognize our confusion, then it is an antidote. If we do not recognize our confusion, then it is the basis for further delusion.

What is the dream state when it is purified? At this point, whatever arises within the dream state is appearance-emptiness, like a rainbow. Dream appearances are mind itself. Apart from being one's own mind, forms, sounds and so forth do not exist in any manner of perceiver and perceived. One's habitual tendency to grasp at appearances as real is cut through. Seeing the true nature of appearances, one gains mastery over one's mind and is neither led where one does not want to go, nor overwhelmed by fear, desire or hatred. Confusion is dispelled and wisdom is accumulated.

In the bardo of dream, the primary methods taught to realize the nature of mind and appearances are the trainings in illusory body, dream yoga and luminosity yoga. Illusory body practice works with the appearances of daytime, and dream yoga with the appearances arising at night in our dreams.[10] Luminosity yoga works with the state of deep sleep. They are profound and sometimes challenging methods, and the understanding that results from this training is extremely useful throughout the bardos of death. Even more than in the bardo of this life, in death, the appearances one undergoes are commonly misunderstood as external phenomena that have no relationship to one's own mind.

TRAINING IN THE ILLUSORY BODY

The first method of dream yoga, training in the illusory body, consists of
two basic elements: training in the impure illusory body and training in
the pure illusory body. In either practice, it is important to maintain a
sense of mindfulness in our everyday life and to remember our motivation
of bodhichitta. We remind ourselves of this by saying: I am training in
these practices in order to achieve enlightenment for all sentient beings.
May they all have the opportunity to experience the illusory nature of our
world.

Impure Illusory Body

First we train in the impure illusory body. At this time, we look at our
world and remind ourselves that it is an illusion, just like a dream or a
rainbow. This world is not ultimately real. The beings inhabiting it do
not truly exist. We remind ourselves that there is nothing to be found in
these appearances; neither metaphysics nor science can find any means of
establishing their true existence. In the end, both approaches lead to the
same conclusion.

One of the ways to understand the dreamlike quality of our present
experience is to look at the experience of yesterday from the perspective
of today. When we do this, we see that everything that happened yesterday exists now only as a memory. Our conversations, actions, thoughts
and feelings, even the sights and sounds of yesterday, are no more real
than the images that appeared to us in last night's dreams. From today's
point of view, there is not much difference between the two. Both are
now memories, although our memory of yesterday's daytime experiences
may be stronger than that of last night's dream. We see, too, that our
immediate experiences of today, which seem tangible and real right now,
will appear dreamlike to us when we look back at them tomorrow.

In the beginning, we must orient ourselves to this view and become
accustomed to looking at the world in this way. We remind ourselves again
and again, in every situation of life, that our experience is "like a dream,
like an illusion." Whether we are in a positive situation and having a good
time, or in a negative situation and having a terrible time, we have to
remind ourselves that all the appearances of our present moment of experience are the illusory display of mind, and that their true nature is appear-

ance-emptiness. When we are having a good time, we are likely to forget to remember; and when we are having a bad time, we may not have the mental strength or presence of mind to remember. However, if we can remember when things are going relatively well for us—neither very badly nor very well—then we can build up a habit of recollection, which will come to us naturally when we need it most. When some terrible thing is happening in our lives, such as the end of a relationship, an accident or illness, or our own moment of death, we will be able to look at it and say, "This is like a dream, like an illusion."

At the same time, the Buddhist teachings tell us that the best, most potent time in our practice is the time when things go completely wrong and we hit rock bottom. It is in such difficult moments that we are most able to look deeply into our lives and find a true connection between what we are experiencing and our practice. It is a powerful time for us because we have given up hope; therefore there is no fear. There is a sense of hopelessness and fearlessness at the same time. We are not clinging so tightly and painfully to this sense of "me," or so absorbed in ego's self-centered concerns. To the contrary, we do not have such a fixed outlook and are less anxious about our self-centered concerns. We can simply say, "Things are not working out as I had planned." Of course, it is the worst time in our samsaric life; but it is a wonderful time for our practice because there is nothing to lose.

What we are experiencing now is an illusion, like a dream. We are in a dream right now. From the point of view of tomorrow, it is not real. When we look at our experience of a nighttime dream from the waking state, we can see how solid and believable those appearances seemed from within the dream state. However, when we wake up from that dream, those appearances are no longer there. It was all just an illusion. In the same way, the illusion of a solid and real world dissolves when we wake up from this dream of samsara into the state of awakening or buddhahood.

Form-Emptiness

The impure illusory body practices include training in three aspects of relative appearance: form-emptiness, sound-emptiness and awareness-emptiness.

When we train in form-emptiness, we are training ourselves to see how the physical world is illusory. The method suggested by Padmasambhava is to look into a mirror and focus on all the reflections in it. You gaze at your face, your body and whatever is visible in your environment: the furniture in the room, the trees outside the window, the mountains beyond them and so on. You focus on these with mindfulness, awareness and a strong motivation to realize the illusory nature of the world. That is the first stage of this practice.

In the second stage, you also begin talking to yourself; that is, you address your reflection in the mirror. The instructions suggest that you focus on two topics: praise and disparagement. First, you praise yourself. You tell yourself, "Yes, you're looking very fine today," and offer other compliments. You praise yourself and then see how you feel. You look at your feelings at that time and see those feelings as illusory. You also see the praise itself and the image you are praising as illusory. That is what we are trying to see. There is nothing there to praise, even though you see the images and feel joy when you hear the praise.

After you have praised yourself, then you change your attitude toward the reflected image and begin to disparage yourself. This technique is not as pleasant. It involves finding fault with yourself, saying unflattering or even harsh words. Here you express whatever you do not want to hear about your physical self. Again, you look directly at that experience and the unhappiness that arises. You see the criticism, the feelings, and the one being maligned as illusory.

Next, you dissolve the illusory body in the mirror into yourself. At this time, the illusory image in the mirror becomes inseparable from yourself—the person standing in front of the mirror. They dissolve into one. Then, you sit and meditate on appearance-emptiness, cultivating the feeling that your body is like the one in the mirror: appearing, yet empty. Just as the image in the mirror is an illusion, simply a reflection of light, in the same way, your own physical form is an illusion, a purely luminous body. Rest in that appearance-emptiness form as much as you can.

Lord Buddha Shakyamuni, in the Prajnaparamita sutras, used a number of examples to teach the true nature of phenomena. He said that everything is like "a magically created illusion, a dream, a mirage, the moon on water, a reflection in a mirror," and so on. Such examples help us see clearly the appearance-emptiness nature of our bodies, our minds and our world. Just as a scarecrow looks like—but is not—a person, just so we appear to be solid and real people, although in truth our bodies are bodies of light—and everything else is the same.

In the beginning, it is important to enhance or augment this experience by saying to yourself throughout the day, "This is a dream; this is illusion. Everything is like images in a mirror or reflections in water." The teachings suggest that you not only remember these words, but also say them aloud to yourself from time to time. Maintaining mindfulness of this illusory nature is crucial for our practice in all six bardos.

Sound-Emptiness

When we train in the impure illusory body practices associated with form-emptiness, we are transforming the appearances of relative forms that are physical. In a similar way, the illusory body practices also include training in the relative appearances of sound, or speech, another fundamental aspect of our existence. When we hear a sound, we also experience it as something that exists in a substantial and real way. For example, when someone curses us, it feels very tangible, almost as if we have been struck physically. We feel no doubt about the reality of the words or their underlying message, which can give rise to many disturbing emotions and mental afflictions. Therefore, we also train in understanding sound and the appearances of all its aspects—spoken word, language and meaning, and the natural sounds of the elements—as sound-emptiness.

When we read a book, the printed words we see are an appearance of form-emptiness. If those words are read aloud, then the sounds we hear are an experience of sound-emptiness. One method taught to train in hearing the spoken word as sound-emptiness is the practice of listening to echoes.

The instruction here is to produce a sound with your voice and then listen to the echo of that sound as it reflects back to you. Just as you used your reflection in a mirror to train with physical forms, here you use the reflection of your voice to train with sound. For instance, if you are in a long hallway or tunnel and you shout out "hello," then you will hear the same sound as it comes back to you. The practice involves listening to your own words and to the echo, noting their respective qualities and similarities. In fact, your voice is as insubstantial as the echo itself. Neither has any solidity whatsoever. While working with this practice, it is important to remain mindful and aware; after all, you are not simply shouting.

This practice can also be done in a cave or valley, and you can work with the sound of chants or mantras.

This exercise is often done in Tibet by monastics who are training to become *umdzes,* or chant masters, for their monasteries. They will often go to a river where there is a waterfall to train their voices. Waterfalls are especially good places for this because they are so resonant. The monks attune their voices to the water's deep, echoing sounds, which go on continuously, and they chant along with them. In this way, their voices become strong and deep. Good umdzes not only become excellent chant masters, but they also become trained in sound-emptiness. Others, who have good voices but proudly think, "I'm the best umdze," only receive ego training.

Training in sound-emptiness relates not only to our understanding of the nature of sound itself, but also to how we understand language as a system for communicating meaning. It is important for us to train in this aspect of sound-emptiness because we experience many disturbing emotions, as well as a great deal of ego clinging and confusion as a result of our misunderstandings of language overall. For example, when we hear a certain word, we tend to connect it with a particular meaning. We project our meaning onto that word and then grasp onto it as reality with great conviction: "This person called me 'arrogant.'" Promptly, that person becomes our enemy, or perhaps an enemy of the state. Consequently, we have to train our minds not only to hear the sound of words, but also to notice how we connect their meaning with our thought processes and concepts. In this way, we will come to see how we mingle sound and our thoughts about sound together to make a solid world, a solid reality. The more evident this becomes to us, the more clearly we will see how sound and meaning arise together in a dreamlike way, as illusory reflections or echoes of the relative world. Therefore, training in sound-emptiness is a fundamental preparation for our journey though all the bardos of life and death.

Awareness-Emptiness

Third, we train in the illusory body practices of awareness-emptiness. In this case, we are working with the relative appearances of mind in the form of thoughts. We are transforming the way we view our thoughts altogether. Instead of regarding thoughts as something to be subdued, tamed and overcome in order to "get to" the essence of mind, we view thoughts themselves as direct expressions of mind's pure, luminous nature. Thoughts themselves become a path to the recognition of the ultimate nature of mind. This level of practice requires tremendous mindfulness and a stable practice of shamatha because our method depends not only on seeing the thought process, but also on seeing instances of single thoughts.

On the relative level, thoughts appear to our minds; they arise, abide for a fleeting moment and then they cease. What is the nature of these thoughts? They are not physical phenomena. They are mental events, the movements of mind itself. While they color and shape our world according to their content, that content itself has no form—no color, size or shape. Their nature and the nature of the mind from which they arise is the same: awareness-emptiness. At this stage, we look closely at our thoughts to personally determine and directly experience their essence.

Generally speaking, perception and thought are closely related. As soon as we see a form, hear a sound, or connect with a feeling, mind registers that perception, and next we have a thought or form a concept about it. This thought appears to our mind, but it is not a solid form; rather, we make it solid, or at least regard it as solid, through our habitual tendency to objectify and impute "real" existence to things. We perennially fall into the same pattern; we solidify the reality of our mind, thereby disconnecting ourselves from the fresh, vibrant energy and wisdom of our thoughts. It does not matter whether a thought is a thought of passion, aggression, ignorance, jealousy, pride or anything else. If we can train our minds now in the recognition of all thoughts as awareness-emptiness, then, at the time of death or in our after-death journey, it will be possible for a single thought or perception to trigger the realization of the nature of mind.

If we look at our thoughts, then we can see clearly how they are awareness-emptiness. A thought simply arises and then dissolves naturally. We do not have to do anything to it to make it go away so there will be room for another thought. We do not have to cure our thoughts or push them away. Each thought arises rainbow-like in the clear, empty space of mind. Each is unique, original and beautiful in its own way. Then it is gone.

Thoughts from this perspective are regarded as mind's ornaments; they beautify the mind in the same way that lilies make the pond they are growing in more appealing. Without the lilies, the pond is rather boring. Thus, when we do not solidify them, thoughts are a beautiful experience;

however, when we do, they bring us pain in unending variations. The choice is ours. According to these teachings, we suffer whenever we solidify any experience of mind, whether it is perceptual or conceptual. When we do not solidify our experience, our thoughts bring us greater clarity. Both thoughts and emotions have the same positive quality of enhancing the clarity of mind, so long as we do not reduce them to labels or freeze them conceptually.

When we train in awareness-emptiness, we simply watch our thoughts. We observe the first flicker of thought and watch it as it arises. We see the quality of that particular thought; yet, we simply watch it the way it is, without trying to change it. We experience it and then let it go when it goes. We do not have to hold onto any thought to prevent our minds from being too lonely because there is no doubt that another one will come. We will not be left without a thought, at least not for very long.

The instruction is to watch the process of thought as naturally and directly as we can, without artifice and without fabrication. This means we are not being too clever, or strategizing how to look at our thoughts, and we are not building our thoughts up further, with layers of new thoughts, labels or concepts. We become removed from our experience by the labeling process. This happens when we see an object, give it a label, and then regard the object and the label as being one and the same. In some sense, the label distracts our mind from a direct experience of the object itself. For example, while we may recognize an object as a table, the label "table" is extraneous to the object itself. It is merely a given name; the object would not change if we called it something else. In a similar way, when a thought arises, we give it a name and try to classify it. This makes it into something that it is not. Thus, in order to understand mind clearly, we should simply experience our thoughts without any labeling. This is the means to recognize thoughts as the awareness-emptiness aspect of mind.

These are the three major phases of the impure illusory body practice: training in illusory form, illusory sound and illusory mind. After accomplishing these three practices, we can see that when we say, "The world is illusory," we do not mean that objects are illusory while the subject is not. We do not mean that there is a truly existing subject that looks out on an illusory world. Rather, there is a dreamlike mind that perceives a dreamlike world: a dreamlike eye consciousness that sees dreamlike forms; a dreamlike ear consciousness that hears dreamlike sounds, and so on. In all these practices, we adopt the view of appearance-emptiness, in which we see all three spheres of our experience—subject, object and action—as illusory.

Pure Illusory Body

Second, we train in the pure illusory body. Here, we are working with pure appearances. These trainings are connected to the practices of deity yoga. There are a great number of deities in the tantric Buddhist tradition, but they are all regarded as embodiments or personifications of the meditator's own enlightened nature. They are not regarded as externally existing gods or supernatural beings. Their physical characteristics, posture and ornaments are symbolic representations of the various qualities of enlightenment—the innate wakefulness, wisdom and compassion that are always present within the nature of mind and that fully manifest when that nature is realized. Through the practice of visualizing such pure forms as the deity and the mandala, or the surrounding world of the deity, we are training ourselves to see the true nature of mind and appearances. We begin by working with conceptually generated forms but these lead us to a nonconceptual experience of sacred outlook, a direct perception of the ever-present lucidity of mind.

When you create such a visualized form in your mind, you should focus on developing an image that is very clear and precise in every aspect. For this reason, you begin by looking at a picture of your chosen yidam—for example, the Buddha Vajrasattva—which is frequently used as a basis for deity yoga visualization practice. Vajrasattva is generally depicted seated cross-legged on a moon disk on top of a lotus. He is white in color and is ornamented with a crown, silk cloths and various ornaments. He holds a vajra and a bell, signifying compassion and wisdom, and is associated with great purity.

There are helpful techniques for developing your visualization. First, you gaze at the picture of Vajrasattva until your eyes become somewhat fatigued or "numb," and your vision blurs slightly. At that point, you close your eyes and allow the image to reflect in space. Then you open your eyes, look at the picture again, and then close your eyes as before. You repeat this process until a rough image of it appears in your mind. It is also helpful to cut out the actual image—remove it from its background—

and place it on a dark background. You continue practicing and refining the image in this way until you have created the clearest, most detailed visualization possible.

The visualized form you are creating at this stage is called a pure illusory body. It is a visualized form of appearance-emptiness. It is clearly appearing, yet insubstantial; it is lucid, vibrant and nonexistent. Therefore your visualization of the deity is like a reflection of the moon on the water. Once you have established this stage of the visualization, that is, the outer form of the deity, then you dissolve the visualization into yourself. At that point, you and the deity become inseparable. You, yourself, are the deity—a pure illusory body. As the deity, the world that you perceive, the surrounding mandala of myriad appearances, is transformed through your pure vision into a sacred world.

In that moment, we are transcending ordinary perceptions and concepts and viewing the world from an enlightened perspective. When we visualize ourselves as a deity, our ordinary pride in ourselves, which is based on ego-clinging and attachment, is transformed into "vajra pride." This is not an attitude of superiority we hold in relation to others, nor is it merely a case of holding a high opinion of ourselves. Vajra pride refers to our pride and confidence in the absolute nature of our mind as buddha: primordially, originally pure, awake and full of the qualities of enlightenment. Thus we can say, "I am the deity. I am a buddha."

The general Buddhist teachings point to the same view of emptiness and our innate buddha nature; however, this nature is taught as a potential to be uncovered as we progress along the path. In contrast, in the Vajrayana, we are buddha *right now*, in this very moment. Taking complete pride in that, we say, "Yes, the nature of my mind is buddha and this is the enlightened world." When we can fully embody this sense of vajra pride, our body *is* an illusory body, and our surroundings *are* a manifestation of enlightened world. This is the essence of deity yoga practice.

The instructions here also suggest that we mix the image of our principal teacher, or root guru, with that of the deity. This is done, for example, with the practice of guru yoga. It is also an essential condition for receiving an *abhisheka*, or initiation ceremony. At that time, the guru appears as the yidam deity and empowers the participants to practice the sadhana of that yidam. Whenever we see our guru as the deity, we are engaging in the practice of the pure illusory body.

These two trainings in impure and pure illusory body are essential for the practices of dream yoga which follow. In fact, they can be regarded as the ngondro, or foundational, practices for the bardo of dream. When we begin to genuinely appreciate the illusory, dreamlike nature of our waking experiences, we are starting to mix those appearances with the appearances of our nighttime dreams. We are bringing those two states closer together.

The practice of illusory body is important for the natural bardo of this life as well as the painful bardo of dying and the two bardos after death. When death occurs, we will be faced with our own fear and uncertainty as we go through the process of the dissolution of our consciousness and the cessation of our bodily functions. Simultaneously, various appearances of luminosity will arise, provoking further confusion and panic. In each of the bardos of the death and after-death states, we will be faced with the challenge of meeting our own mind at every turn in the form of unfamiliar and vivid appearances.

At these critical times, we can transcend our suffering instantaneously through the practice of seeing them as empty-appearing forms arising from the luminous nature of our mind. If, in this life, we make a connection with the illusory body practices, then we will be well prepared for any bardo situation or experience of nowness. Whenever we feel there is no solid ground, we will be in familiar territory—in the space of complete openness that invites the arising of pure appearances.

TRAINING IN DREAM YOGA

Within the bardo of dream, the second and main method of training taught by Padmasambhava is the practice of dream yoga. This set of practices includes training in recognition of the dream state, also called "lucid dreaming"; transforming the dream state once recognition is gained; and the enhancement practices, by which obstacles are overcome.

It is said that our dream experiences, like our daytime experiences, arise from our habitual tendencies. The formation and reinforcement of these tendencies is linked to the accumulation of karmic seeds acquired in the past that condition our way of perceiving, thinking and acting in the present. All the positive and negative seeds we have gathered remain within our mindstream in latent form until we meet with new causes and conditions that support their ripening in a specific form. The momentum of this cycle is usually uninterrupted because as soon as one seed ripens, yields its result and is then exhausted, that action becomes the cause for the planting of another seed, perhaps an even stronger one.

During the day, it is important to maintain the mindfulness and awareness that we have developed through the illusory body practices. We remind ourselves, over and over: "The ultimate nature of all appearances is emptiness and their relative expression is appearance-emptiness inseparable. Therefore, this is like a dream, like an illusion." Then at night, when the time for sleep comes, we practice dream yoga, which begins with recognition of the dream state. This means that we become conscious that we are dreaming within the dream state. We know that we are dreaming but we do not wake up. Padmasambhava's instructions say that before going to sleep we should generate bodhichitta with words such as: "In order to free myself and others from the ocean of samsara, I would like to engage in this practice of dream yoga, which has the power to liberate the suffering, fear and confusion of samsara. May all beings achieve perfect happiness and complete awakening." With that as your motivation, you fall asleep with the strong intention that, when a dream arises, you will become aware that you are dreaming.

Recognizing The Dream
First Method: The Guru

After establishing our motivation and intention, we assume a certain posture. We do not simply go to sleep. The text suggests that we adopt the posture of a sleeping lion. This is the posture assumed by Buddha Shakyamuni at the time of his *parinirvana*. This term refers to the passing away of a buddha or fully accomplished master. Such a death is regarded as entry into the state of enlightenment. There are sculptures depicting the Buddha's parinirvana and you can see from pictures that he is lying down on his right side. His right hand is positioned under his cheek, and his left arm rests naturally along the top of his left side. We use this same posture. You can also close your right nostril by pressing very gently with a finger on your right hand, and then breathing in a relaxed way through the left nostril. We then sleep in that posture.

In addition to the posture, there are also instructions for generating specific visualizations. If you are a Vajrayana practitioner, then you first visualize yourself as a yidam deity with which you have a practice connection, such as Vajrasattva. If you cannot create a clear visualization, then you simply adopt the vajra pride of that deity. Next, you visualize your root guru sitting above your head. It is said that you can sometimes visualize your pillow as the lap of your guru; so, in this case, you are falling asleep in your guru's lap. Following this, at your throat center, you visualize a small form of Vajra Guru, or Guru Rinpoche, that is approximately one inch tall. "Vajra Guru" and "Guru Rinpoche" are epithets for Padmasambhava, who is regarded as inseparable from your principal or root guru. These visualizations are generally oriented in the same direction as you are. It is said that you should visualize them all as appearance-emptiness: appearance-emptiness deity, appearance-emptiness guru—like the reflection of the moon on water. There is nothing solid in them.

As you are falling asleep, you should maintain vajra pride and focus on the visualization at your throat center. Also, continue to hold in mind your aspiration to have a lucid dream, to recognize dream as dream. You want to avoid getting into your usual, confused dream state. This is also a time when you can make supplications, such as, "Grant me blessings so that I can recognize dream as a dream, illusion as illusion, confusion as confusion, and see the reality of all—the absolute nature of mind." Supplicate in this way from time to time. You do not need to engage in complicated forms of chanting or sophisticated prayers. Simply make the basic point, and supplicate in your own words, in any way that feels comfortable to you.

It is most important at this time not to become distracted or be interrupted by random thoughts about tomorrow's schedule—what time you have to get up in the morning, or what you need to do tomorrow that you did not do today. Being interrupted by thoughts is generally the main obstacle to successfully recognizing your dreams. It is also an obstacle to recognizing your involvement with confusion in your everyday life, where you are constantly becoming distracted from your present awareness. You usually do not stop and notice, "I am getting confused," "I am getting angry" or "I am getting jealous." You don't see it at all. Instead, these thoughts and emotions all seem very natural and normal.

The main point here is not to become too distracted by any kind of thoughts. During this practice, focus your thoughts one-pointedly on the form of the guru at your throat center, and your desire to have a lucid dream.

For many people, such recognition does not happen on the first or second attempt. You need to repeat this method again and again with some diligence until eventually it becomes very natural to you. You are able to concentrate without distraction, to fall asleep easily and to enter a state of lucid dream without great effort.

If, upon waking, you realize that you did have a dream, or dreams, which you failed to recognize, then you should acknowledge that, and try to see that such dreams are not really separate from this life's appearances. In the postmeditation state, in this case the state after sleep, you can try to reinforce your perception of the dreamlike, illusionlike nature of the world. You can also strengthen your motivation to free yourself and others from confusion, and renew your aspiration to recognize the dream state.

Second Method: The Yidam

After working with this method for a while, if you are unable to accomplish recognition of the dream, then the teachings suggest a second method. As before, you lie down in the sleeping lion posture. Then visualize your root guru above the crown of your head, and yourself as a yidam. At your throat center, however, instead of the guru, you visualize a small form of the same yidam as your self-visualization. For example, if you are visualizing yourself as Vajrasattva, then at your throat center you also visualize a small Vajrasattva.

If you do not immediately begin to have lucid dreams with this method, try to persevere for a while. It is important not to hop from method to method. Begin by training in only one method, and train in it for a long time before trying another one. Otherwise, you will never know whether a particular method would have been effective if you had tried it for longer, or whether it would not have produced any result and a change was truly required. You cannot find that out if you change methods too frequently. You have to stick with one for a while. Apply the method again and again until you are very certain about it and can say, "I tried this very diligently for weeks, and I am still not recognizing my dreams." Then you can move on to the next method. This is a good guideline in general.

Third Method: The Unexcelled Syllables

In the next method, again as before, you take the correct posture and then visualize yourself as the yidam deity with your root guru seated above your head. Next, you visualize a red, four-petaled lotus at your throat center, on which are arranged the syllables OM AH NU TA RA. Begin by holding your mind focused on the lotus. Then place the syllable OM in the middle, AH on the front petal, NU on the right petal, TA on the back petal and RA on the left petal.

Hold the full visualization clearly in your mind; then gradually shift your focus to the syllables, moving your attention from one syllable to another as you go through the stages of falling asleep. First, you focus on the OM, simply placing your mind on it for a while. When you begin to feel drowsy and notice your senses starting to withdraw from outside contact, you focus on the syllable AH in front. As you begin to feel a sense of heaviness and your body starts to relax, you focus on the syllable NU on the right petal. When you feel yourself falling more deeply into a sleep state and your body feels heavier still, you focus on the back syllable, TA. Finally, just before falling asleep, when you think, "I'm just about to go . . ." you focus on the syllable RA on the left petal.

The text says that when you are really about to fall asleep and you think, "Now I'm going . . . I'm going . . . " you go back to the OM. At the very last moment before losing waking consciousness, you should reinforce your aspiration once again, saying, "I want to recognize my dreams." If there is no thought that intervenes between that aspiration and sleep, then your aspiration is more likely to take hold and you will be successful.

Fourth Method: Bindu

If you are unable to visualize the syllables, Padmasambhava gives one final method. Here, you create the basic visualization as before and then simply visualize a pale red bindu, or sphere of light, at your throat center. A bindu is always vibrant, sparkling, shining and transparent, like a rainbow. Visualize the bindu in this way and place your mind on that as you fall asleep. Immediately before losing consciousness, you reinforce your aspiration to recognize your dreams.

Individual Differences

One of these methods should work for you. However, because each of us has a different physical makeup, our experiences will be individual. Some people dream very little, and therefore they find it difficult to recognize their dreams. In some instances, it is a physical issue, in which case there is no need to worry. Other people simply have an easier time recognizing their dreams. This does not necessarily mean that they are more realized than those who find this sort of recognition harder to achieve. Whatever the case may be, we must make our own effort; we can also consult with our individual masters who can offer more personalized guidance on how best we can relate with the various practices.

In some cases, however, this situation may arise from certain obscurations, or stronger defilements. For a Vajrayana practitioner, it could possibly indicate a samaya problem. In such circumstances, it is suggested that one go back to the Mahayana practices of refuge, bodhichitta and working with the *paramitas* in order to accumulate more merit and wisdom. The practices of guru yoga also will be very beneficial in helping to reconnect with the Vajrayana path in a genuine way. In particular, for Vajrayana practitioners, the *ganachakra,* or feast practices, provide a method of purification.

Transforming Dream Appearances

Once we can recognize our dreams—when we have a dream and can say, "I am dreaming now. I know I am dreaming"—then what do we do? Padmasambhava's teachings tell us that we need to transform our dreams. Therefore, the second training or set of practices is transformation: transforming the appearances we encounter in our dreams.

When you become conscious that you are awake in a dream and can maintain that awareness for some time, you have an opportunity to change what you are seeing and doing. In our daytime experience, it would take more power of mind than we have normally to change one thing into another, such as a table into a flower. You would need the power and realization of a great yogi like Milarepa in order to do that. However, in this practice, within the dream state, you are training your mind to develop that power. So, for example, when you dream of a flower, you try to transform it. You change the flower into a bird or a cloud or a kite— you make it into any thing you can. Or, when you meet up with a fearsome being, a wild animal or someone who is trying to kill you, you transform that being into an enlightened form, such as a yidam deity— and let it kill your ego. When you are in a chaotic and confusing situation, you try to transform that samsaric condition into an experience of sacred world, such as the mandala of a deity. The text also says that, gradually, you can try such things as flying. However, you should not attempt this too early in your practice. If you try too soon to jump from a cliff to practice flying, then your fear will probably just wake you up. At that point, you will have lost the recognition of the dream and therefore a very good opportunity. You will have to try again later. When you are more accustomed to the practice of transformation, there will be no fear of such actions.

After you have practiced transformation for a while, you can play around in your dream world. Padmasambhava's text says that if you have a strong aspiration to experience the sacred world of the buddhas, then before going to sleep you should express that aspiration by saying, "I not only want to recognize my dreams, but also I want to travel in my dreams to the buddha fields to hear the profound teachings of different buddhas." In transforming your dream into the experience of sacred world, you can meet with the buddhas and bodhisattvas and have a nice chat, as you do with your friends around your coffee table. Then you can come back.

One day I was with my teacher, Khenpo Tsültrim Gyamtso Rinpoche, in the Annapurna coffee shop in Kathmandu, Nepal. We were sitting there and then Rinpoche started teaching. Following my habitual tendency, I pulled out my notebook and started writing down what he was saying. I was asking questions and writing away, and then Rinpoche began to sing one of Milarepa's songs. I was writing this down, too, along with other things. We were both singing and chanting at one point and talking pretty loudly when suddenly I realized where I was. I had been totally oblivious of the fact that we were in a public place—a busy coffee shop. I looked around and everybody was staring at us! That was like the experience of waking up in a dream. There I was, having a nice chat with Buddha in a coffee shop in Kathmandu. If we recognize our dreams, then we can do the same thing with the buddhas and bodhisattvas of the three times.

Ultimate Transformation

Ultimate transformation in the bardo of dream is the transformation of confused appearances into the experience of wisdom. Our ability to transform our dream appearances relates directly to our ability to maintain a nondistracted, stable mind. This ability is the essence of shamatha practice. When we look at an image in a dream, we try to see how clearly our minds can focus on it and how stable our concentration can be. We also try to see to what degree our minds can experience the genuine reality, or true nature, of these appearances. That is our goal in this practice. It is not merely to enjoy ourselves—to have a nice dream and play around in it. The goal here is to realize absolute reality—the true nature of our minds—through the direct apprehension of these three things: appearance-emptiness, sound-emptiness and awareness-emptiness.

If you have a hard time recognizing your dreams, then the text advises that you should train more in the illusory body practice. While you are practicing, maintain strong mindfulness and try to avoid interruptions by thoughts and by your habitual tendencies. For example, you may be thinking, "This is illusion. This is a dream," when suddenly, a thought of anger arises and, in the next moment, you find yourself shouting at somebody. With that thought, you, your anger, and the object of your anger feel suddenly very solid and real. It is not that you should never shout. You can shout—but do it with mindfulness. That will change your way of thinking. You could think: "I am shouting in a dream." That is a better way to shout. If you gain some realization out of that experience, then the person who made you shout also receives a share of that positive karma—he or she was instrumental in provoking your insight.

Overcoming Obstacles

As the third aspect of the instructions for dream yoga, Padmasambhava provides several enhancement practices that relate to our basic patterns of dreaming and the obstacles that may arise for us.

The first pattern is waking up as soon as we recognize a dream; our recognition rouses us from our dream and brings it to an end. The second pattern is forgetfulness. We recognize our dream at first, but then we lose our awareness and are caught up in the dream once again. We forget the instructions about recognizing that we are dreaming and then transforming our dream appearances. The third pattern is one in which clarity and confusion alternate. First, we recognize the dream state, and then, due to our habitual tendencies, we lose our awareness and fall back into non-recognition. After that, we have another glimpse of recognition, but then we become confused again. Thus we experience an alternating cycle of recognition and non-recognition. The fourth pattern is remaining completely awake. Because we are anticipating our practice, we cannot fall asleep at all.

For each of these problems, Padmasambhava provides us with particular remedies. The instruction for waking up after recognizing our dream is to change the focus of our attention during the visualization. Instead of focusing on the image at the throat center, we should lower our focus and place our attention on our heart center. We can also visualize two dark bindus at the soles of our feet; although these bindus are dark, they are still a form of a light—bright and velvety. Focusing on these will help us to remain asleep. This may also be helpful if we are having trouble with insomnia.

Another method, which equally applies to and counteracts all of these problems, is to train more in the illusory body. When this training begins to have a genuine impact on us, we will overcome both forgetfulness and confusion. When we have developed more mindfulness and awareness of the illusionlike nature of our daily life experience, that awareness will continue through to the point of sleep and into the dream state. It will not simply stop when we close our eyes. Therefore, we should make a special effort to cultivate our awareness a few hours before going to sleep, and to heighten that awareness right when we are going to bed. Usually, we go to bed without any intention to observe our minds. We are happiest when we can just "drop off" in an instant, like turning off a light switch. When we do that, there is no awareness whatsoever.

It is taught that the last thought you have before falling asleep becomes very powerful in affecting your mental state during sleep and dream. If you fall asleep while you are being attentive to your mind and experience, then, at the very least, the quality of mindfulness that continues will positively influence your dream experience. Accordingly, it is also very important not to fall asleep when you are under the influence of strong emotions. If you find that such emotions are coming up, then you should apply whatever remedy is effective in subduing them. Look directly at their nature, or simply cut through them. Do not let them go wild; if you do, then that disturbing energy will continue and negatively impact your dream experience.

Training in Luminosity Yoga

The third main method given by Padmasambhava for taking the bardo of dream onto the path of enlightenment is the training in *luminosity yoga,* or the *yoga of deep sleep.* The state of sleep occurs when the six consciousnesses dissolve into the all-basis consciousness. This means that they are no longer directed outward; they are no longer moving toward or making contact with their objects.

For example, the eye consciousness does not perceive external forms. Thus, when we fall deeply asleep, the clarity aspect of the movement of the six consciousnesses disappears, and sleep is the unclear aspect of consciousness that abides after dissolution takes place. When we say the clarity aspect is absent, we are only saying that it is absent from the six consciousnesses, not that it is absent from mind as a whole, because the ultimate nature of mind is clarity. The essence of deep sleep is, in fact, great luminosity, the true nature of mind. It is utterly bright and utterly vivid. It is a dense clarity, and because its clarity is so dense, it has a blinding effect on the confused mind. When we purify the ignorance of deep sleep, when we transcend that delusion and further penetrate the intense clarity, then we experience the clear, luminous nature of mind.

When do we meditate on this luminosity? Primarily, we should try to directly experience the true nature of mind at the very moment of the dissolution of the waking state. At that time, we generate bodhichitta and, without being interrupted by other thoughts, we look with mindfulness and awareness directly at mind itself with the intention of observing its aspect of clarity. At the very moment of dropping off to sleep, it is taught that pure awareness shines clearly, full of vivid and bright qualities. This is a very short moment. Although we may miss it the first time, and the second, and so on, if we become accustomed to looking in this way, then eventually we will be able to see this luminosity. By not allowing our mindfulness to wander, we will be able to sustain the experience as we transition from a conscious state into the state of sleep. Furthermore, if we gain stability in this practice, then we will be able to sustain this experience into the dream state as well, and we will have control over our dreams. In addition to being mindful, we also need to be relaxed, or we will not be able to fall asleep. Therefore, we need to have a balance between tight and loose, and look at luminosity from within that balance.

If we train successfully in the luminosity of deep sleep and become capable of transcending our confusion during sleep and dreams, it is said that we will then be able to apply this ability at the stage of death. If we can mix the luminosity of deep sleep with the luminosity of death, we will then be able to arise in a pure wisdom body that is free of confusion.

The meditations on luminosity are an aspect of the training known as the Six Dharmas of Naropa. The extensive methods of practice need to be engaged under the guidance of your personal teacher. Trying to practice them by yourself, using only the descriptions you find in books, is not beneficial, and may in fact be harmful.

FRUITION OF TRAINING

Through the practices of illusory body, dream yoga and luminosity yoga, we transform and completely transcend the ordinary delusions of the bardo of dream. It is taught that perfect accomplishment in these trainings results in the attainment of two of the three aspects of the enlightened nature of mind: the *dharmakaya* and the *sambhogakaya*.

The *dharmakaya* is the empty essence of mind, the fundamental nature of all phenomena. It is nonconceptual awareness, and therefore beyond all speech, thought and expression. It is the true experience of the naked state of alpha pure mind. When we purify the confusion of deep sleep and recognize mind's empty, luminous nature, we attain the state of dharmakaya.

The *sambhogakaya* is the radiant, blissful energy of this fundamental nature of mind, which possesses tremendous power to manifest in a variety of pure forms. This nature is spontaneously present and inseparable from dharmakaya wisdom. When we purify the dream state and the confusion of taking something that does not exist to exist, we attain the state of sambhogakaya and perceive the pure, symbolic forms of enlightened mind and world.

The third aspect, the *nirmanakaya*, is the uninterrupted display, in physical form, of these two energies: mind's empty essence and its unceasing creative power. It is the unity of the alpha pure and the spontaneously present luminous nature of mind manifesting in a variety of pure and impure forms. When we purify the delusion of the waking state of mind that imputes true existence to phenomena and then engages in dualistic fixation upon the triad of subject, object and action, we attain the state of nirmanakaya.

These three aspects of the enlightened nature of mind are inseparable; they are inherent qualities of mind itself. They correspond to the experiences of the three bardos of death: the painful bardo of dying, the luminous bardo of dharmata and the karmic bardo of becoming. If we do not attain enlightenment—the state of complete awakening to the actual nature of reality—during the bardo of this lifetime, then, as mentioned previously, we have an even greater opportunity to do so when we enter and cycle through the bardos of death. During each of these transitional states, there is the potential to transform our confused experience into its enlightened counterpart. When we are at the death point, if we recognize the clear light nature of mind, then we will attain the realization of dharmakaya. If we recognize the true nature of the pure visions of the luminous bardo of dharmata when they arise, then we will attain the realization of sambhogakaya. If we recognize the true nature of the confused appearances of the karmic bardo when they become manifest, then we will attain the realization of nirmanakaya and be assured of an auspicious rebirth. Since the three kayas are inseparable, attaining the complete realization of any one brings the experience of all three. Thus we have three opportunities or means of connecting with the complete realization of the three-kaya nature of mind.

These situations will be discussed later in greater detail. However, in the bardo of dream we have a chance to train for the experiences we will meet in the bardo of dharmata. At that time, the sambhogakaya luminosity manifests in vivid forms that seem to be outside of oneself and beyond one's control. It is therefore essential to recognize that the forms and sounds appearing at that time are the creative display of one's own mind. This training is perhaps even more essential for the karmic bardo of becoming. This is because at that time one meets with powerful projections of one's own mind that are confused and could lead to intense states of suffering as well as to an unfavorable rebirth.

Once we understand this view, both theoretically and on the basis of personal experience, and we develop facility with these practices, we will be able to take care of ourselves in the bardos of death. We will be able to take death as the path. We will see that death too is a dream. If we gain mastery over the mind of dreams, then we will also have mastery over the mind of death. When we attain mastery over the dying mind, we are able to go wherever we wish when we die, just as we can in our dreams. Conversely, when we do not have mastery over our dreams, we are led powerlessly around by the dream itself. All the practices of the bardo of dream serve as methods for us to achieve this control and mastery over our mind.

Dreams and Dreamers

One experience of dream is the state of illusion we enter when we are sleeping. However, when we look at the notion of dream more broadly, it encompasses the whole of our experience, all aspects of our reality. Traditionally, dreams can be classified in three ways: by the dream's level of reality; by the dreamer's level of realization; and by the duration of the dream.

LOOKING AT THE DREAM

When we look at the dream state from the perspective of the bardo of dream, we find that we experience three kinds of dream realities: the example dream, the actual dream and the dream at the end of time. What we usually refer to as "a dream"—our nighttime experience of appearances that is connected to the dream yoga practices—is known as the *example dream.* The *actual dream* is regarded as the daylight experience of our ordinary day-to-day life, which is connected to our practice of illusory body. The *dream at the end of time* refers to the experience of death that marks the end of one particular cycle—the end of that particular appearance of life and that set of life experiences. This dream is connected to the bardos of death and the after-death intervals. These three types of dreams are the experience of all beings that possess sentience, or mind, whether they are human, animal or exist in some other form. Right now we are human beings, and in this realm, we have sensory experiences that we label good and bad, tasty and tasteless and so on. The same sensory experiences take place in every realm. For example, now you enjoy going to restaurants and choosing from a great variety of cuisines; however, if you had been born as a donkey, then you would view a green pasture as a great, delicious banquet. All such appearances occur within the actual dream of a particular realm—and when that dream ends, the experiences of the final dream begin—the dream at the end of time.

LOOKING AT THE DREAMER

The dream can also be classified by the degree of realization possessed by the dreamer. Viewed from this perspective, there are also three types of dreams. In Buddhist language this is expressed as the *dreams of ordinary beings*, the *dreams of yogins*, and the *dreams of the bodhisattvas on the bhumis*. An ordinary being is someone who perceives the world conventionally and is fully subject to ego-clinging and habitual tendencies; therefore, the dream of an ordinary being is seemingly very solid, very real, and, accordingly, very confused. In contrast, a yogin or yogini is someone who follows the spiritual path and has some level of realization of the nature of mind. From a Tibetan Buddhist perspective, this path is the Vajrayana path. The dreams of such practitioners will therefore be very different; they will, to some degree, be experiences of appearance-emptiness. The third category refers both to the most highly realized beings, the bodhisattvas on the bhumis, who have fully realized emptiness, and also to the postmeditation state of a buddha. Needless to say, the dreams of such beings are totally in the nature of transcendent experience. Thus, these three types of dreams are classified from the point of view of internal, personal development.

LOOKING AT THE TIME SPAN

A third classification views dreams according to their duration. These three types of dream are known as the *lesser*, the *middling*, and the *greater* dream. Here, lesser means shortest, not inferior; middling, or intermediate, means its duration is a little bit longer; and greater refers to dreams that can last for quite a long time.

The *lesser dream* refers to the appearances that arise when we go to sleep and enter the bardo of dream. These nighttime dreams are generally quite short. We may have twenty different dreams in one night, each lasting only a few seconds, or we may have a dream that lasts for five minutes. These dreams are temporary appearances—so temporary that sometimes we scarcely remember them. We might wake up and say, "I know I had a dream, but I can't remember it." That shows how ephemeral these appearances are, and how shallow in terms of the impression they leave on our mindstream.

The *middling dream* refers to the dream we have after death. In particular, it relates to the karmic bardo of becoming, which is said to last for approximately forty-nine days—much longer than our nighttime dreams. Although this dream endures for several weeks, our mind is not at all stable at this time; our perceptions and thoughts are fleeting and erratic. There is a sense of groundlessness, because there is no solid, physical form anywhere, and we ourselves possess only a mental body.

The *greater dream* refers to the dream of our day-to-day experience in samsara, which is the natural bardo of this life. This dream seems to us to be much more grounded, or rooted in a substantial reality, because it has the appearance of being solid and real. This does not mean that it *is* real; only that it appears to us to have greater qualities of solidity, existence and continuity. For example, when we wake up tomorrow morning, it is likely that we will still be where we were when we went to bed. However, when we wake up from a dream, we are no longer where we were. In one night, we may have a series of dreams in which we travel to many places. Things move very fast in dream. In one, we are trekking in the Himalayas; next we are flying off to Mardi Gras in New Orleans; then we are relaxing on a beach in Mexico; then again, we may be sitting on our meditation cushion in our own home. But when we wake up from all of these, we will not find ourselves in any of these places; we will be in the same place where we closed our eyes. The same reality appears to us each time we wake up into this daylight dream.

Padmasambhava explains the actual meaning of greater dream as the state in which we have the most stable or grounded confusion. In contrast, in other dream states, our confusion is fluctuating and unpredictable. For example, in the after-death experience of the bardo, we only intermittently comprehend that we no longer exist in physical form. When this reality dawns on us, we feel extremely afraid. However, in the bardo of this life, we always feel that we are here, so there is a stronger sense of ground or a stronger foundation for our confusion. In a sense, this greater confusion is good news. It provides us with a reliable base from which we can transcend our confusion altogether. In contrast, when our experience is more fleeting, it is very difficult to transcend anything because we cannot focus on it; that is, unless we have developed stability of mind through our practice of shamatha meditation.

Lighting a Torch in the Darkness

The instructions that guide us through the bardo of dream are known as "lighting a torch in the darkness." The darkness is ignorance, and to enter the states of sleep and dream is to enter a very deep experience of that ignorance. The torch that illuminates that darkness is our own pure, radiant awareness, which dispels the confusion that ordinarily engulfs us. When we recognize that awareness, the light of that realization infiltrates every aspect of our confused, samsaric states of sleep and dream.

The teachings on the illusionlike, dreamlike nature of appearances are basically related to the teachings of the Mahayana dharma. It is therefore extremely important to study the Mahayana view of emptiness as taught by the Buddha in the Prajnaparamita sutras, and later by his followers Nagarjuna and Asanga, the founders, respectively, of the Middle Way, or Madhyamaka, School and the Mind Only, or Chittamatra, School. The Mind Only view is very helpful in understanding relative reality. This school presents various detailed classifications of consciousness that are descriptive of how mind creates its projections. From studying these teachings, we learn how it is that these seemingly solid illusions arise and how it is that they are actually phenomena of mind. On the other hand, by studying the view and analytical methods of the Middle Way School, we gain an understanding of the absolute nature of all relative phenomena, their absence of true existence.

When we bring these two views together with the Vajrayana methods of illusory body and dream yoga, our practice becomes quite easy. If we do not have the view of emptiness, then we will struggle, feeling that we have to suddenly see our solid world in a non-solid way, like a rainbow.

That would not be very easy. However, if we continually remind ourselves during the day that this is an illusion, a dream, then, at night, we will have lucid dreams and we will be able to transform the appearances in those dreams.

Mastering The Mind
The Bardo of Meditation

4

WHEN WE RECOGNIZE the true nature of mind, we see not only its empty essence, but also its quality of wakefulness, of lucid awareness that is fully and vividly present. That awareness is the naturally abiding wisdom and compassion of the enlightened state. It is primordially present within the nature of mind. It was not created in the past by a divine being or act; it is beginningless and endless, beyond concept and philosophy. It is the nature of our mind and of the universe. Whatever state of mind we have, whatever thoughts or emotions we experience, all of these are in the nature of this wisdom. The whole experience of the samsaric world is simply the expression, or play, of this all-pervasive and uninterrupted wisdom. Fundamentally, there is nothing to fear; there is nothing that is not in the state of liberation. All forms, sounds, thoughts and emotions are appearance-emptiness, like the moon's reflection on water. In this utterly pure space, there is a sense of joy, freshness and total freedom, which naturally radiates outward. We accept and appreciate who we are and whatever arises in our experience. We are not bound by grasping at or rejecting appearances. Therefore, there is a state of genuine peace, of cessation of struggle.

> E MA
> At this time, when the bardo of meditation appears to you,
> Abandon the accumulations of distractions and confusion.
> Rest in the nature of nonwandering and nonfixation free
>   from extremes.
> Achieve stability in the development and fulfillment stages.

The *bardo of meditation* refers to the meditative state of our mind. It begins whenever we are resting our mind in the present, the state of nowness, in a clear, aware and undistracted manner. It ends whenever we are distracted from that state. Therefore, the length of time we spend in this bardo is very individual; it depends on how long we are able to remain focused and relaxed, aware and at rest.

Meditation as Bardo

The meditative state in which one rests directly in the nature of mind is the experience of genuine bardo; it is the experience of "gap"—the non-conceptual awareness that is beyond samsara and nirvana, or confusion and liberation. It is a moment of truth when we are at a fork in the road. When that moments ends—no matter how long that moment is—we exit either in the direction of liberation or confusion. To recognize the nature of mind is to take the fork in the road that leads us to liberation; to fail to recognize mind's nature is to follow the way of confusion.

If we have followed the latter course, then we must continue to deal with impure appearances in the form of duality: we feel a solid sense of "me" that is separate and distinct from an equally solid "you" or "it," or a cumulative "other." The ever-questionable and shifting relationship between these two breeds a state of constant struggle. We are moved now by hope, now by fear. Dissatisfied with who we are, we react toward the "other" with aggression, passion or a dismissive indifference. One moment we are happy, but in the next, we may be perturbed, angry, desirous, or simply dull and blank. In the space of this environment, we feel oppressed and burdened to the degree that our minds are obscured or constricted by confusion.

The simple difference lies in our habituation either to states of awareness or states of ignorance. It is a difference that marks our experience of this life as well as our experience of death. When we die, our habitual mind continues. We may be beset with fear and overwhelmed by the reflections of our own mind that appear to us, reflections from which we cannot escape. There is nowhere we can go to hide from our mind. If we have glimpsed the nature of mind and trained ourselves to rest in its nature, then we will recognize those appearances as the self-display of mind. They will help us to further recognize and realize mind's nature. We will have an opportunity to attain complete liberation; failing that, we will at least know with confidence that we possess the skill to direct our passage through the bardos of death. We can master any moment of uncertainty. Whatever thoughts, emotions or appearances arise, we will not be pulled in the direction of confusion or fear. Our training in vipashyana meditation is a direct means of entering into and stabilizing that experience.

Vipashyana

When you return home exhausted after a long day of hard work, you are usually very ready to take a break from that work and simply rest. If you have been engaged in particularly arduous physical labor, such as construction, cleaning, or even exercising on a treadmill, then you will naturally feel extremely tired. When you have reached the very peak of your exertion, when you have expended every ounce of energy you have, you reach a point where you simply take a deep breath and sit down. When you allow yourself to wholly let go and relax in that moment, your mind becomes completely nonconceptual. You do not have a thought in your head; body and mind start to calm down and loosen up, and yet you are not distracted. There is a sense of being fully present and appreciating that moment. That experience of resting after hard work, along with the relief that accompanies it, is given as an analogy for the bardo of meditation.

The bardo of meditation in Padmasambhava's teaching is connected to the experience of vipashyana. Vipashyana means "clear seeing," or "superior insight," and what is being seen at this point is the nature of mind, that is, the nature of ordinary mind, our naked awareness. Thus, vipashyana refers to the insight that directly realizes this nature of mind. This is sometimes expressed as "insight into emptiness," and this superior realization relates to the emptiness of both self and other, or mind and its phenomena.

The key point in vipashyana meditation is, therefore, awareness. What is awareness? It is simply a state of mind that is not distracted from the present moment. When we bring the mind to rest in its own state, in its own nature, without distraction, then we are in a state of awareness of the present moment. Regardless of our outer circumstances or inner state of mind, if we are present within the very experience of nowness, if we are fully experiencing the moment, then that is nondistraction. That is awareness. That is meditation. Thus, awareness, nondistraction and meditation are one and the same.

Vipashyana meditation in the Vajrayana sense begins with the practice of meditation on emptiness. When we practice from this perspective, the object upon which we focus is the nature of mind itself, its aspect of clear emptiness. However, in order to be able to rest our mind in this way, we must rely on the ground of shamatha, or calm abiding meditation, as discussed in chapter 2. If we are well trained in shamatha, then we can place our mind on any object—a pebble, an image of the Buddha or the sky— and it will rest there unwaveringly. Thus, the mind of shamatha has two aspects: it is not only calm, but also it abides wherever it is placed. Once we have developed this skill, we will also be able to rest our mind in the state of emptiness, in which there is no tangible focal object.

Without shamatha, there is no possibility of developing vipashyana. However, if we do not go on to develop vipashyana, then our shamatha cannot help us very much. While it will calm our mind, it cannot ultimately cut through and eradicate our disturbing emotions. Only the superior insight of vipashyana can do that. In a classic example of the relationship between the two, shamatha is compared to a pond, and vipashyana to the flowers that grow in and beautify the pond.

The great yogi Milarepa said:

Not being attached to the pond of shamatha
May the flower of vipashyana bloom.

Accordingly, vipashyana, which cuts both suffering and the causes of suffering, is seen as the more essential aspect of meditation.

It is important to understand that the bardo of meditation is where we train our minds to deal with the challenges and opportunities of the transitional experiences of all six bardo states. We are not simply trying to have a good meditation session or to become a calm person. We are not only working to improve our conditions or psychological state in the bardo of this life. The benefit of our training goes far beyond that. If you view your training here as the means to acquire the tools and precious possessions you will carry with you wherever you go—even in your journey beyond this life—then you are hearing the message of Padmasambhava and the lineage. The message is clear: to recognize the nature of your mind is to possess the key to liberation. All the trainings we undertake in the bardo of meditation lead to this point. Because the explanations of the meditations can be detailed and lengthy, it is possible to lose sight of the larger context in which they are presented. It is therefore essential to remind ourselves of the connection between our trainings in vipashyana and our journey through the bardos. Whatever bardo we may be passing through, it is transcended when we wake from our confusion and recognize the nature of mind.

Domesticating Wild Mind

The purpose of vipashyana is to tame our minds, to transcend our ordinary, dualistic consciousness. An example often used to describe this process compares the mind to a wild horse. In order to tame a wild horse, you first have to catch it, which requires considerable thoughtfulness and skill. You cannot simply run up to it and grab it. You have to approach it with great care. These days, wild horses are often rounded up with helicopters, a method that requires little skill and is quite unnatural. A more natural way is to develop a personal connection with the horse that you want to catch. After all, you are not in the business of mass-marketing wild horses. Your motivation is more personal; you have watched this beautiful wild horse from a distance and have fallen in love with it.

If you are able to approach and capture the horse on the basis of your personal connection and use of skillful means, then there will be the appropriate psychological space or environment for training it. Slowly and gradually, you get to know the horse, and the horse gets to know you. Through this contact, mutual understanding, connection, closeness and love develop. Eventually, your horse will be docile and trained enough for you to ride; however, when you ride it for the first time, you will still need to be very mindful. Even though you know your horse is now tame, you do not really know what it is going to do. Even a few months or a few years later, you will still need to be careful and alert.

We have to train our minds in a similar manner. No matter who we are—American cowboys or cowgirls, Tibetan yakboys, Indian buffalo boys—we are each training the wild horse of our mind. We are all doing the same thing. First, we have to make a personal connection with our wild mind and learn to appreciate its untamed, natural beauty. Then we have to capture it with mindfulness, and finally we have to tame and train this mind with further skillful means. One day, we will be able to ride it and direct it wherever we please. The Rolling Stones have a song that goes,

> Wild horses couldn't drag me away.
> Wild, wild horses, we'll ride them some day.[11]

That is the level that we have to reach, where wild horses cannot drag us away from the present moment of awareness. Once we have reached that level of training, then even in the bardos of death we will be able to guide our mind steadily past all difficulties toward awakening, toward freedom from samsara.

There is another well-known image; it compares our wild minds to a mad elephant in a china shop. When untamed, this elephant can very easily destroy many things in the shop, and even the shop itself. With one move, the elephant can destroy a wall; and with another move, another wall. In only four moves, this elephant can destroy the whole structure. In the same way, if our minds are not tamed, they can easily destroy our whole collection of virtue—all the merit and wisdom we have accumulated through the accomplishment of countless positive deeds.

Vipashyana meditation is the process of taming and training our minds. How do we do it? We catch our minds with shamatha and we train them with vipashyana. Then we ride our minds with mindfulness while remaining aware of the greater environment. Following these methods, we will reach our goal quite quickly—especially when we remember the thought of impermanence, which works like a whip.

Stages of Training in Selflessness

The meditations on emptiness are taught and practiced in stages, with each stage reflecting a particular view of self, mind and world. In the Hinayana and Mahayana stages of practice, vipashyana meditation on emptiness begins with analytical meditation, which looks at the notion of "self," or identity, from the vantage of absolute truth. When we speak of absolute truth, or ultimate reality, we must understand what is meant by *twofold emptiness:* the *selflessness of persons* and the *selflessness of phenomena,* or the emptiness of the self of persons and the emptiness of the self of phenomena. We approach this understanding through a systematic reasoning process, which leads us to glimpse emptiness directly. However, to really connect with such a glimpse means that we connect with our heart and intellect joined, so that we are not merely engaged in dry reasoning. While such a process might sound very conceptual and dualistic, if we engage in it properly, then it will bring about the experience of emptiness—it will produce the echo of emptiness. If we can rest within that experience, then it will deepen and become more profoundly present in all of our experiences.

In meditation, the actual practices involve actively looking for a truly existing self to see if it can be found. We first reflect on the self of persons and analyze our experience to see where it might be located and what, exactly, it is. When we set about looking for this self, which feels so solidly present and unquestionably real, where do we look? We look at what we cling to most strongly: body and mind. However, when we look more closely at these two, we find that they are not singular entities at all but are themselves collections composed of many parts. In Buddhist terminology, these collections are known as *skandhas,* or "aggregates," of which there are five, and which, when taken together, make up the totality of what we regard as a "self." They are the basis upon which we think, "This is me," as well as "That is other." The five skandhas include the skandha of form, which relates to body, as well as the four skandhas of feeling, perception, formation and consciousness, which relate to mind. The functioning of the skandhas is the means by which we know and grasp at the world in increasingly conceptual and solidified ways.

First, we look among these five skandhas to see if the self is located in just one of them, or if it is found in the sum of all five. If, for example, we conclude, "This self must be somewhere in the skandha of form," then we look at our body to see what part of our body can be identified as the self. Is the self the whole body, or one of its parts? If it is a part, then which part is it? Is it the brain? Is it the heart? After looking for some time, if we conclude that there is, after all, no self in the skandha of form, then we apply the same line of investigation to the remaining skandhas. The analysis proceeds in this way until we have reached certainty in finding, or not finding, the self.

Once no personal self has been found in the skandhas, we look for the self of phenomena, the true existence of "other." In this way, we exhaust all possibilities—we leave no stone unturned—in our search for what it is we cling to as "I" and "you," or "me" and "mine." The result of such investigations is the discovery that no inherently existing self can be found anywhere, either as a personal form of identity, or as a characteristic of external phenomena. In this way, we are led to the realization of selflessness: all phenomena are empty of a truly existing self. At that point, we relax and rest our mind with no further thought.

A true understanding of emptiness—one which does not distort its meaning into nihilism, the extreme and total negation of relative appearances—comes from understanding the Mahayana Madhyamaka view of the great master Nagarjuna. When the full teachings of such a master are comprehended, we appreciate emptiness as a unified state of being that surpasses and is devoid of the dualistic split of self and other. That state is called by various names. In the Mahayana tradition, it is called "ultimate truth," "buddha nature," and also "genuine reality"—all of which refer to the truest, deepest and most genuine level of reality. It is a state of wisdom that is inconceivable, beyond the reach of concept; therefore, when conceptual mind looks for it, nothing is ultimately found.[12]

In the traditions of Mahamudra and Dzogchen, vipashyana meditation consists of resting in the nature of mind, or the ultimate state of reality, that has been pointed out to you by your guru. In Mahamudra, the awareness that is pointed out is called "ordinary mind," or *thamal gyi shepa,* and in Dzogchen, it is "naked awareness," or *rigpa.* While the primary practices of these two traditions are nonconceptual resting meditations, there are also some practices that are more conceptual. In Mahamudra, there are specific practices for investigating the nature of mind, and in Dzogchen, there are methods for differentiating rigpa from consciousness.

The details of these practices should be received from your individual root teacher. When you have a strong heart connection to your guru and then receive these instructions directly from him or her, it is a much more personal and powerful experience because the guru knows you and you know your guru. The moment of transmission, of pointing out the nature of mind, becomes a strong meeting point—a genuine meeting of minds. The instructions are far more effective than when one receives a general introduction to vipashyana from a teacher.

POINTING-OUT MIND'S NATURE

Sometimes we put our glasses in our pockets or on our heads and later we ask, "Where are my glasses?" This is quite common. We look everywhere else without finding our glasses. That is why we need the guru, who can say to us, "There are your glasses." That is all that the Mahamudra and Dzogchen teachers do: they simply point out. What they are pointing out is something that you already have. It is not something that they give you. They do not give you new glasses. They cannot afford to give you new glasses, but they can afford to point out where you can find your own glasses.

When we receive pointing-out instructions from our root teacher, we are being introduced directly and nakedly to the reality of mind's nature. These instructions become very effective if we have prepared ourselves to receive them. That preparation consists of the training in the three prajnas. As described earlier, the training consists of studying the philosophical view of the path, contemplating that view in order to integrate it into our understanding, and subsequently engaging in both the preliminary and main practices of the stage of meditation.

Pointing-out is similar to pointing to the sky when it is very cloudy and saying to someone, "There is the blue sky." The person will look up and say, "Where?" You may reply, "It is there—behind the clouds." The person to whom you are pointing out the blue sky will not see it at first. However, if even a patch of blue sky appears, then you can say, "Look— the blue sky is like that." The person then gets a direct experience. He or she knows experientially that there is blue sky, which will be fully visible when the clouds are gone.

In the same way, if you have developed an understanding of the profound view through study and reflection, and some level of meditative stabilization through your practice of shamatha, then that experience of peace and clarity is like a glimpse of the nature of mind. When the teacher points out the nature of mind to you, you will recognize it in the same way as the person seeing the patch of blue will recognize the blue sky. You will say, "This is the nature of mind." When you can rest freely, everything becomes like that glimpse, just as the whole sky is blue once the clouds have gone. Therefore, in order for the pointing-out to be effective, the text says that we need to prepare the ground by developing a stable practice of shamatha meditation.

LOOKING DIRECTLY AT MIND

The whole point of our practice in the bardo of meditation is to see clearly the nature of mind that has been pointed out to us. It is not sufficient just to notice the presence of thoughts and emotions. We need to recognize their true nature and then rest within that experience.

In the Dzogchen tradition of Padmasambhava, "clear seeing," or vipashyana meditation, is accomplished by simply resting in naked awareness without any concepts or thoughts. How do you do this?

First, bring your awareness to your eye sense consciousness and place your gaze into the empty space in front of you. Then, simply relax at ease without fixation. The instructions say:

> Direct your awareness to the eyes.
> Direct your eyes into space.
> By resting loosely, wisdom will naturally arise.

While remaining in a state of nondistraction, you look with a mind that is vividly and sharply focused, and you rest within that. You do not bring any thoughts into the experience. It is not necessary to remember to be calm or clear or to remember any instructions. You simply look without any thoughts at all.

The text says that if you look straight ahead into space with your eyes wide, it will bring the experience of nonconceptual rigpa. When practicing the methods of the general Hinayana-Mahayana path, the gaze is downward. When practicing Vajrayana methods, we look up into space. In both Mahamudra and Dzogchen practices, it is important to look straight into space.[13] The text also says that it is important to do short sessions, repeating them again and again. Once you become more familiar with this practice and it has become more natural, you can extend your sessions.

The true nature of mind that you are looking for is found simply in whatever you experience "now," in this very moment. There is no "true nature" beyond that. This is what the guru points out. Our usual problem is that when an afflicted mind arises, we do not recognize its ultimate nature, its fundamental state of emptiness. We do not see its vividly arising energy as the display of our own primordially pure awareness—our innate wakefulness. We think that it is purely a poison, a klesha.

If it is aggression that appears, we think, "I should not have this aggression! I should be experiencing the nature of mind." Consequently, we push the aggression away and try to find the nature of mind elsewhere. However, there is nothing to be found elsewhere. There is nowhere we can find the nature of mind outside the aggression we are experiencing now. Therefore, we have to look at that aggression as straightforwardly as possible. We have to look at it directly—just as directly as our eye consciousness looks at space.

In the same way, we penetrate all the disturbing emotions that arise for us. We look straight at whatever is there in any moment of consciousness, without labeling it or altering it. It is important to experience the texture of aggression, of passion, of jealousy in its natural, raw state. How does it feel? What does it taste like? Usually we do not fully grasp such experiences. Instead, just as we are beginning to get into the experience, we run away from it, or else we completely change it into something else through concepts and thoughts. As a result, we miss the fullness, the entirety of the experience.

If aggression arises and you conceptualize it—that is, you label it and think, "This is aggression"—then it seems very solid and real. However, if you experience it freshly, just as it is, then it naturally dissolves into space and is self-liberated. Nothing has made it dissolve—neither you nor any other factor present at the same moment has caused that transformation. It changes by itself. It dissolves into space naturally. That is its primordial nature.

If you are a Buddhist, the way in which aggression arises in you has not changed since you became a Buddhist. It arises in exactly the same way as it did before you became a Buddhist. Whether you are a religious person of another tradition, or a person without any religious beliefs, it is also the same. Moreover, it is the same whether you are a human being or another form of sentient being. The nature of mind is the same. It arises and it manifests within the space of your awareness in its own natural state. Thus, the genuine state of aggression is not aggression; rather, "aggression" is a label that we give to a particular experience. Passion is a label that we give to another experience. When you look at the raw, vivid and sharp

experiences of passion and aggression, you realize that they are inseparable. From the point of view of the experience, there are no distinctive
labels that identify something as passion and something else as aggression, ignorance or jealousy.

How do we bring this understanding into our personal experience? We
will realize the nature of mind only when we have the courage and awareness to look directly at the present moment of our experience—whether
it is a virtuous thought, a perception or a negative, disturbing emotion. It
does not matter. The nature of mind is right here. The reason that we do
not recognize it is not because it is not here, but because we are looking
somewhere else.

In order to realize the nature of mind and stabilize that recognition, we
must persist in looking at our experience, constantly, moment by moment,
with a sense of discipline; yet at the same time we need a sense of humor.
We need a sense of spaciousness and relaxation. Many people think of
meditation as hard work. That is not meditation. Meditation is learning
how to let go of stress and striving. We have to learn how to rest. That is
what we are doing here: resting in the nature of mind. All Mahamudra and
Dzogchen teachers have said that the only way to recognize the nature of
mind is to relax fully. The Mahamudra instructions say that those who can
relax the most have the best meditation; those who have an average ability to relax have mediocre meditation; and those who cannot relax at all
have the least meditative experience. This has been repeated again and
again by other masters. The ability to rest within our immediate experience is especially important at the time of death and when we are entering the after-death bardos.

When we can relax in that experience of nowness—whatever that
is—there is hope. It may be just a glimpse of that experience, but if we
can sustain that glimpse, then it becomes realization. We will discover
how insubstantial and ephemeral the appearances of mind are—how
our thoughts and emotions are simply beautiful experiences. There is
nothing to frighten or threaten us. However, if we go beyond the actual experience and label our emotions, then we will lose our opportunity. If we think, "This is anger, and I feel this way toward so and so
because…" then we will find many reasons to support and increase our
anger. As our thoughts proliferate, we will experience more pain, confusion and suffering. If, on the other hand, we allow ourselves to sim-

ply rest relaxed for a moment, then that moment becomes an experience of freedom.

Gaining Certainty in Liberation
THREE WORDS THAT STRIKE THE VITAL POINT

The great mahasiddha Garab Dorje, the original master of the Dzogchen lineage in this world, transmitted an exceptionally clear instruction on the essential points of liberation that came to be known as *Three Words That Strike the Vital Point.*[14] It was taught repeatedly by Padmasambhava and commented upon very beautifully by Patrul Rinpoche. The vital point we are trying to strike is enlightenment, the experience and realization of the true nature of our mind, and the three words are the pith instructions that carry one straight to that point.

The first word is to *decide directly on one thing*. What are we deciding on? We are deciding that this very moment of consciousness is self-liberated; these very experiences of emotions—of suffering and happiness that are arising—are the expression of rigpa, our naked awareness. We have to ascertain this. We are at least affirming our intention to understand the nature of mind and work toward genuine realization. This decision is the first word that strikes the vital point.

The second word is to *directly recognize one's nature*. We become directly introduced to rigpa, the essential nature of our mind. We recognize that, apart from this very experience of nowness, this very mind, there is nothing to be pointed out. We recognize that *this is it*. No matter who appears in front of you—all the buddhas of the ten directions and the three times, or an ocean of bodhisattvas, dakas and dakinis—there is nothing more to point out. Coming to that kind of recognition is the second word that strikes the vital point.

The third word is to *gain confidence in liberation*. This refers to confidence in self-liberation. We gain confidence that this very mind that we are experiencing now, in this present moment, is self-liberated. When we look directly at that mind, we spontaneously know it as unborn, and we can taste the experience of realization. Developing confidence in that is known as the third word that strikes the vital point.

These instructions are taught through the "four great modes of liberation" in the Dzogchen tradition.

Dzogchen's Four Great Modes of Liberation

In the Dzogchen tradition, the state or process of liberation can be viewed from several aspects. These are known as the *four great modes of liberation*: primordial liberation, self-liberation, naked liberation and complete liberation. These are summarized here, using the example of passion. When we gain confidence in liberation, we develop certainty in these four aspects of liberation.

Primordial Liberation

When a moment of passion arises in a vivid and sharp manner, the nature of that passion is primordially liberated. In this sense, "primordial" refers to the ground, to the fundamental state of emptiness of that passion. At the moment when passion arises, it is already in the state of selflessness, or shunyata. Its nature has never been tainted by any trace of samsaric confusion. It is already free from concepts; therefore, it is primordially and utterly free. We do not need to re-create that ground of emptiness, because it is already there. That basic state is simply a brilliant experience of unceasing clarity. That is primordial liberation.

Self-liberation

With regard to self-liberation, that vivid passion is not liberated by anything outside of itself. Like a snake that simply uncoils itself from its own knot, passion returns to its natural state independent of any external antidotes. It is self-liberated. It is already in the nature of transcendence, of rigpa, the true nature of mind. Even in the relative sense, passion arises, changes constantly and ceases by itself. As much as we may desire to solidify and hold on to it for another moment, it will not stay. That is why, from the Vajrayana perspective, it is taught that we cannot purify or transform passion except through passion itself. This is also the meaning of self-liberation.

Naked Liberation

Naked liberation occurs when the mind observes itself. When passion arises and we look at it nakedly and straightforwardly, we do not see anything that truly exists in a substantial way. The bare experience of passion is simply the "isness" quality that is left when we look at passion without concepts. It is called naked liberation because when we look nakedly and directly at the passionate mind, that very process of looking liberates the experience of passion. The true nature of rigpa is naturally free from the dualistic experience of consciousness. In the absence of our solid concepts, there remains a sense of vivid energy and movement, like the flickering of a flame. That vibrant, radiant quality shows us the actual insubstantial nature of mind, which is not what we generally experience in our mundane, relative world. That is what we call naked liberation.

Complete Liberation

Complete liberation occurs when passion is further liberated as mind observes the experience of passion again and again. In the first moment of the arising of passion, we look at it directly, and it liberates itself. In the second moment, we look directly again and it liberates itself further. As we continue to look nakedly and straightforwardly at this world of passion, moment after moment, it liberates itself further and further, or more completely. This method needs to be applied repeatedly and in short sessions. In this way, we can see that the essence of rigpa does not abide in any of the three times—past, present or future—and is perfectly free. This process is similar to working with "the watcher" in shamatha practice. The watcher is the self-conscious aspect of mind that participates in our practice as an "observer." When we look at the watcher, it dissolves. Then it returns again, and we look it, and it dissolves again. Eventually, the watcher does not return. That is complete liberation.

Fundamentally, these are the instructions on the nature of mind and how we look at it. As far as primordial liberation is concerned, it is important to look without artifice or further fabrication. For self-liberation, it is important to look without engaging too much in concepts and mental discernments, such as labeling thoughts "good" or "bad." At certain times it is necessary to engage conceptual mind, or to apply analysis, and at other times it is important to withdraw from that activity. Knowing the right time for each is what we call skillful means. When you are actually in a session of Dzogchen or Mahamudra meditation, it is important to disengage completely from all movements of conceptual mind and simply rest. For naked liberation, it is important to observe the nature of mind while resting naturally. Whatever arises, let it rest in its own place. For complete liberation, it is necessary to go through all the stages of the path and their meditation practices. Therefore, the pointing-out instructions for these practices become essential. These should be received directly from your individual teacher, a master who holds the genuine lineage transmission of those teachings.

Taking the Message of Liberation to Heart

When we look closely at our thoughts and emotions, we can see their quality of self-liberation. When we see their nature of appearance-emptiness, we see that they have no inherent existence. They are unborn and, therefore, they neither abide nor cease. They spontaneously appear from the nature of mind and naturally dissolve back into that nature. When we realize this, we can see that thoughts and emotions do not impose anything on us or bind us in any way; therefore, they are not truly a cause of suffering. When we see that they are naturally free, we are free as well. We do not need to follow after them, solidify them, act on them or create a world around them. That is true for the bardo of this life as well as for the bardos of death, where the projections of mind become quite vivid.

If we can get closer to the ultimate nature of our emotions and rest directly within that nature, then we can see that self-liberation is taking place all the time. We can see that no other method of liberation is necessary and also that no other method could possibly work. If you are experiencing anger, for example, you may feel that you need to apply an external antidote to that anger, so that you do not have it anymore. However, if you simply rest in that anger, then it liberates itself. You do not need to think, "First, I need to destroy this anger that is bothering me and then I will rest in the nature of mind." Often our minds are habituated to that way of thinking. That is the same as thinking that first we will destroy our enemy and then we will have peace. However, we never know if we are going to have peace after destroying our enemy. What assurance do we have of this? Another enemy, another moment of anger, might arise.

Ultimately speaking, any method outside of self-liberation does not destroy anger. If we decide to "count to ten," or replace an angry thought with a happy thought, or sit on our meditation cushion and follow our breath, those are relative methods that will help us temporarily. However, we are only suppressing our anger, not uprooting or eradicating it. In order to uproot our anger, in order fully to transcend it, we need to be present with the full experience of that emotion and penetrate its essence. We need to see its true nature, its genuine state. Then we will see that we are not actually liberating our anger, nor are we liberating ourselves. Our anger is self-liberated because it is primordially liberated. That is its nature. It is not newly liberated. There is no need to liberate anger from being anger, and change it into something we think of as pleasant or positive. What we call "anger" has in fact never been anger; its fresh and vividly arising energy has never been bound by our concept of anger. When we recognize this—the natural process of self-liberation—then we will find a complete and deep sense of peace.

The vipashyana methods of Madhyamaka are an equally important and powerful tool for recognizing the self-liberation of emotions. Using the method of contemplative analysis, we first look at the arising of anger. When we find that there is no arising of anger, then naturally there can be no abiding of that anger. When we find that there is no abiding of anger, then there can be no cessation of that anger. This holds true for all emotions. Therefore, Madhyamaka continually emphasizes "no arising," which cuts the process at the very beginning.

Like Mahamudra and Dzogchen, Madhyamaka does not apply any antidotes to suppress or destroy the arising of emotions, other than the analysis that produces insight into their nature. When we analyze the emotions in this way, they are self-liberated. It is important to understand that these methods are not mere philosophy. In Tibet, there are many stories about monks who attained realization in the midst of very aggressive debates. At some point, they had a gap experience—something clicked and they said, "Ah!" Such philosophical debates are not a simple matter of refuting your debating partner. The point is going beyond philosophy to gain direct insight into the nature of mind.

ACCEPTING AND REJECTING

The key to resting in the nature of mind, whatever upheavals we may be going through, is simply to be in the moment. This means that we accept who we are, we acknowledge our experience and we appreciate its fundamental value. In order to do this, however, we need to overcome one of our greatest problems, which is our habitual tendency to dwell in a poverty mentality—a state of perpetual dissatisfaction.

When we feel we are lacking in good qualities, we want to reject who we are and be someone else. We think, "I want to be a yogi. I do not want this old me; I am tired of myself. I want to be Milarepa." However, that is a very unrealistic and extreme desire. How can you be Milarepa? He was who he was. What we are aspiring to here is his realization. We are aspiring to his awakening. Of course, we want to achieve enlightenment. We want to achieve realization of the nature of mind—but whose mind? Do you want to realize the nature of your mind or Milarepa's mind? You do not need to realize the nature of Milarepa's mind because he has realized it already. Not only are such desires irrational and impractical; they are not genuine, either. They lack clarity and discrimination.

There is a story about Mahatma Gandhi, who, some time after achieving independence for India, visited a mental hospital. Among the many people he met was one particular inmate who sat and talked to him. He sounded quite sensible. He displayed no signs of insanity, but talked very naturally and normally. Gandhi-ji began to wonder why this man was locked up. At that very moment, the inmate asked, "What is your name?" and Gandhi-ji replied, "Gandhi." The inmate said, "Oh, yeah, everybody who comes here says that! You will learn." Just as everyone there wanted to be Mahatma Gandhi, we want to be someone other than ourselves. That is the problem obstructing our realization of the nature of mind.

One aspect of the desire to be someone else is the tendency to reject our own experience. When we are angry, we struggle with ourselves, thinking, "I don't want to feel this anger! I would rather feel anything else! Even jealousy would be better than this!" When we try to escape our emotions by changing them into something else, then the experience is no longer genuine. The key is to be who you are, which involves both courage and wisdom. We do not just heedlessly accept who we are and jump into our confusion. On the contrary, we relate to the basic state of our being with mindfulness and awareness, and we appreciate that. Whether you are an angry person, a jealous person, a passionate person or a slightly ignorant person, that is who you are. It does not help to try to be someone else.

It is like the story of Gandhi-ji talking to the inmate. Gandhi-ji thinks that he is "Gandhi," but in absolute reality he is not. From an absolute point of view, he is shunyata, emptiness. We may think "I am so and so," but when we analyze the basis of that thought, we find we are not that person. It is quite ironic. When we look at the story of Gandhi-ji, the inmate is like a yogi who is telling us something, trying to wake us up. Who knows which one is the crazy person? The story is very interesting from an absolute point of view as well as from a relative perspective.

When the Buddha characterized the six realms of existence in the sutras and tantras, he described the suffering of the human realm as the tendency to be perennially caught up in states of dissatisfaction and distraction, what we would call "poverty mentality" and "busyness." These are the primary characteristics of human suffering, of human life. Somehow, we must find a way to transcend that suffering, to find our own experience of realization that will transform these basic tendencies of the human realm.

When we experience the actual nature of emotions, perceptions or thoughts, they do not have the characteristics of poverty mentality and busyness, which are purely mental fabrications. Therefore, in order to transform these fabrications now as well as in the bardo states to come, we must take to heart the teachings on self-liberation. When we can rest our mind in the present moment of our experience—without being distracted by thoughts and without altering the experience in any way—then we can penetrate all fabrications. They will simply dissolve in the space of nonconceptual awareness. All thoughts and emotions are naturally self-liberated when we accept who we are, accept each experience as it arises and genuinely appreciate the opportunity that such experiences provide.

SELF-EXISTING WISDOM

There is no wisdom higher than present mind itself. The opportunity to connect with our inherent, self-existing wisdom is present within every level of our experience. Whether we are exhibiting positive or negative qualities, whether we are being mean and spiteful to others, or kind, gentle and sympathetic, we must acknowledge and be present within that. When we look straight at an emotion such as anger, no matter where or how we look, we cannot pinpoint anything that is solid or real. Our anger appears to us like the reflection of the moon on water—clearly apparent, yet utterly selfless. It is nothing more than the display of mind's luminous energy arising from empty awareness wisdom.

We can see the illusionlike quality of anger by looking at yesterday's anger from today's point of view, or today's anger from tomorrow's point of view. This method was mentioned earlier in conjunction with the illusory body practice. For a moment, pretend that it is tomorrow and you are looking back at today, at any moment of anger or strong emotion that you remember. What appears to us now as so real and compelling, such that we speak and act in certain ways, can appear from tomorrow's point of view as no more substantial and significant than a mirage. When we truly look at our emotions, we find that they are simply a display—the expression of self-existing, self-arising wisdom. They are the expression of the nature of mind, of ordinary mind, of rigpa. They are nothing but the manifestation of mind's inherent clarity.

All of our efforts on this spiritual journey are aimed at the realization of this self-existing wisdom, which is the wisdom of buddha, our own innate wakefulness. Since these emotions are an expression of that luminous mind, how could we and why should we reject or abandon them? From the Mahamudra, Dzogchen and Vajrayana points of view, there is no need to relinquish or abandon the emotions. They are regarded as ornaments of our realization—they enrich and beautify mind. It is neither possible nor necessary to abandon them. Even if we wished to find something that would put an end to them, so that we would never have to experience them again, we could find no such thing. How can we destroy our own wakefulness? It is possible to eradicate confusion, but even in death the expression of wisdom cannot be stopped or destroyed.

LETTING GO OF FREEDOM

Generally speaking, when we want to acquire liberation, it is impossible. However, if we can let go of the concept of enlightenment, then liberation comes naturally. Accordingly, we should not hold too tightly on to the concept of liberation or freedom. Holding rigidly to any view or belief usually results only in more suffering, as we can see from many examples in our world today.

Even in our own lives, there are times when we want something so much that we cannot let go of the thought of it. Whether that is an object, a person or a state of mind, whatever it is, we long for it, but it remains out of reach. Then, at the very point where we totally give up and let go of it, we get what we have been wishing for.

In the same way, when we can finally let go of our efforts to achieve liberation, when we can simply relax and experience our emotions nakedly, that is the point at which we can experience the freedom that has been there all along. From the Vajrayana, Dzogchen and Mahamudra points of view, when we can recognize the nature of mind, of rigpa, and relax in that nature, we do not have to seek after freedom—enlightenment comes to us. That is possible in this very lifetime.

It is said clearly in these teachings that, aside from "this very thought," there is nothing upon which to meditate. There is no object other than the present moment of mind that can help us bring about the state of non-thought—of nonconceptual, nondual wisdom. Likewise, there is no means of arriving at that state other than the direct and naked experience of the genuine nature of emotions. When we experience that nonconceptual wisdom, we are beyond hope and fear. What would we hope for or fear? Actual liberation is already right there within that experience. When there is no hope and no fear, that is what we call freedom. That is what we attain through the practices of the bardo of meditation.

THE NATURE OF ALL

Once we have realized the nature of mind through determining the nature of a single thought or emotion, then we have realized the nature of all thoughts and emotions. You will definitely not have to work your way through all the others. You do not have to think, "Well, that is one down, now on to the next one." This view is also the view of Madhyamaka: "The emptiness of one is the emptiness of all."

This means that, when you realize the emptiness of the self of persons, you also realize the emptiness of the self of phenomena. The emptiness of these two is no different. For example, the emptiness of an object, such as a table, is no different from the emptiness of an individual person. The reality of shunyata or egolessness is the same. In a similar way, the nature of mind remains the same whether it is manifesting as passion, aggression or ignorance.

Therefore, the text says that it is important for us to look at each arising of thought or emotion, to accept that experience and to be clear about its nature. Once we have realized the nature of the angry mind, then, when jealousy arises, we will already have realized the nature of the jealous mind. The text says that this is similar to realizing the nature of water.

If you analyze a single drop of water and consequently come to understand its make-up—that it is composed of two parts hydrogen and one part oxygen—then you will know that any water you see is composed in the same way. You will not have to go through the analysis all over again. You will realize that all water is the same, whether it is in a bottle, a glass, a tap or a toilet. Therefore, it is important not to skip the opportunity that is right in front of you. Penetrate the experience, whatever it is.

Although we may realize this theoretically, it is natural for us to set aside difficult experiences. If we find anger difficult, then when anger comes, we might say, "Anger is very difficult, so I cannot deal with this now. I will work with my passion when it comes because I can deal with that much better." However, when passion arrives, it will be the same story. At that time we will think, "I thought passion was easier than anger, but now I realize it is not. I can deal better with anger after all, so I will look at the nature of mind when anger comes." In this way, we continue to jump back and forth. We switch our focus from anger to jealousy, jealousy to passion, passion to pride. We go around and around and around. This is what we call cyclic existence. It is not the path to liberation. That is why it is crucial to be with whatever is in front of us: Be diligent, precise and clear, and cut through it on the spot.

Therefore, if, through any emotion, you can get a good grip on the nature of mind—just one good grip—that is all you need. It is even more effective if you can pinpoint your most challenging emotion and work with it. If other emotions arise intensely, then you have to work with them also; but primarily, try to get a good grip on the most obstinate one. Then you will have a good grip on all your emotions. At the same time, if you jump around and try to grab too many things at once, then you end up with nothing. You find that everything has slipped away. You have no experience and no realization. You are back at square one.

Guarding Awareness

The bardo of meditation is, in brief, the state of meditative concentration, or samadhi, in which the mind is at rest and is not distracted from its object—in this case, the nature of mind. The mind therefore rests in the state of union—the inseparability of awareness and space. The main practice of the bardo of meditation is vipashyana, the method that produces the superior realization or insight that directly sees the nature of mind. Here we have discussed several approaches to the cultivation and realization of vipashyana, including the view of the tradition of Dzogchen. Whichever method we use, it is important for us not to become distracted. Nondistraction is the actual body of meditation; it is the most essential support for our practice.

According to these instructions, in terms of any emotion that arises in meditation, it is important not to become distracted by anything outside of it. Do not lose the energy of that emotion, whatever it is. Simply rest your mind and look at it.

In terms of the thoughts that arise during meditation, you should recognize that there are two kinds: coarse and subtle. It is important to attend to both kinds of thoughts. It is said that coarse thoughts are like robbers and subtle thoughts are like thieves. Coarse thoughts are easily noticed. They are like careless bandits that come and rob us of our awareness, right in front of our eyes. Subtle thoughts hide beneath the surface of our attention. We are often not aware of their presence. They steal our awareness in a more furtive way. They can distract us without our even recognizing their presence. If we notice them for a moment, they run and hide again. They steal our mindfulness, our concentration and the focus of our meditation. The instruction is therefore to always guard our awareness.

PATH OF SKILLFUL MEANS

In addition to the instructions for shamatha-vipashyana, the instructions for the bardo of meditation include the practice of deity yoga of the Vajrayana path of skillful means. In general, there are two stages of deity yoga practice, known as the "creation" and "completion" stages, or *utpattikrama* and *sampannakrama*. In order to engage in this practice, you need to receive individual instruction from your teacher, as there are many forms of deity yoga, and each is specific to a particular deity. Deity yoga is the main Vajrayana practice for the bardo of becoming, the interval that precedes one's rebirth and the continuation of samsaric existence. Therefore, this practice will be discussed along with the bardo of becoming. However, the methods of nondistraction and recognition of the nature of one's mind apply in the same way. Whichever methods we use, whether it is shamatha-vipashyana or deity yoga practice, we should always remember that all are used simply to bring about the experience of the nature of mind.

Connecting the Bardos of Life and Death

The first three bardos—the natural bardo of this life, the bardo of dream and the bardo of meditation—all relate to and can be included within the natural bardo of this life, since both dreams and the state of samadhi occur within this life. Because we are in this bardo right now, the instructions for all three are our main practice, and they are crucial for the development of our path. However, during this life we should also reflect on and familiarize ourselves with the next set of bardos we will experience. From the ultimate point of view, this life's training is important because it determines whether we will achieve enlightenment in this lifetime; from a relative point of view, it is important because it determines how we will meet our death and navigate the after-death intervals.

In some ways, we may find it difficult to see a direct connection between these first three bardos and the remaining three. We may not see the connection between our life now and what happens after we leave this life. However, there is a connection. If, in this life, we habituate ourselves to these practices, then our experience of the bardos of death and after-death will be familiar to us, and they will be much more powerful tools for us to recognize the nature of mind. Hence, our practice in this life supplements our practice at the time of death and beyond. If you are a skillful practitioner in this life, then your training now will bring you a powerful and vivid experience of the nature of mind. As a result, when you enter the bardos of death, you will not feel that you are in completely unknown territory. Rather, your encounter with death will feel like you are meeting someone you already know—an old and trusted friend from your past life.

Evaporating Reality
The Painful Bardo of Dying

5

IN THE BARDO of this life, we may be very earnest in our contemplation of mind's ultimate nature, and try with great effort to gain some experience of it through meditation. At the time of death, however, this very experience arises effortlessly. When we finally reach the point of the dissolution of all dualistic appearances, we experience a moment of complete awareness, a moment of vivid clarity. It is like a shift in the weather, when the sky clears up; the dense covering of clouds is gone, and suddenly we see the vast sky. At this moment, mind arrives directly at its own ground. It is just like coming home.

We are usually so distracted by the appearances of the outside world that we never notice mind itself. Now all that remains is mind. We may feel trapped, in a sense, as there is nothing to carry us away into perceptions of past and future. However, if we can relax and appreciate the peace and freedom of the present moment, it is a great experience. There is a teaching in the Mahayana tradition: if you can change a situation, then why worry? If you cannot change a situation, then why worry? Just relax.

When mind returns home to its original state, our experience is completely natural. In contrast, in our ordinary life, we often feel somewhat constrained and artificial in our behavior. When we go out to a social event, we choose our clothes carefully. We do not simply wear whatever we please. When we arrive at the home of our host or hostess and remove our shoes at the door, we do not simply throw them anywhere. We take them off and carefully put them in a certain place. When we sit in that person's house, we do not sit in too casual a way; we sit carefully and properly. However, when we return home, we feel more at ease. We throw our shoes and clothes wherever we please. We sit down and relax. When dualistic appearances dissolve, it is just like that. The mind simply relaxes and lets go of everything. In the same way, when we come to observe mind's ultimate state, its empty-luminous nature, it is like relaxing in our own home—it is quite a pleasant experience. Therefore, dying is not necessarily only a time of physical suffering and mental agony. We also meet with many powerful moments of clarity.

Consequently, if we have had some amount of practice in this life, then this will be a good time. It will be a time to celebrate, instead of a time of suffering. On the other hand, for those who have had no practice, it will be time to pack up the party. Therefore, yogis and yoginis are not afraid of death. For them, death is a time to recognize the guru's pointing-out instructions on ordinary mind, or naked awareness. The experience of death is the same as the moment in which you received pointing-out instructions from the guru. The same! When you are sitting in the presence of the guru receiving those instructions, it is a very enlightening, uplifting and joyous moment. The death experience is identical to that moment.

On the basis of that moment, we can be liberated. If we are not able to be liberated at the time of death, then it is necessary to have the instructions on the after-death bardos. But if we do achieve liberation, then those bardos do not arise.

> E MA
> At this time, when the bardo of death appears to you,
> Abandon attraction, attachment and fixation to all.
> Enter into the nature of the clear oral instructions without
>   distraction.
> Transfer into the unborn space of self-arising awareness.

The *painful bardo of dying* begins at the time when we are struck with some unfavorable condition that causes the dissolution of the appearances of this life, whether it is an accident, a terminal illness or any natural cause such as old age that results in the exhaustion of our body. It ends with the cessation of our inner respiration, just before the dawning of the bardo of dharmata, which follows it.

For realized beings, such as Padmasambhava, the painful bardo of dying does not exist; consequently, the two subsequent bardos also do not exist. However, when you are not a realized person—even though you may feel that you know enough, or just enough, to get by and escape those experiences—you must go through the interval called the painful bardo of dying. It is said to be painful because, at the time of the dissolution of the elements when we begin to lose contact with the appearances of this life, we experience some degree of physical and psychological pain and suffering.

Attachment to This Life

At the time of our death, we may become overwhelmed by feelings of sadness, fear and pain. What is the source of that pain and suffering? Its origin is our attachment—our grasping at and holding on to the appearances of this life. We are simply unwilling to let go of them, whether our attachment is to our spouse, family, home, work, wealth or reputation. That is the primary cause for the pain of this bardo.

Even now, when we remember death, we may feel that fear and attachment. Whenever these feelings arise, we can remind ourselves again and again that such emotions are of no help to us. If we find ourselves lingering in these states, we can recall that we are not the only persons who are dying. Everyone who has taken birth will die. Everyone who was born long ago has died. Everyone living in the present is dying now or will die. Everyone who will be born in the future will also die. No one is left behind to go on living. We cannot find anyone who is twenty-five hundred years old. We might live a long time; perhaps we will live past a hundred but then we will be gone.

If it were the case that no one but you had to die, that no one but you were to be punished by death, then, of course, it would be reasonable to feel sadness or fear. You could say, "Why only me?" However, even though we know this is not the case, when death approaches we continue to ask, "Why me?" and "Why now?" As there is no one who can tell us the length of time we have to live, the point is to be ready. In first aid training, we learn emergency techniques like CPR, so that when a crisis comes, we are prepared to save someone's life. Although we never know exactly when it will happen, whenever we do get that call, we will be ready to apply our training helpfully. Similarly, if we receive a call that tells us our death is approaching, then we need to be ready with these instructions. We must be ready to use the tools in our first aid kit as effectively and as forcefully as we can. That is the whole purpose in working with these instructions. If we can let go of our attachment, then this bardo is no longer the "painful" bardo of dying. It is simply "the bardo of dying," which we can then experience clearly. Otherwise, our minds are so overwhelmed by our clinging and grasping that we miss the whole experience. We lose our opportunity to notice what is actually taking place; we overlook each occurrence of the manifestation of the nature of mind. Then we are unable to take the experience of this bardo fully onto the path. In order to counteract this tendency and create a more positive situation, we can practice letting go of our attachment to this lifetime.

When we look closely at our attachment, we see that it is nothing more than habituation. We have developed certain patterns that we persist in. We have become caught up in a pattern of clinging and grasping that has become so entrenched and solidified that we have ceased to notice it. Therefore, we have to reorient ourselves; we have to habituate ourselves to a new way of relating to our experience that will help undo our old patterns and extricate us from our attachment. The most effective means for doing this is to become habituated to the practice of mindfulness and awareness. Thus, it is important to remind ourselves repeatedly to apply this practice in every situation. We do not wait until we are sitting on our meditation cushion. If that were the case, then a lot of time would be wasted. If we can undo our habitual clinging and attachment now, in this lifetime, then we can transcend the suffering of this bardo.

THREE CAPACITIES OF PRACTITIONERS

The traditional teachings say that individuals have differing experiences of this bardo according to whether they are practitioners of great capacity, middling capacity or lesser capacity. The way each type of practitioner dies and how they experience the bardo is somewhat different.

Great Practitioners

The greatest practitioners, those who have gone beyond all dualistic grasping and fixation, transcend the normal process of death and achieve the state known as the *rainbow body*. At the point of death, their pure minds dissolve back into ultimate reality, or dharmata—the completely pure nature of mind and all phenomena—and the gross elements of their bodies dissolve back into the basic reality of shunyata. As an outer sign of accomplishment, their body will shrink, and, if left undisturbed, it usually disappears; they do not even leave their body behind. They may leave only their hair and nails, which are the coarsest parts of the physical body, and these relics are collected and enshrined by their students.

Padmasambhava achieved the rainbow body, and many of his disciples also left this world in that form. These things can happen. Such physical transformations are not a matter of great importance. Much more amazing things can happen: the transformation of our confused mind into the state of enlightenment. That is something that should really amaze us. Rainbow bodies and other such physical manifestations, on the other hand, should be understood simply as signs of good practice.

Middling Practitioners

When practitioners of the middling capacity die, they meet their death without fear or struggle. Because they have transcended their attachment to the appearances of this life, they are able to simply rest in the nature of mind, in the *samadhi of dharmata.* Practitioners of this level do not dissolve their physical body into the rainbow body. They leave their bodies behind, as many great masters have done. Nevertheless, they realize the true nature of mind at the time of death.

Practitioners of these two capacities do not go through the experiences of the bardo of death, and so they do not need to be concerned with the teachings and instructions on those bardos. Death, for them, becomes the experience of great samadhi, of profound realization. Yogis such as Milarepa and Padampa Sangye sang about this again and again. They said that death is not death for a yogi; it is a little enlightenment. That is the song of these masters, repeated and echoed throughout the centuries. That is what we will experience if we can die in such a manner.

Lesser Practitioners

Practitioners of a lesser capacity, those who do not possess a strong and stable realization of the nature of mind, will go through the experiences of the bardo at the time of death. Therefore, the instructions of Padmasambhava are crucial. They are like an emergency kit for use in the event that everything does not go as planned. In that case, we have a backup plan: If Plan A does not work, then at least we can go to Plan B.

Reading Minds

How do we measure who is of great capacity, who is of middling capacity and who is of lesser capacity? We cannot judge according to appearances. We cannot judge according to how they sit, or according to how
long they do—or do not—practice. We can judge someone's capacity only
on the basis of inner development: What is going on in that person's
mind? That is the only way a person's level of practice can be known.

When we look back into history, we can find examples that vividly
show us this truth. If we were to go to India today and we happened to
meet the great mahasiddha Tilopa, it is very likely that we would mis-
judge him. Even if someone there told us, "The yogi Tilopa is a great spiritual being," we would see his filthy appearance and observe his actions
and think, "That grimy-looking fisherman by the Ganges River cannot be
anyone great; he is catching and killing fish and eating them right there!
How crude!" If we were to consider only Tilopa's appearance, then our
judgment would be totally wrong. This is why the teachings say that
appearances are deceptive. Our minds are habituated to judging others all
the time. We look at one person and we say, "Yes, I can trust her." We look
at another person and we say, "No, I cannot trust him." One person is
good; another is bad. We also make judgments about who is a good
teacher, a bad teacher, a good student or a bad student.

Until we are realized beings ourselves, we cannot judge the spiritual
state of others. We can make such judgments only when we have the realization to directly read someone else's mind. Then we can say, "Yes, this
person has many negative thoughts," or "This person has many positive
thoughts." Only then can we say whose mind is calm and whose is agitated; who is a developed practitioner and who lacks training. It is not sufficient to say, "I *think*" this or "I *think*" that. We must be able to see
clearly.

Similarly, the only way that we can judge our own practice is by reading what is going on in our own minds. We cannot judge according to
how long we practiced meditation today or how well we seemed to conduct ourselves. These are not the factors by which to judge. The only
meaningful way to assess our practice is to read our own mind and see our
thought patterns, our emotions and overall habitual tendencies. We need
to read our own mind in order to see how much we are grasping at this

world and how attached we are to it. To what degree could we let go of the world right now and simply sit in a state of calmness and clarity? Only we can make these judgments about ourselves. Nobody else can make them.

In school, a teacher may give us a quiz to see how well we are doing in a certain subject, but this kind of examination is not the ultimate test. The real test is the one we give ourselves. We look at ourselves—our emotions, our thoughts—to see how we are doing. The point is to get to know both our strengths and weaknesses realistically. Then we make adjustments wherever improvement is needed. Since this self-assessment is of benefit to us, we should take real care in doing it. We should attend to it and develop our own practice.

Preparing For Death

When we see that the time of our death is approaching, coming closer and closer, we can prepare ourselves by making the aspiration to remain calm. We can tell ourselves: "Now death is coming. It is my time to die. This is a very important moment for me." At this point, we should focus on our intention instead of thinking about things left undone or ways to extend our life. We should not forget that when our time to die comes, nothing will change that.

There is a story about the death of the young daughter of a Tibetan king. This young girl died in the lap of Padmasambhava. The king was suffering terribly, and he pleaded with Padmasambhava to do something to bring his daughter back. Padmasambhava had great power; he had performed many inconceivable feats, such as subduing all the *maras*, the powerful negative energies that were obstructing the practice of the dharma in Tibet. But even Padmasambhava could not grant the King's wish.

Once the moment of death has arrived for us, no matter how desperate we may be to prolong our life, nothing can be done. Nobody can alter our karma; we have no choice but to follow it. What will help us is to begin preparing for that moment now by setting a firm intention to meet our death with calmness and mindfulness. We prepare ourselves mentally by becoming familiar with the stages of death, and then affirming our intention to remain calm and present, alert and mindful throughout these stages. It is very important to give rise to this aspiration now and to train in it; then, at the time of death, it is essential to reaffirm that aspiration and to maintain our motivation, our one-pointed determination, to remain in a peaceful yet alert state of mind.

At the same time, we must understand that our intention will be interrupted at times by pain and fear; so it is important to reinstate our intention again and again. Sometimes we think that doing something once is enough. For example, we may have taken the bodhisattva vow and generated bodhichitta—the aspiration to liberate all beings—at that time. So, we think that is enough. But it is not. We need to generate that aspiration every day; and not just every day, but at least three times a day. Similarly, at the time of death, we will need to voice our intention again and again until we are firmly rooted in it. When we are one with that intention on the levels of both body and mind, then that alone is a very good and powerful practice.

Dissolving of the Elements

According to these teachings, our bodies are composed of five elements: earth, fire, water, air, and space. When we are born, these five elements come together and our bodies come into existence. At the time of death, these elements are departing, dissolving or falling apart as opposed to coming together. Before discussing the details of the dissolution of the body, however, it will be helpful to have a general understanding of the notion of the coarse and subtle bodies.

Coarse and Subtle Bodies

From the perspective of Mahamudra, Dzogchen and the Vajrayana traditions, our ordinary physical body, composed of the five elements, is the "coarse body." The "inner essential body," also known as the "subtle body," or the "vajra body," is not visible to the eye. The subtle body is composed of channels, or *nadis*, winds or energies, *pranas*, and essences of the physical body, or *bindus*. The channels are pathways through which the subtle energies, or winds, move. The winds carry the essences of the physical body. There are several examples that illustrate how the channels, winds and essences relate to one another. In one, the channels are like a house, the winds are like the people in the house, and the essences are like the

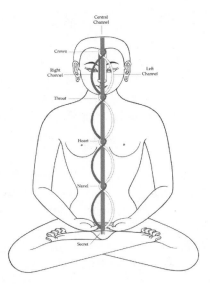

minds of those people. In another, the channels are like the body, the winds are like the breath, and the essences are like the mind.

From the perspective of these teachings, the inner essential nature of mind, which is referred to as the *connate wisdom of bliss-emptiness,* is the basis for the development of the inner essential body (the subtle body). The inner essential body is in turn the basis for the development of the coarse body. Thus the physical body arises from mind like the rays of sunlight arise from the sun. In terms of the elements, the body's development follows a progression that originates with the element of space. From space, the element of consciousness arises; from consciousness, the element of wind arises; from wind, the element of fire arises; from fire, the element of water arises; from water, the element of earth arises. The correspondence between the body and the elements is as follows: flesh corresponds to the element of earth; bodily fluids correspond to the element of water; bodily warmth corresponds to the element of fire; breath corresponds to the element of air; mind consciousness corresponds to the element of space. The coming together of all these elements results in the complete formation of body and mind on both the coarse and subtle levels.

If one understands the nature of the coarse body, it will help one to understand the nature of the subtle body; and if one understands the nature of the subtle body, it will help in realizing the ultimate nature of mind. Therefore, the coarse body, the subtle body and the nature of mind are all interdependently connected. For this reason, it is important to study the way the body is established, or the way the body comes into being, as well as how it dissolves. This view is different from the Hinayana view that regards the formation of the physical body as the result of negative karma and as a basis for suffering, and also from the Mahayana view that regards the body as illusionlike, and as a confused appearance of relative truth.

In general, in the Vajrayana, it is said that there are three main channels within the body. There is the central channel, called the *avadhuti;* the right channel, or *rasana;* and the left channel, or *lalana.* The central channel is located in the middle of the subtle body, extending in a line from the crown to a point that is approximately the width of four fingers below the navel. It is described in slightly different ways in the various scriptures and instructions. For example, it is usually said to be light blue, but is sometimes described as being a bright, light yellow or golden color. At certain points along the central channel, other channels of the subtle body intersect with it to form "wheels" or *chakras,* and within each of these, the vital energy, or *prana,* moves. While there are many different chakras, four primary chakras lie along the central channel of the subtle body at the head, throat, heart and navel. In addition, there is another main chakra located just below, but not touching, the central channel. This is called the "secret chakra," and it is located at the genital area.

There are also many classifications of the energy currents, or winds; for example, there are five root and five branch energies. Each of these is associated with a particular element, bodily function, skandha and wisdom, and each has a particular seat or location in the body. During the process of death, the energies of the channels, winds and essences in the body dissolve, as do the five elements; as a result, the systems of the body begin to function less and less effectively.

As each element dissolves, the sense consciousness and wisdom to which they correspond also cease. Of course, wisdom itself does not cease, as the ultimate nature of the five wisdoms is transcendent and changeless; however, the relative or dualistic manifestation of the wisdoms ceases along with the elements with which they are associated. For example, when mirror-like wisdom dissolves, we lose the capacity to clearly see multiple images distinctly and at once.

The details of these systems and processes may be learned through a study of the Vajrayana teachings.[15]

THE COARSE DISSOLUTION PROCESS

The Signs of Death

From a coarse perspective, the elements of the body dissolve in the following four stages: Earth dissolves into water, water dissolves into fire, fire dissolves into wind and wind dissolves into consciousness. As each element dissolves, we first experience an increase and then a loss of its particular qualities. This process is accompanied by the signs of death, which manifest on the outer, inner and secret levels. The outer signs relate to the experience of the body; the inner signs to the experience of mind, or our cognitive functioning; and the secret signs to the experience of luminosity. At the time of the appearance of the outer signs, there will also be the appearance of inner signs, both of which may be perceptible to others.

Along with those signs, there is also the appearance of the secret signs that "flash" at this time and are only perceptible to the one who is going through this bardo. The outer and inner signs are indications of the diminishing connection between our mind and our physical body, as well as the external, relative world; the secret signs, on the other hand, are an indication of the approach of the experience of the ultimate nature. At the same time that ordinary perception is dimming and becoming more confused, mind's aspect of clear emptiness becomes increasingly apparent. From the empty essence of mind, the radiance of pure awareness begins to manifest as inseparable luminosity and emptiness. This occurs in stages. The secret signs manifest first as "the luminosity of example," foretelling the dawning of the actual luminosity that arises at death and in the after-death states. Altogether, these are the signs of death that commonly occur for all beings.

The detailed descriptions of these stages may at first seem confusing. However, when we look at the basic experience of each, they are fairly simple and straightforward. They correspond to experiences of body and mind that are common in our day-to-day lives. For example, our bodily sensations fluctuate according to environmental conditions and to our own state of health and age. Our mental states also vary. We may feel cheerful when the sun is out and lethargic when it is raining. We may wake up in the morning feeling muddled, but be alert and clear-headed by evening. At the end of the day, when we are exhausted, we may lose awareness by spacing out. We may forget things, like a friend's name, or where we parked our car. If we are suffering with an illness or coping with personal problems, we may experience more acute outer and inner signs of physical or cognitive distress. Often we do not attend to these alternations of the body-mind experience. However, if we become familiar with the deeper nature of mind and phenomena, then, when the various levels of signs arise in this bardo, we will recognize in them an opportunity to perfect our understanding and realization of mind's reality.

It is helpful to hold in mind the primary experience of each stage, and not to get lost in the secondary or more minor effects that accompany it. The most common of the primary physical and cognitive signs for each stage are given in brief here. They are then followed by a more inclusive description.

First stage: As the earth element dissolves, we experience a loss of physical strength and agility; mentally, our perception becomes less clear.

Second stage: As the water element dissolves, we experience a sense of dryness and increasing thirst; mind is more easily agitated and susceptible to confusion.

Third stage: As the fire element dissolves, we begin to feel cold; our perceptions of external appearances alternate between being clear and unclear.

Fourth stage: As the wind element dissolves, we experience difficulty breathing; our thoughts become vivid and we may feel disoriented.

The secret signs that accompany these stages may or may not be noticed. However, they are simply experiences of mind's ever-present luminosity.

The First Dissolution: Earth into Water

The first dissolution occurs when the chakra at the navel center starts to dissolve. This corresponds with the dissolving of the earth element into the water element. The outer sign manifests initially as an experience of growing heaviness. As the dissolution continues, we may begin to feel that our body is dissolving, or becoming less solid. At the same time, our physical strength, resilience and sense of balance show signs of diminishing. For example, a spoon might feel heavy in our hand, or we might find it difficult to lift our head or stand on our feet. At the same time, our bodies may appear to become smaller or thinner. There may also be leakage of some bodily fluids. At this time, the eye sense consciousness, the skandha of form, and the mundane level of the mirror-like wisdom are also dissolving.

On the cognitive level, the inner sign is that our mind feels heavy and listless; our perception dims, and appearances become unclear or murky, as though there were not enough light in the room.

The secret sign that arises now is connected to the experience of emptiness. As the more coarse-level appearances begin to recede, you may perceive mirage-like or dreamlike phenomena for an instant, or for several moments. Such appearances, though clearly illusory in nature, are still considered to be an experience of the relative truth level of appearance-emptiness.

The Second Dissolution: Water into Fire

The second dissolution occurs when the heart chakra begins to dissolve. At this time, the water element begins to dissolve into the fire element. The outer sign manifests first as the sensation of being inundated by water. Subsequently, our bodies begin to dry out. For example, our mouth, nose and tongue may feel dry and uncomfortable as our body loses fluids. At this time, we may feel very thirsty. The ear sense consciousness, the skandha of feeling, and the mundane level of the wisdom of equanimity are also dissolving.

The inner sign is that our mind becomes increasingly unclear. Since the heart chakra has a strong relationship to the functioning of the mind, our consciousness becomes vague and foggy as the heart chakra dissolves. At the same time, our mind may become restless and agitated. The emotions may be easily provoked, and we may become upset or angry quickly. We often see this reaction in people when they become ill. At the stage of death, the experience is stronger and more intense.

The secret sign that emerges now is the perception of an appearance like smoke, clouds or steam. In contrast to the previous experience of mirage, this visual aspect is less solid, less tangible or real. It is a deeper and clearer experience of emptiness, one that is closer to the ultimate truth level of reality.

The Third Dissolution: Fire into Wind

The third dissolution occurs when the throat chakra dissolves, and the fire element dissolves into the wind element. The outer sign is that first we experience an increase of warmth in our bodies, followed by a loss of bodily heat. The heat of our bodies escapes by means of the breath, which progressively becomes colder, and it is also lost through vapors released through the pores of our skin. This heat loss begins at the extremities and moves toward the heart; first, our hands and feet become chilled, and then our limbs start to feel stiff and uncomfortably cold. We sometimes experience the same symptoms when we are very sick. From the perspective of Tibetan medicine, such symptoms will arise if you have a wind disease, or *lüng* imbalance. To counterbalance this, certain medicines are rubbed on the soles of the feet to help bring heat back to the body. At this point, the nose sense consciousness, the skandha of perception, and the mundane level of the discriminating awareness wisdom are also dissolving.

The inner sign is that the clarity of the mind fluctuates; it is alternately clear and unclear. We switch between the two states of clarity and dullness. It is as though we sometimes "wake up" and sometimes fall back into a state that is devoid of perception. At this point, it becomes very obvious to us that we are losing touch with conscious experience. This inner sign manifests outwardly in an occasional inability to recognize people. In general, external appearances are not perceived distinctly.

The secret sign is sparks of light that have the appearance of fireflies. The smoky appearance of the last stage now becomes brighter and sharper as a sign of the rising of mind's luminosity. Prior to this stage, the secret signs were expressions of the empty aspect of mind's nature. Now the luminous aspect of mind's nature is manifesting more clearly and distinctly. These flashes of luminosity manifest just for a moment, followed by another moment, and another, like the blinking of fireflies. It is there and then gone.

The Fourth Dissolution: Wind into Consciousness

The fourth dissolution occurs when the secret chakra at the genitals dissolves, and the wind element dissolves into consciousness. Again, at first the wind element intensifies, and then weakens. The outer sign is that the breath becomes markedly shorter. Breathing becomes more difficult and, eventually, the exhalation becomes longer than the inhalation and is sometimes accompanied by a rattling sound. At this time, the eyes start to roll upward. Each time this happens, they remain in that position longer. The tongue and the tactile sense consciousnesses, the skandha of formations, and the mundane level of the all-accomplishing wisdom are dissolving.

Eventually, breathing stops, and from the perspective of the coarse dissolution process, this is the time when death arrives. However, according to these teachings, this is only the cessation of the outer respiration. It is followed by the dissolutions leading to the cessation of the inner respiration, and the actual point of death.

The inner sign is that our minds become extremely confused and unstable. Previously, our ability to recognize familiar people and things had already begun to fail us. Now, at this stage, with our mind becoming increasingly unclear, we begin to hallucinate. According to these teachings, the hallucinations we will experience depend on our karmic seeds, the habitual tendencies we have developed in the past. For example, if we are habituated to negative thoughts and imaginings, such as thoughts of causing harm to others, then we will have similar thoughts at this stage of the dissolution process. If, on the other hand, we are habituated to positive thoughts, then they continue, and the illusions that appear to us will be positive in nature. Either way, these mental phenomena will arise more vividly and appear more solid than ordinary thoughts; therefore, they will exert an even more powerful effect on our mind. Although we call these appearances "hallucinations," they are no different than from the absolute point of view than the thoughts we have now; they are just more intense.

In the natural bardo of this life, when negative thoughts arise, they are not necessarily a big deal. However, at the time of the bardo of dying, we are gradually losing our connection with our bodies and the physical world and finding ourselves closer to the phenomena of mind. If our mind is calm, then we will be able to focus it and place it where we want it to be. Otherwise, we are likely to feel disoriented and unbalanced, as if under the influence of a drug.

For those who are habituated to the deity yoga practices of the Vajrayana, which rely on the visualization of enlightened forms, appearances of the sacred world will manifest at this time. For example, if you have been practicing a particular yidam deity and your mind is stable and focused, then you will see the empty yet vividly appearing forms of the mandala of that meditational deity. If you follow the path of devotion, then you will see the manifestation of the guru mandala that you have been supplicating. Whatever arises at this time will be a pure appearance that communicates the essence of the wisdom of enlightenment. You will be able to rest your mind peacefully, just as you do now in the bardo of meditation. However, the experience of resting mind in this bardo is much more powerful. The blessings of the sacred world manifest more intensely, making it possible to see the spontaneous play, or *rolpa*, and unobstructed energy, or *tsal*, of the nature of mind. When you can rest your mind within that experience, just as in the practices of Mahamudra and Dzogchen, this time becomes genuinely auspicious. It becomes a powerful opportunity to realize the nature of mind.

The secret sign is said to be like a brightly shining torch or lamp. Its arising portends the appearance of the actual ground luminosity, although it is not quite yet the actual luminosity itself. It is very important to attend to and rest in these secret signs when they arise. Once again, it is important not to get disoriented or lost in the outer and inner signs.

The Subtle Dissolution Process

The Fifth Dissolution: Consciousness into Space

The first four dissolutions can be grouped together, since they are the dissolution of the four basic elements comprising the coarse body; earth, water, fire and wind. However, the fifth dissolution, which is the dissolution of consciousness into space, occurs on the level of the subtle body and is categorized separately. According to the Buddhist view, "consciousness" is not a single entity, but a collection of consciousnesses, from coarse to very subtle, which function together to produce a basic sense of self and other, as well as our common experience of the world.

The more coarse or superficial aspect of consciousness is known as the "sixfold collection of consciousnesses": the five sense consciousnesses, which directly perceive their objects, and the mental consciousness, which is mental perception and cognition. The mental consciousness is basically the "thinking" or discursive mind. More subtle is the aspect known as the afflicted consciousness, or "klesha mind," which is the instigator of mistaken thoughts, conceptions and disturbing emotions. It perceives the basic mind and then mistakenly fixates on it as a truly existing "self" and on objects as "other," or truly existing external phenomena. This basic mind itself is the most fundamental aspect of consciousness. It is variously known as the storehouse, all-base, or basis of all consciousness, or by its Sanskrit name, the *alaya-vijnana.* It is the stream of consciousness that continues from moment to moment and carries the karmic seeds or trace impressions from past actions, as well as the potentialities for their ripening into positive and negative actions in the future.

Altogether, these comprise the aggregate or skandha of consciousness, which in a more general sense is regarded as the realm of thoughts and emotions. With the dissolution of consciousness, the dualistic mind—the ability to perceive, conceptualize, grasp on to objects, give rise to kleshas, to project a self and other—is ceasing, just as the external breath ceased previously.

In life, we experience cessation all the time, as the final moment of the development of every mind state: a thought dissolves, there is a gap, and then a new thought is born; it develops, fades and is gone, and so on. Here, however, when this process ceases, it is ceasing for this lifetime. Thus, what we are looking at is the way the appearances of this life dissolve.

Appearance, Increase and Attainment

The dissolution of consciousness into space occurs in a process with three stages, called *appearance, increase* and *attainment.* Before describing the mode of dissolution, it will be helpful to look at the meaning of these expressions. In a general sense, these terms refer to three stages in the evolution of conceptual mind, from its original state of nonconceptuality through to the exhaustion or cessation of that process. One could say they refer to the arising, abiding and cessation of conceptual mind.

Briefly, from the ground luminosity, an aspect of consciousness arises, moves toward an object, apprehends it, engages with it conceptually, produces thoughts and emotions about it, and then dissolves naturally back into the ground luminosity. In the next moment, the process is repeated. This movement is compared to waves arising on the surface of an ocean and subsiding back into it. From this perpetual movement of mind outward towards various external objects, the samsaric appearances of this life are born.

At the time of the bardo of dying, this process reverses. The functions of relative, conceptual mind are ceasing; consciousness is ceasing to apprehend objects and ceasing to engage conceptually with them. Finally, the samsaric appearances of this life evaporate with the actual cessation of dualistic consciousness.

In the context of our ordinary experience in the bardo of this life, when we identify these three aspects of conceptual mind—the mind of appearance, the mind of increase and the mind of attainment—we are identifying three distinct moments in the functioning of the perceptual-conceptual process.

The mind of appearance refers to the moment of apprehension by conscious mind of an object by one of the sense faculties; for example, a visual object. The first contact of conscious mind with its object is a bare perception, a moment of direct seeing, and it is therefore nonconceptual. There is no thought about it whatsoever. In general, most mental states first abide in a nonconceptual manner. For example, when we wake up in the morning, we first awake with a nonconceptual mental state, and then slowly thoughts become involved. In the first stage of the dissolution of consciousness, our capacity to perceive objects ceases due to the dissolving of the mind of appearance and its absorption into the mind of increase.

The mind of increase refers to the time when the conceptual mind meets and mixes with the bare perception, and concepts and thoughts are produced. There is an increase of the mind's involvement with the object. We begin to cling to and fixate on the nonconceptual appearance. At this point, we think, "This is a tea cup. It was made in China." In contrast, when the mind of increase dissolves and is absorbed into the mind of attainment, our capacity to engage with objects conceptually—to grasp onto and label them—also ceases.

The mind of attainment has several explanations. In one, it refers to the moment when conceptual thought has developed to its fullest point and has begun to dissolve. This shows that thoughts and concepts cannot remain involved with appearances forever, since those appearances are momentary and continually changing. Therefore, in this explanation, attainment refers to the dissolution or disintegration of concepts.

In another explanation, attainment refers specifically to the maximum development of conceptuality, and the term "full attainment" is then used to refer to the moment when conceptual thought has disintegrated and dissolved back into luminosity. Here, we are following the latter explanation. When the mind of attainment dissolves, it dissolves into space, the element associated with consciousness. At this point, the cognitive capability of mind ceases; there is no possibility for thought or emotion to arise.

Traditionally, it is taught that there are eighty types of innate thought states or conceptions—manifestations of the three root poisons—that are stopped during these three phases of dissolution. Of these eighty, thirty-three are associated with aggression, forty with attachment or passion, and seven with ignorance. These are deeply ingrained tendencies carried within the all-base consciousness. There is a cessation of all movements of mind connected to thoughts of the disturbing emotions. Thus, the activity of the disturbing emotions, or kleshas, ceases at this point as well.

Subsequently, space itself dissolves into the ground luminosity. At that time, we arrive at the stage of full attainment. All notions of self and other, existence and nonexistence, good and bad are completely dissolved into the expanse of dharmakaya, and nonconceptual awareness wisdom manifests fully. All aspects of consciousness return to their original nature, which is beyond all speech, thought and expression.

There are other explanations of this triad as well. In the detailed Vajrayana teachings, there are explanations of appearance, increase and attainment with respect to outer, inner and secret, and also to the creation stage and completion stage practices. Nevertheless, it is a progression whereby all consciousnesses engaged with perception and conception, with thought and emotion, become weaker or more subtle, while the essence of these consciousnesses, the wisdom aspect, becomes clearer and stronger. In other words, the dualistic aspect of the consciousnesses diminishes, and the nondual wisdom that is the essence of those consciousnesses becomes clearer and more manifest.

The Manner of Dissolution

During our life, the generative essences that we have received from our parents abide within the central channel in the form of two spheres of luminous bright light, or bindus. One of these dwells at the top of the central channel at the crown chakra in the form of an inverted white syllable HĀM, and the other abides at the lower end of the central channel in

the shape of a red ASHE, or A-stroke, which is like a candle flame.

The white bindu corresponds to the element of masculine energy one inherits from one's father, to the expression of compassion or skillful means, and to the form aspect of the union of form and emptiness. The red bindu corresponds to the element of feminine energy one inherits from one's mother, to wisdom, or prajna, and to the emptiness aspect of the union of form and emptiness. All sentient beings have a mixture of these masculine and feminine energies. At the time of conception, the white and red elements of masculine and feminine energy join and we come into existence. In a similar way, these elements reunite during this dissolution.

When death is about to occur, the two bindus begin to move toward one another. First, consciousness dissolves into appearance as the white bindu at the crown chakra begins to descend down the central channel toward the heart chakra. At this point, a luminous white appearance arises that is said to be like moonlight shining in a cloudless sky. Simultaneously, the thirty-three kinds of thoughts connected to the first root klesha, aggression, cease.

In the second stage, appearance dissolves into increase as the red bindu below the navel chakra begins to ascend toward the heart chakra. At this time, a luminous red appearance dawns that is said to be like sunlight shining in a cloudless sky. Now, the forty aspects of thought related to the second root klesha, passion, utterly cease.

In the third stage, increase dissolves into attainment as the two bindus meet at the heart center and merge, squeezing consciousness between them. At this time, the seven thoughts pertaining to the third root klesha, ignorance, cease, and a completely dark appearance arises that is said to be like a cloudless sky without sunlight, moonlight or starlight. This is the point where the inner respiration ceases, and, in the context of samsara, this moment is given the name "death." If we have not trained our mind through practice, then we faint and lose all awareness at this point.

Full Attainment

In the description of the triad of appearance, increase and attainment, the final phase of the dissolution of consciousness is the stage of full attainment. This occurs after the white and red bindus meet at the heart center and envelop one's intrinsic awareness, giving rise to the "black experience." Then consciousness dissolves into space and space itself dissolves into luminosity, into the buddha wisdom, or *alaya-jnana,* at the heart center. If we have stabilized our mind and developed some insight into its nature, then we will recognize the arising in the next moment of the ultimate nature of mind. We will see its empty essence, its suchness, which is nothing other than the dharmakaya, or ground luminosity.

In either case, this signals the end of the bardo of dying. With the dissolving of the elements of the physical body and mind consciousness, we cross the line that divides life and death. Whatever confusion or clarity we have been going through up to this point belongs to the bardo of this life. Now, with the arising of the luminosity, we actually depart from this life and enter the bardos that are a part of our next life's journey.

From its description, it may seem that this process lasts a long time, but the entire dissolution occurs quite quickly. The actual time frame is not set, however, and it varies from individual to individual.

THE STAGES OF LUMINOSITY

At this point, with the dawning of the ground luminosity at the time of death, we have described only the first of three stages in the complete manifestation of mind's luminous nature. The ground luminosity manifests in different aspects as we move from the bardo of dying to the bardo of dharmata, and from that state to the bardo of becoming. Traditionally it is taught that the ultimate nature of mind has three inseparable aspects of enlightenment: dharmakaya luminosity, sambhogakaya luminosity and nirmanakaya luminosity. Altogether, these express mind's empty essence, its radiant energy and its unceasing display of appearances.

As noted earlier, the first indications of this luminosity appear in the form of the secret signs that arise during the dissolution of the elements. The secret signs, as well as the luminosity that is experienced during stages of appearance, increase and attainment, are known as the "luminosity of example" because they are not yet the true luminosity. Those signs, which may arise vividly and very sharply, are nothing other than the expression of ordinary mind or naked awareness, the same mind with which we witness everyday scenes, such as people moving about or the traffic on a highway. Normally, we see such things in motion without being aware of their details. However, there are moments when time seems to slow down—for example, when we have an accident; such a shock knocks us out of distracted mind and hurls us into the present. The very moment that we actually fall down some stairs, or when a car we are riding in strikes a tree, that experience unfolds moment by moment, as though we were watching a movie one frame at a time. In retrospect, we may recall many vivid details about the experience. In the same way, at the time of death, these appearances of luminosity arise much more vividly and clearly. Our minds slow down and we see many of the details we would normally miss.

The genuine luminosity arises at the time of death, with the dissolution of dualistic consciousness. When space dissolves into luminosity, we first experience the clear light of dharmakaya, which is known as the "luminosity of no-appearance." This is an experience of pure awareness in which mind has no object; one's awareness is simply vast and open, like a clear sky. Subsequently, the "luminosity of appearance" manifests. This refers to both the pure, unconditioned appearances of the sambhogakaya luminosity that arise at the time of the bardo of dharmata, and to the impure, or mixed pure and impure, appearances of the nirmanakaya luminosity that are associated with the bardo of becoming.

The experience of the ground luminosity that is the dharmakaya nature of mind is sometimes classified as being within the bardo of dying. The Dzogchen teachings, however, classify this appearance as the first stage of the bardo of dharmata. Accordingly, it will be discussed in further detail in the chapter on that bardo.

Practices For Dying

During the stages of dissolution, and especially at the moment of blacking out, or when nonconceptual luminosity starts to flash, we should apply whatever methods we have been practicing in this life, whether they are Mahamudra, Dzogchen or Vajrayana. It is important to understand, however, that not everyone has exactly the same experiences. Although we all undergo these dissolutions, each of us experiences the process in a slightly different way. For example, when the inner signs arise, they might not confuse or agitate the mind of a practitioner who has established some basis of calmness, while they may be disturbing for someone who has not developed any mental stability. We should never say that there is absolutely only one way to experience the dissolutions. Sometimes we are overly meticulous, wanting to document everything very precisely. We would like to know in advance just how many hours, minutes and seconds each of the stages will last. However, it is important for us to understand that this experience is not precisely the same for everyone because we are talking about mind experience—not just what happens to our bodies.

If you are accustomed to Mahamudra or Dzogchen, then you can employ the various enhancement practices of those traditions, which are taught for the purpose of stabilizing insight, improving the recognition of the nature of mind and developing love and compassion for all sentient beings. If you have trained in Vajrayana deity practice, then you can rely on the Vajrayana practices of prana, nadi and bindu at that time.[16] However, the teachings also say that we can use devotion as a path. When we connect with our heart of devotion, then, in that moment, we are connecting very powerfully, immediately and directly with the awakened heart of the guru and the lineage, as well as our own inherently awakened state.

PATH OF DEVOTION

When we use devotion as a path, we remember our guru and visualize his or her form at the chakras where the dissolutions are taking place. For example, when you recognize the signs that the navel chakra is dissolving, you visualize your guru clearly at the navel and, placing your mind one-pointedly on his or her form, you supplicate the guru and the lineage. While making positive aspirations, you should reiterate your intention to realize the nature of mind *now*. The process is the same for the dissolutions at the heart chakra, throat chakra and secret chakra. Then, when the white and red bindus move toward the heart center and meet, you should place the guru there also.

Working with our devotion means that we are not just relying on our own efforts. We are opening ourselves to a source of blessings that is an embodiment and a reflection of our own fundamental nature. When we genuinely supplicate the guru and the lineage, we feel the presence of the sacred world; the qualities of clarity, gentleness, peace, joy and equanimity are naturally with us. Therefore we are confident, relaxed and fearless. If you practice deity yoga, such as Vajrasattva, then you can supplicate the deity as well. It is no different than supplicating your guru and the lineage. In general, in the traditions of Mahamudra, Dzogchen and Vajrayana, devotion is seen as a key that unlocks the doorway to the most profound experiences of mind.

There are many beautiful and inspiring supplication prayers that we can recite, such as the supplication to Padmasambhava called the "Guru Rinpoche Prayer." Such practices should be done regularly in the bardo of this life and also at the time of death. We recite these prayers now with the intention of transforming the fear and suffering we experience in this life, and at the same time, we maintain an awareness of our impending death and its potential for suffering. Accordingly, we form the strong intention to supplicate in the same way at that time. We say to ourselves, "In the bardos of death and after-death, I will supplicate just as I am doing now." In this way, we develop a habitual connection with the practice so that when we enter those bardos, our supplication comes easily; it is very natural, genuine and relaxed.

Recognizing a Last Chance

Because all of our disturbing emotions have ceased at the time of the subtle dissolutions, they do not manifest in us as they usually do. Since we are finally rid of our kleshas, we should be happy. We should make every effort to connect with that pure space and attain some profound realization. If we have failed to recognize the nature of mind beforehand, then at the time of death we have one last chance to recognize it and attain liberation on the spot.

That is why, each time you practice meditation, it is important to sit with confidence and to arouse the intention to achieve enlightenment in that very session. If you become accustomed to generating such confidence now, then at the time of death you can manifest the same level of confidence and trust in your practice. You have one last chance—for this lifetime, at any rate. It is not your last chance ultimately—there is no sense of being doomed forever. However, the time of death is our last opportunity to achieve enlightenment *now*. Thus, your attitude toward your practice makes a great difference. If you do it halfheartedly, thinking to yourself, "These are the instructions, so I will try them. Who knows— maybe this will work, and maybe it won't," that is still better than not practicing at all. There is a faint sense of trust and hope. However, it is not very strong and it will not be very effective.

Although the details of these dissolutions may sound quite complicated, all we need to do, whatever is taking place, is to simply rest in an open, spacious and relaxed mind. There is not much more that we can do beyond that. Thus, our preparation for death does not involve searching for any new methods. We simply use the methods we have been practicing in our everyday lives: the vipashyana practices of Mahamudra and Dzogchen and the Vajrayana deity practices. These are the methods that will cut through our suffering and fear at its very root, and that is what we need at the time of death—an ultimate remedy. It is the only thing that is definitely going to work for us. We may try other remedies, but they will be questionable. How long will they work? How long will they suppress our suffering and terror? Therefore, at the time of death, we should rely on the practices we have trained in. Our habitual connection with them will help us transcend any conditions we might face.

THE PRACTICE OF PHOWA

Phowa is a practice that is especially connected to the time of death, when our minds and bodies start to separate and begin to lose the connection that they now have. The term *phowa* is often translated as the "transference" or "ejection" of consciousness. It is taught using a number of classifications; dharmakaya, sambhogakaya, nirmanakaya, guru, and pure realm phowa. These will be described in some detail below. However, it is important to have a general understanding of what phowa is. What we are essentially doing at this time is transferring our consciousness from an impure, confused state into a pure and unconfused state. We are transforming consciousness and connecting with the true nature of mind and the reality of all phenomena on the spot.

In general, the phowa teachings are not much different from those of Mahamudra and Dzogchen. The intention of Mahamudra and Dzogchen is to penetrate our confusion and see its ultimate nature of nonconfusion, or wisdom. The purpose of nirmanakaya phowa is the same, but it uses the Vajrayana methods of visualization practice. All are practices that are used to transform a confused state of mind into an unconfused state. Of the five types of phowa that are taught, it is nirmanakaya phowa that is practiced by ordinary beings at the time of death, and it is this type of phowa that is most often thought of in connection with these practices.

In brief, the fundamental goal of nirmanakaya phowa is the sudden ejection or release of the consciousness through the crown chakra, and its transference into an enlightened state or realm as represented by a visualized image of a buddha or yidam deity. The teachings say that when we are approaching death, when our consciousness is leaving our body, our consciousness senses that there are nine gates through which it can leave. Of these nine, eight are gates that will lead us to take rebirth in one of the three realms of samsara: the desire realm, form realm or the formless realm.[17] In speaking of these gates, we are referring to body orifices; the eyes, the ears, the nose, the mouth, the navel, the urethra, the anus and the spot between the eyebrows.

The one gate that will lead us to liberation is located at the crown chakra at the top of the head. It is the door of the central channel, and it is this opening that is regarded as the gateway to the direct realization of Mahamudra. We want our minds to leave our body from that gate and no other. Accordingly, the instructions on phowa say that as you begin to experience the signs of the dissolution of the elements, you should try to focus your mind upward, rather than allowing your attention to fall to the lower parts of your body.[18] First move your focus toward the upper part of your body, about the level of the shoulders, then slowly move it up to the head and then to the crown. If you place your mind closely there at the early stages of the dissolutions, it will be easier to place it there again later when it is time to do phowa.

Although we must train in the practice of phowa, its actual application is always a last resort. Perhaps, throughout our lifetime, we have tried various methods to attain realization and nothing has worked. In addition, at the time of death, we have also applied the same methods with no success. In that case, it is appropriate to use phowa, but strictly as described in the instructions for the practice. Phowa should only be done at the last minute. We do not do phowa when we become ill, or when we are experiencing the suffering and fear associated with our illness. We should not lose our composure in such circumstances. Instead, we should continue with our practice. Only when it becomes very clear that we are at a certain stage of the dissolution process and in the final moments of our life do we use phowa.

When phowa is taught as one of the Six Dharmas of Naropa, it is taught as the sixth and final yoga.[19] It is presented last because these instructions are unnecessary if one has already accomplished the realization of Mahamudra or of Dzogchen. However, there are realized masters known to have practiced phowa at the time of their death: for example, the great translator Marpa, father of the Kagyu lineage, and the great siddha and Dzogchen master Melong Dorje both practiced phowa. These masters did the practice symbolically: first, to teach their disciples, and second, to remind them about phowa. When masters like this have demonstrated phowa, some people have seen certain outward signs, such as lights rising from their heads; however, this depends entirely on the individuals present at the time. It is said that the way such masters perform phowa is nearly identical to the display or manifestation of the rainbow body.

The Training Stage

When mind can no longer inhabit its accustomed dwelling place and the next phase of our journey begins, our body becomes symbolic of the whole world we are leaving behind. The way we make any journey depends on the type of ticket we have—first class, business class, economy class or main coach—and on the type of transportation we use—airplane, train, bus, car, motorcycle or bicycle. We may even have collected mileage points. We may be eligible for an upgrade to first class, which will make our journey easier, more relaxed and comfortable.

The bardo journey is similar, in that the way we travel depends on what we have accumulated in this life—our collection of karmic actions. Thus, the quality of our practice now affects the quality of our journey when we die. If we have a good accumulation of prajna and upaya, then we get a kind of upgrade. Our trip goes more smoothly and is more comfortable overall. If we know that our journey is going to be comfortable, that it is going to be fun and that we will have a nice time, then we will look forward to it. It will be an effortless experience, yet one of great significance. On the other hand, if we have no training and no mileage points, so to speak, then there may be some rough rides here and there.

The actual performance of phowa at the time of death is not something that will come easily to us if we have not familiarized ourselves with it beforehand. Therefore, the key point here is to train now for the real operation, which we will execute later. In other words, there is a training period, and then there is the real mission. First we train, and then we go on the mission. The actual mission can be very dangerous. Enemies are going to attack us, and we must use our skills carefully.

Who are these enemies? They are our own projections, the appearances of our mind. There are no external enemies. There are no "bad guys" outside. At the time of this bardo, all that we perceive as external phenomena are nothing other than projections of klesha mind, ego mind. What we are actually fighting against are our own projections. In fact, we ourselves are a projection as well. Thus, a projection is fighting against a projection. One manifestation of mind is combating another manifestation of mind. That is a beautiful way to look at it. From the absolute point of view, there is nothing to fear, nothing to get uptight or emotional about. Ultimately, there is nothing there, although in the relative sense, there is.

If we can step back and view this display of mind from that perspective, it is like being in the audience at a theater and watching two actors on a stage. As they play different roles, we experience various emotions. At one moment, we feel good and are happy. At another moment, we feel bad and are angry. Then passion arises, then foreboding, and so on. We enjoy this display because we know it to be illusion. The drama may touch us, but it does not fool us. In the same way, at the time of the bardo of death, we will also experience a range of vivid emotions. We must find a way to relate to these colorful manifestations and to accomplish our mission with the least collateral damage.

The time we spend training in phowa is the most important time we spend with these teachings. We must become very skilled in these methods. When the actual time for phowa comes, we should not be thinking that we need to re-read our notes or listen again to tapes of teachings. By then, it will be too late. Once we are on our mission, we cannot go back to the instructor and ask, "What do I do?" If we are in that situation, we may panic. Instead, we have to understand the instructions thoroughly and be able to apply them precisely. When we have practiced doing something over and over, the process becomes instinctive and automatic.

This is similar to shamatha meditation. The first time we sit down, we may feel a bit lost, not knowing what to do. We may have to remind ourselves of the instructions and then proceed to apply them in a conceptual way. Eventually, however, the conceptual process fades away and our practice becomes natural. We no longer have to think about what to do or recall what our teachers said. As soon as we take our seat, we are right in the space of shamatha. Phowa should be like that. Due to our training, it should be as familiar and effortless as shamatha practice. That is not to say that it becomes altogether effortless. However, we will not have to struggle to recall the basic instructions and procedures.

METHODS OF TRANSFORMATION

Dharmakaya Phowa

Dharmakaya phowa is the vipashyana meditation practice of Mahamudra and Dzogchen. It is formless practice and therefore does not employ any visualization. When we realize the nature of mind through the penetrating insight resulting from this style of vipashyana meditation, the confused mind is transformed on the spot. The process is not a gradual one. This is the best form of phowa because there is an immediate transference of consciousness from the state of confusion to nonconfusion. At the time of death, one simply rests without distraction in the nonconceptual wisdom nature of mind.

Our ordinary notion of phowa is that one ejects one's consciousness out of the body to a pure or enlightened realm. However, once we have realized the nature of mind, we have accomplished the purpose of phowa. Mind is already in a state of perfect purity. Whatever state of mind we have—a discursive mind, a mind bound up in passion, anger or ignorance, or simply a mind engaged in the perception of an object—the moment we realize mind's nature, consciousness is released from any obscuration or confusion and transformed right on the spot. That is dharmakaya phowa. Simply hearing Mahamudra or Dzogchen teachings and lightly contemplating them is not dharmakaya phowa. Dharmakaya phowa requires us to thoroughly chew and digest the instructions that we have been given and then to manifest them as realization. This is the type of phowa practiced by yogis such as Milarepa and all of the great Mahamudra and Dzogchen siddhas.

Sambhogakaya Phowa

Sambhogakaya phowa is based on the deity yoga or yidam practices of the Vajrayana. When we can clearly visualize ourselves in the form of the deity we are practicing, and when that experience is stable and accompanied by the realization of the purity of appearances and sacred outlook, then we are engaged in the practice of Vajrayana phowa. This means that we have unshakable vajra pride in our own being as enlightened. We directly experience the nature of our mind as sacred buddha mind and the nature of the world as a sacred mandala. It is the perfection of the realization of appearance-emptiness; thus, the practice of illusory body also aids the accomplishment of this yoga. When we can arise as the deity naturally, spontaneously and vividly, with vajra pride and sacred outlook, that is Vajrayana phowa. It is not necessary for practitioners of this type of phowa to visualize the detailed imagery of the nirmanakaya phowa, such as the central channel in which consciousness travels up and out of the body. At the time of death, one simply manifests as the deity and no other method of transformation is needed.

Nirmanakaya Phowa

Nirmanakaya phowa is also based on the deity yoga or yidam practices of the Vajrayana. This is the transformation practice most often done by ordinary beings and is therefore the method commonly associated with these teachings. It employs a more detailed form of visualization than other methods. Formal sessions begin with taking refuge in the Buddha, Dharma and Sangha and generating bodhichitta. Additionally, the practice utilizes three postures known as the posture of body, the posture of the breath, or *prana*, and the posture of the focus, or visualization.

The Three Postures

The posture of the body is the Seven Postures of Vairochana, as described earlier.[20] The posture of the breath, or *prana*, refers to our concentration on the breath and to the methods of bringing the energy of prana into the central channel of the subtle body. First we perform the exercise called the cleansing of the breath, either nine times or as described in the instructions for the practice we are doing.[21] These instructions will vary. Additionally, we practice "vase breathing," a technique in which the breath is held lightly in order to help us concentrate our mind. The posture of focus refers to the development of a clear visualization, which is used as the basis for the practice, and to our one-pointed focus on that. These three postures constitute the foundation upon which we can establish a perfect practice of phowa.

Instructions for the Main Practice

The nirmanakaya phowa most commonly trained in is the Amitabha phowa. Therefore we will use this form as the basis of our description here.

Once we have taken our seat and assumed the correct postures, we first visualize the syllable HRI as blocking each of the eight impure gates, or orifices, from which our consciousness could exit the body, and which lead to rebirth in a samsaric realm. Next we visualize the central channel, which extends in a straight line from below the navel to the crown chakra at the top of the head. The central channel is visualized as being wide open at the point at which it meets this chakra, which is the ninth gate. At the heart center, in the middle of the central channel, we visualize a red bindu that is bright, shining and transparent like a flame. In the middle of this bindu we sometimes visualize the syllable HRI, the same syllable that is blocking the eight gates. At other times the bindu alone is enough. Either way, we focus on the bindu, which is the inseparability of prana and mind. It is said that the bindu shines, flickers and sparkles, and sometimes emits sounds, as burning candles occasionally do. We utilize this image so that our minds will be focused more clearly and precisely.

Next, seated on the crown of our head at the opening of the central channel, we visualize the Buddha Amitabha, who is red in color. During our training sessions, we visualize that Amitabha's feet are blocking this opening, thus preventing our consciousness from leaving our body.

There are many different phowa practices associated with different bud-dhas and yidams. Although the structure of the practices is basically the same, each has a different visualization that incorporates imagery con-nected with that particular buddha or yidam. Accordingly, sometimes a bindu is visualized at the heart center, and sometimes a syllable is visual-ized instead. At other times, the two are visualized together. Other images, such as hand implements, are also employed. For example, when the main figure is the deity Vajrasattva, a vajra is visualized instead of a bindu or HRI. The vajra may be marked at its center with the syllable HUM. If your main practice is Vajrasattva, then you will be very familiar with this image, and it will be easy to visualize. Like the bindu or HRI, the vajra symbol-izes the subtle mind.

The training consists of repeatedly sending the bindu we have visual-ized at our heart center up through the central channel to our crown chakra, where it lightly touches the feet of Buddha Amitabha and imme-diately returns to our heart center. The rising and falling of the bindu is coordinated with our breathing. The bindu "rides the breath," so to speak. This is affected by our practice of vase breathing, in which we gently hold our breath, or prana, in the abdomen and then release it so that it moves upward through the central channel. When we release our breath, this causes the bindu at the heart center to move upward. What we are doing is working with the upward wind, which is one of the five primary winds, or pranas. In forms of the practice that employ the HRI visualization, you might actually utter the syllable aloud, "HRI, HRI, HRI..." while it is ascending. With the utterance of the final HRI, the syllable leaps and touches the feet of Amitabha and then immediately descends to the heart center once again. Like a ping-pong ball, it goes up and down, up and down. We repeat the full visualization again and again. This is phowa training practice, not the actual phowa for the time of death.

Postmeditation

It is sometimes said that the practice of the transference of consciousness can shorten one's life span, since we are working with interdependent phe-nomena. We are practicing ejecting our consciousness and creating a ten-dency for that to occur. To overcome this, before concluding our session, we visualize the syllable HĀM or a vajra clearly blocking the opening at the crown chakra. It is important that we maintain that visualization during postmeditation as well.

Another means of protecting one's longevity is to visualize at the conclusion of our session that Buddha Amitabha transforms into Amitayus, the buddha of long life. Amitayus is seated in the same posture as Amitabha and is also red in color, but he appears holding the vase of long life. While in some Dzogchen and Nyingma teachings, Amitabha is seen as a dharmakaya buddha, here he is seen as a nirmanakaya buddha, and Amitayus is seen as a sambhogakaya buddha. Since this particular phowa practice is connected to Amitabha as the nirmanakaya buddha, it is known as nirmanakaya phowa.

Application at Death

When we practice nirmanakaya phowa at the time of death, we visualize that Amitabha is seated about one foot above our head, leaving the opening to the central channel unblocked. We also do not place any syllable or other obstruction at this orifice. It remains wide open. This time, when shooting the bindu or syllable up the central channel, our intention is to cause it to leap with its final movement into the heart center of Buddha Amitabha, where it dissolves. Our mind becomes inseparable from the heart of Amitabha, which is nothing other than the essence of our own nature of mind. The visualization practices of Vajrayana phowa are simply the means we use at this time to remind ourselves that the enlightened wisdom and compassionate qualities we see in Buddha Amitabha are a reflection of the nature of our own mind. There is no Amitabha waiting for us outside.

When do you actually perform this ejection? It is necessary to be familiar enough with the stages of the dissolution process so that you will recognize them. When the early signs appear—the coarse dissolutions of earth into water, water into fire, and so forth—that is the time to prepare. You should be ready. In general, phowa should be performed at some point during the stages of appearance, increase and attainment; that is, after the external respiration has ceased and before the internal respiration ceases. Some instructions state that phowa can be done as late as the second stage of the mind dissolution, at the time of increase and the manifestation of the red appearance. Remember that when the red and white bindus merge at the heart center, they encase and squeeze the subtle consciousness between them, and consciousness dissolves completely into space, at which time the black appearance arises and we go unconscious. The inner respiration ceases at this point, and then it is too late.

What happens if we perform phowa at the correct time but our practice is unsuccessful? We are still "there," so to speak, and did not realize the nature of mind. In that case, the dissolution proceeds in the same way. We have to reinforce our attention and try to maintain awareness so that we will recognize the luminosity that arises in the next bardo, the bardo of dharmata.

That is the third type of phowa and the main practice for ordinary beings at the time of death.

Guru Phowa

Guru phowa is similar to nirmanakaya phowa, but it is a much less common practice. Whereas there are Amitabha phowa retreats where we can train together with other students, and there are the Amitabha practices that are done by the sangha when someone dies, guru phowa is something that we do privately. While it is not generally emphasized or practiced widely, many Mahamudra and Dzogchen practitioners perform this method of phowa.

In guru phowa, instead of visualizing Amitabha above our heads, we visualize our guru. Otherwise, the visualizations are the same. We may also forgo the detailed images of the central channel, chakras and so forth, and simply visualize our guru above our heads. That is the main instruction and the most essential aspect of the visualization. If that is difficult, then we can visualize our guru at our heart center. Whichever method we use, it is important to practice it.

Pure Realm Phowa

Pure realm phowa is connected to the practice of dream yoga. It involves directly transferring our consciousness at the time of death to one of the buddha realms, such as the pure land of Amitabha or Akshobya, or to any of the sacred realms of the dakas, dakinis or bodhisattvas. The capacity to effect such a transference is developed through training in dream yoga. In that practice, not only do we learn to recognize the dream state, but also we develop the skill to transform our dream appearances. When we have developed that degree of control over our minds, then we can travel in our dreams to any buddha field we wish. According to these teachings, if we can exercise that kind of power in our dreams, then we will be able to exercise the same power in this bardo. We can use our understanding and experience of dream yoga to spontaneously transport ourselves to any sacred realm with which we have a heart connection. For example, you do not have to be a realized being in order to take birth in Amitabha's pure land. Ordinary beings with a strong aspiration and good accumulation of merit can also take birth there. If we can achieve such a positive situation, then we will have the optimum conditions to continue our spiritual training. Our practice will be supported by the blessings of buddhas and bodhisattvas.

These are the five basic types of phowa, all very powerful practices. However, when we train in phowa, it is usually in the third type, which is nirmanakaya phowa. Of course, if we have a stronger connection with another type, then we train in that. We each practice according to our individual makeup. The reason that nirmanakaya phowa is most commonly used in training is because it involves visualization, which almost everyone can do. In contrast, there are more differences in the capacities of individuals to work with their dream experiences. Therefore, the method we choose should be based on our personal connection to that practice.

SUDDEN DEATH

The descriptions of the dissolution process and meditation practices we have just outlined are for a natural death, which allows us some time to work with our experiences. Our bodies are giving up slowly and all of the dissolutions will inevitably occur, whether we recognize them or not. A sudden death experience is completely different. It is sometimes said that the dissolutions are not experienced at all in those cases—one just "blacks out" and goes straight into unconsciousness. The instruction for this situation is to simply remember one's guru or deity and instantly flash the image that comes to you in the space above your head.

The most powerful way to prepare for such an eventuality is to bring to mind repeatedly the glimpse of Mahamudra or Dzogchen awareness that has been pointed out to us in this lifetime. We do not do this twenty-four hours a day, of course, but if we can practice clicking into this awareness even once or twice a day, it is better than nothing. It is better than once a week.

You can remind yourself by setting your digital watch to beep at a certain time—even every hour. When you hear the beep, you say to yourself, "Now I will look at my mind." Then you look. You can use anything convenient as a reminder. For example, if you commute to work by car, then you can say, "Whenever someone honks at me, I will look at my mind."

All Practices Are Phowa

If we broaden our understanding of phowa, then we see that it includes all those practices that have as their goal the realization of the true nature of mind. Mahamudra, Dzogchen and Vajrayana practices all accomplish this purpose—ultimate liberation through the transference of consciousness from a state of samsara to a state of nirvana, or from a condition of ego-centered suffering to one of profound peace, openness, joy and unceasing compassion.

Likewise, our conventional understanding of the term "bardo" is quite narrow and typically associated only with death. However, now we know that there are six bardos and many kinds of bardo experiences. This life itself and the states of meditation and dream are bardos, as well as the intervals belonging to death and after-death.

What will really open our eyes and help us practice these instructions effectively is to develop this broader understanding. We do this by going through the stages of hearing, contemplating and meditating. As a result, we will appreciate the intention and power of each practice and avoid becoming stuck in a poverty mentality—a desire for something we assume to be better than what we enjoy now. Generally, we quickly become dissatisfied with our own practices and want "higher" ones. We think that the teachings on bardo and phowa are more transcendent than our shamatha-vipashyana, ngondro and deity practices. When we are a little more savvy about our practice, we will change our attitude. Then we will know, "This resting meditation given to me by my teacher is a great form of bardo practice," or, "This analytical meditation is also phowa."

Poverty mentality results in our mind becoming distracted and neurotic. The whole point of this spiritual journey is to develop a sense of sanity and to have a clear, one-pointed mind as opposed to having a mind that is split into many directions due to our narrow understanding. That is why the development of a deeper and more refined knowledge of the path will help us to accomplish the ultimate goal of our practice.

PLANNING OUR LAST THOUGHT

When the bardo of dying appears, it is important to remain as calm as possible, and to maintain a peaceful and positive state of mind. This is critical because the very last thought that appears to our mind exerts a powerful influence on our after-death journey and our next rebirth. That thought creates a certain atmosphere that affects the environment of our journey. If our last thought is negative, then we will find ourselves dealing with a negative environment. If our last thought is positive, then we will find ourselves supported by an environment in which we feel confident and relaxed. If we practice phowa, then our final thought will be of Buddha Amitabha or another representation of enlightened mind, such as the luminous bindu at our heart center. In all of these ways, we are essentially focusing on the nature of mind, which is a very positive and liberating thought.

If our mind becomes disturbed by conflicting emotions or strong attachments to this life and our possessions, then we can practice the methods for working with these states that have already been described. For example, we can practice detachment. We can also look at the nature of the emotions that are arising in that very moment, according to the instructions of Mahamudra and Dzogchen. If we can simply cut right through them, that is best. If, however, we are not successful in practicing any of these instructions, then the appearance of many disturbing thoughts, emotions and ego-clinging will obscure our experience of the bardo of dharmata, which comes next. Because our mind is agitated instead of clear and calm, we will also experience confusion and difficulty in the bardo of becoming.

We must work with our own state of mind, but it is very beneficial to have the support of a positive environment around us while we are facing death. In Tibetan practice, it is traditional for someone to request on our behalf the presence of our teachers or lamas, as well as our spiritual brothers and sisters, who will come to visit and practice with us. A gathering of

such friends over a period of several days can exert a tremendously positive influence on the environment.[22]

LOOKING AHEAD

Training in phowa during this lifetime and practicing it at the time of
death are two very different situations. When we are training, our practice has a quality of playfulness. We are merely imagining what happens
at the time of death. We are thinking, "Now, the bindu at my heart center is rising. It is flying up to meet the very heart of Buddha Amitabha...."
However, when we do phowa at the time of death, it is the real thing.
Consciousness is moving, exiting from our bodies into another realm of
experience. This is very different from our experience of training. Nevertheless, if we have cultivated a sense of calmness, clarity, and stability in
our phowa practice, then, when it is finally happening, there is a very
good chance that we will recognize the nature of mind. This is so because
the actual experience is much more intense and powerful.

Our practice becomes doubly effective when we possess both the view
and practices of Mahamudra and Dzogchen along with the ability to perform phowa. Then we have both the taste and experience of the genuine
nature of mind, as well as the Vajrayana method of transferring our consciousness into that state. In the event that we do not achieve liberation
in this lifetime through the first method, we will have another tool to use
as a last resort.

Being trained in phowa is like being prepared to meet an emergency.
For example, if we are packing our suitcase for a long trip, it might occur
to us to bring along a first aid kit. However, as our suitcase gets heavier
and heavier, we may wonder if it will really be needed. Our suitcase is
already quite full. In fact, we can barely lift it and may have to pay for
excess baggage. We may decide not to take it. Later, though, when we are
in the countryside, we may fall and suffer painful cuts and bruises. Then
we will think wistfully about the little first aid kit back in our apartment.
We will remember how small it is and how easily we could have packed
it after all.

It is true that a first aid kit is not something that we will use every day
while traveling. It is not like our clothes and toothbrush. Still, it is good

to pack such a kit so that we will have it if we need it. Although we may feel that we are sufficiently prepared for our journey through the bardo of dying, having accumulated many wonderful practices, any phowa training we do in our life will be beneficial. Whether we have trained extensively or only in a single session, that preparation will help us transcend our confusion at the time of death when we need it most.

AIMING FOR THE HIGHEST

Somebody who has achieved Mahamudra or Dzogchen realization does not have to worry about leaving the body through the crown chakra at the time of death. They do not have that kind of exit problem, so to speak. Realized beings are not trapped in the body, even though they are using the nirmanakaya body to manifest. They have already transcended the distinction between samsara and nirvana. They have fully realized appearance-emptiness: the inseparability of form and emptiness, sound and emptiness and awareness and emptiness—all of those. For them, there is no solid body to begin with. There is no solid world called samsara and no solid world called nirvana. Therefore, they have no need to look for a way out.

However, an exit is needed for those who do not have such realization and therefore do experience a solid world. When phowa is not performed and we have also failed to recognize the ground luminosity, our consciousness will still be within our body when we reawaken from our unconscious state. In some descriptions, this is likened to the feeling of being confined inside a house and wishing to escape. The consciousness sees doors and windows—the body's orifices—as possible exits and slips out through one of them.

It should be mentioned that there are different descriptions of exactly when consciousness exits the body. Some say it exits immediately after waking from the black experience, having not recognized the dharmakaya luminosity, and the brilliant visions of the bardo of dharmata arise after that. Others say that consciousness may still be within the body during the appearance of these visions. From another perspective, we could say that when we awaken to these vivid appearances, it is as if we are standing on a borderline between two countries. If you are standing on the border between Canada and the United States, for example, then where are you? To which country does the border belong?

Nevertheless, there are graphic descriptions of consciousness's exit from the body, and at this point, we have little control over the process. It happens very quickly. In contrast, through the practice of phowa, we can direct our consciousness to exit through the crown chakra, the doorway to liberation or rebirth in a pure realm.

Sometimes, however, there are questions about this. For example, if you have the aspiration to be reborn here, in this world, in order to help sentient beings, or if you feel great devotion to your teacher and wish to remain with him or her, then how does that fit with the practice of phowa? If you leave through the crown chakra, are you definitely off to Amitabha's realm? Is there no possibility of returning here for eons?

According to the teachings, you should always aim for the highest goal. Then, even if you cannot reach that high, it will be high enough. For example, when you shoot an arrow, you shoot it at full strength so that even if it does not reach the ultimate target, it goes quite far. In a similar way, even if you aim for rebirth in a pure realm, it does not necessarily mean that you will accomplish that. It depends on your practice. You should try your best to direct your consciousness to leave your body from the crown chakra, but that could mean that you will take a higher birth in samsara, *or* that you will be reborn in a pure realm or a buddha field. While there are no clear assurances that you will actually get to a pure realm, you will definitely achieve a higher, or more auspicious, rebirth.

For ordinary sentient beings without stable realization, it is always good to aspire to reach to a pure realm, such as that of Amitabha or Vajrasattva. This is not simply to save oneself from samsara, but to benefit other beings as well. Our intention is to achieve enlightenment there and then return. When we come back, we do not come back powerless. We have a much greater ability to help sentient beings and much more control over how we accomplish that. If we come back confused, then we will only create more suffering and confusion for others. If, on the other hand, we return in possession of greater clarity and wisdom, then we can offer that to the world, just as Buddha Shakyamuni did. Even now, we are still benefiting from his enlightenment.

What is an enlightened being? It is simply someone who fully realizes the true nature of mind and phenomena. Buddhists call such a person "buddha," a Sanskrit term meaning "awakened one." However, if a Buddhist were to call a great master from another spiritual tradition "a buddha," then the followers of that tradition might be offended. They might say that their teacher is not a buddha, but is someone or something else. However, such labels do not matter. We do not need to impose our ideas or terms on other philosophical or religious systems. If someone possesses genuine realization, then that person is an enlightened being. That person has the capacity to act with boundless compassion and wisdom to bring great benefit to beings, to manifest a pure realm of experience that will support the realization of enlightenment in others.

A pure realm is not necessarily an actual world or a planet; it is a state of mind where we can achieve enlightenment. It can be on this earth or in a different universe. It does not matter. We aspire to that. That is always the best thing for us, and it is also the best thing for all other sentient beings.

Egoless Journey
The Luminous Bardo of Dharmata

6

IN WHATEVER WAY we have met the moment of our death, the journey of mind continues. We leave behind our physical body and all the appearances of this life and move on to our next stopping place and our next set of experiences. All that we have gone through up to this point, including the dissolution of the elements and of consciousness itself, belongs to the bardos of this life. Now we enter the luminous bardo of dharmata, which is the beginning of reaching the destination known as our next life. At this time, we have a perfect opportunity to achieve enlightenment and so we should look forward to these experiences. Rather than feeling, "Oh no, I don't want to be here," we should be full of enthusiasm and curiosity. We should resolve to remain calm and to be courageous. It is like exploring any new place. While there is a sense of anticipation, there are also strong feelings of hope and fear.

> E MA
> At this time, when the bardo of dharmata appears to you,
> Abandon all shock, terror and fear.
> Enter into the recognition that whatever arises is pristine
>   awareness.
> Recognize the appearances of the bardo in this manner.

The luminous bardo of dharmata begins when the element of space dissolves into luminosity, or dharmata. It ends after the various appearances of this bardo are not recognized and one faints or goes unconscious. According to the Dzogchen or Nyingma tradition of presenting these teachings, this bardo arises in two stages. In the first stage we experience the "ground luminosity," or the "luminosity of no appearance." In the second stage we experience the "spontaneously arising luminosity," or the "luminosity of appearance." It is in the second stage that the various displays of forms, sounds and lights are experienced. These appearances are explained as unfolding in a series of three distinct phases.

Exploring New Experiences

We often place high value on travel, especially to foreign countries with exotic landscapes. If we live in the West, then we may dream of going to the East, and so on. When we visit a foreign land, however, it is our attitude toward that landscape that determines the nature of our experience. We may give in to fear or we may choose to trust our environment. Either way, our response to the world in which we find ourselves shapes our whole experience.

For example, if you are in India and you are too scared to leave your hotel, then you will not see India. You will see only the Holiday Inn in New Delhi before going back home. Many people who go to unfamiliar places do that. For instance, if you are Chinese and you look only for Chinese restaurants in India, then you will have no genuine experience of Indian cooking—or you may have a disappointing experience of it! If you are Japanese, then why look for a Japanese restaurant in India? If you are American and you look for a McDonald's there, then you are not experiencing India.

Rather than wanting to be at your usual restaurant, you have to make a leap—into the hot and spicy curry sauce. You have to taste the bitter and sweet flavors of Indian food. Then you can say that you tasted it and that you did or did not like it. That is no problem. You can have your opinion and then make a choice, but at least you should taste it once with an open, inquisitive mind. With the same frame of mind, you should be willing to venture out into the streets and the slightly polluted air, where you can mix with the people and visit the shops, museums and monuments. Later, when you return home, you will feel as though you have seen and tasted something. You can say that you have walked the streets of New Delhi; you have been to the National Museum, where you saw the sacred relics of Buddha Shakyamuni.

If you can approach the bardo of dharmata with the same sense of openness and willingness to explore your experiences, then that attitude

PLATE I   GURU PADMASAMBHAVA

PLATE 2   SAMANTABHADRA AND SAMANTABHADRI
PEACEFUL MANIFESTATION OF THE PRIMORDIAL BUDDHA

Courtesy of Shelley and Donald Rubin
http://www.himalayanart.org

PLATE 3   MAHOTTARA HERUKA AND KRODESHVARI
WRATHFUL MANIFESTATION OF THE PRIMORDIAL BUDDHA

PLATE 4   SHITRO THANGKA
PEACEFUL AND WRATHFUL DEITIES

will not only help to ease potential difficulties, but it will also help you to recognize the nature of mind. If you are genuinely inquisitive about these unfamiliar experiences and are willing to taste them, no matter how spicy or mild, sweet or sour they may be, then you can relax. You can tell yourself, "I am willing to face this. I am willing to experience this as genuinely as possible."

If we are Americans in India, then we do not want to try to be in America. Pretending will not change anything. We will still be in India and we will still be confronting the same things. In the same way, if we try to be in the bardo of this life when we are in the bardo of dharmata, it is not going to work. No matter how hard we try, that is not where we will be. We are in the bardo of dharmata, and therefore we have to be there.

The key to understanding and working with the bardo teachings altogether is being in the present, being in the state of nowness. Being genuinely present with our experience of the bardo is a very productive and fruitful approach in terms of our practice. On the other hand, being there yet wanting to be elsewhere is very regressive; it is going backwards in terms of practice. It is as though we have gone forward on our journey to a certain point, and then we try to turn around and go back. In terms of our bardo journey, this will not work. At this point, the mind's dissolution has already taken place. There is no going back. Since it is not going to work, it is better to let go of all resistance and be fully there.

Dharmakaya Luminosity: *The Luminosity of No Appearance*

Ground Luminosity: The Wisdom of Dharmata

At the end of the bardo of dying, when all of the elements of the physical body and mind consciousness have dissolved, we leave the bardo of this life and enter the bardo of dharmata. This experience arises for us after our consciousness has dissolved into space, and space has dissolved into luminosity, into the buddha wisdom, or *buddha jnana,* at our heart center. The completion of this process takes place with the arising of the appearance of the "black light," which is the dawning of the ground luminosity. As described previously, for those without a stable practice of meditation and some experience of mind's empty-luminous nature, this is the moment that we hit the "off" button of our television set—there is a flash of light and the screen goes dark.

The arising of the ground luminosity signals the first stage of the bardo of dharmata. It is our first experience of the genuine luminosity of mind, its full state of wisdom. Viewed from the perspective of our practice and our spiritual journey, it is an extraordinary moment. It is the time when every aspect of the "all-basis consciousness," the *alaya-vijnana*, has dissolved into the fundamental state of wisdom, and we return to the original space of mind—its starting point. Since all aspects of our relative, conceptual mind have ceased, mind's absolute nature of mind is revealed. Because that absolute nature is buddha nature, or *tathagatagarbha*, our experience in this moment is a vivid experience of enlightened mind. Even if we did not "get" the nature of mind in this lifetime, it manifests so powerfully now that we have a much greater opportunity to recognize it.

The Dzogchen teachings call this the arising of the alpha pure wisdom of dharmakaya. If we can maintain our awareness now, then we can rest our mind in the ground luminosity, in the state of dharmata itself, which is said to be like a clear, cloudless sky—without sunlight, moonlight or starlight.[23] It is a naked experience of awareness without any reference point, a pure experience of shunyata without a speck of obscuration.

Instead of going unconscious at this point, those who have a developed practice of meditation and have attained some realization of the nature of mind will recognize the ground luminosity as the fundamental nature of reality and the essence of their own minds. They will be able to rest in this luminosity. However, whether one is a practitioner or not, this experience of luminosity manifests unfailingly for all beings.

Dharmata Obscured

Normally, we do not experience our buddha nature clearly. It is obscured by the all-basis consciousness, the alaya-vijnana. This is the basic mind that continues from moment to moment, and functions as a storage facility for all our karmic seeds. Every action we engage in, whether positive or negative, leaves its impression there, much like data is stored on a hard disk drive. Each impression is like a seed. It is a form of potential for these impressions to ripen into another set of actions similar in nature. If we routinely repeat certain actions, then stronger impressions are made. This store of karmic seeds, then, is the source of our habitual patterns, our tendencies to act in certain ways, over and over again. The "actions" that make an impact on our mind are mental actions to begin with, the movement of thoughts, as well as our intentions and motivations. These mental actions lead to physical actions—either the actions of speech or body.

It is this aspect of mind that obscures our perception of genuine reality. Consequently, we fail to recognize "our own face," the wisdom that is our original and true nature—our buddha nature. Instead, we take ourselves to be the ongoing stream of thoughts and emotions that arise moment to moment from this storehouse consciousness. The whole purpose of the path is to correct this misperception and uncover our self-existing wisdom. At the time of death, with the dissolving of consciousness into space, and space into luminosity, nothing of this stream remains to obscure mind's empty radiance.

Samadhi Days

Our intention as practitioners is to be able to rest in the ground luminosity, and so reach our destination of enlightenment via the shortest and least difficult route. Accordingly, we rely on our practices of shamatha and vipashyana to develop the strength of mind and the power of our practice to be able to accomplish that. How long will we be able to rest when the time comes?

It is generally taught that you will be able to rest in the ground luminosity for approximately five "samadhi days." One samadhi day is equal to the length of time an undistracted state of meditation can be sustained on a regular basis. This means that if you can rest in the nature of mind without becoming distracted for one hour now, then you will have the ability to remain resting in the ground luminosity for five hours. If another person can maintain a state of nondistraction for five minutes now, then he or she will be able to rest in the luminosity for twenty-five minutes. And if someone else can rest for only five seconds now, then that person will have only twenty-five seconds of resting then. Therefore, the length of a samadhi day varies from person to person.

If, on the other hand, you are a developed meditator, a yogi or yogini who can rest in samadhi effortlessly, you will attain enlightenment at the time of the bardo of dharmata. When you see the luminosity, you will recognize it. You will think, "Aha! This is it! This is what I have seen in my practice and what I have been trying to experience fully." This sudden recognition is similar to a moment when we grasp the real meaning of something we have been thinking about and contemplating for a long time. We are unable to fully "get it" until something we see or hear suddenly triggers our understanding. Then we have an "Aha!" experience.

From this, we can see the importance of the shamatha and vipashyana practices and the development of calmness, clarity and mindfulness for attaining liberation in the bardo of dharmata. If we have no experience of samadhi, then there will also be no resting during that time and no recognition of the ground luminosity. We will certainly faint and fall into a state of unconsciousness.

MEETING OF MOTHER AND CHILD LUMINOSITIES

That "Aha!" experience is what we call the meeting of the mother and child luminosities. The motherlike luminosity is the ground luminosity, the basic reality of all phenomena. The childlike luminosity is our individual experience of that nature. In reality, these two are not separate; they are separated only by our perception of being apart. When the two meet and then merge into one, we have a nondual experience of luminosity. It is at this very moment that we can attain liberation in the bardo of dharmata. If we can recognize and rest in that experience, then liberation is certain. There is no doubt. When accomplished yogis rest in that samadhi and realize the nature of mind, there is no time limit on how long they can rest. Once we realize the nature of mind, then that is our enlightenment, and it has no measurable time. We can only measure the time we have rested in a nondual state if our resting is short and unstable. Then when we come out of that resting state, we can look back on it. We can say it was five minutes, ten minutes, one hour or two hours. Therefore, it is very important to train in meditation practice now and make every effort to recognize that luminosity in the bardo of this life. Even if we fail, our training may enable us to recognize it in this bardo.

When the mother and child luminosities meet, it is not like the meeting of two separate and unrelated people. There is a powerful and instantaneous recognition of connection. When a child meets its mother, it knows, "This is my mom." There is no question. The child does not have to think about it and ask, "Is this my mom or not?" Generally speaking, you grow up with your mother, and so you naturally recognize her whenever you see her, no matter where you are. And you naturally recognize her voice, even from a distance. You can even recognize her footsteps.

Motherlike luminosity is the wisdom, or prajna, element—the empty aspect—of buddha wisdom, or *buddha jnana.* In terms of ground, path and fruition, it is the ground aspect of the nature of all phenomena. It is the "basis of all" wisdom and the source and heart of our sacred world. Childlike luminosity is the path, or *upaya,* aspect of our experience of this basic wisdom. *Upaya* refers to the methods we use in order to bring about the experience of that wisdom—from shamatha and vipashyana all the way to the deity practices of the Vajrayana. We exert ourselves in all of these methods to try to experience the reality of the ground luminosity.

The childlike luminosity is said to be slightly impure in the sense that it is still conceptual. For example, when we first start to experience self-lessness on the path, it is still theoretical. We rely on study and contemplation as well as analytical meditation to help us grasp it intellectually. Then, when we practice resting in the nature of mind, we have various hopes and fears about whether or not we can accomplish the state of non-thought, or nonconceptual wakefulness. However, whatever glimpse of realization we successfully generate on the path is the childlike luminosity, the immature awareness that nevertheless will recognize its mother, its source, with which it has a heart connection. As our realization matures, it becomes progressively less conceptual.

When mother and child luminosities merge, ground and path become one. There is recognition and realization of the ground, the basic nature of all phenomena. At that time, wisdom, or prajna, and method, or upaya, become one. Their merging brings the experience of nonduality, which is said to be like rivers from different mountains flowing into the ocean. The rivers may come from different mountains, but they dissolve into one basic element when they finally meet. In the same way, these two luminosities come together.

The terminology for this experience of luminosity varies according to tradition, but all names for it point to the same reality. In the Sutrayana, this experience is called *prajnaparamita,* the perfection of wisdom, also known as the "great mother." In Madhyamaka, it is called "ultimate truth" or "absolute truth." In Mahamudra, it is called "nonconceptual wisdom," which in Tibetan is *thamal gyi shepa,* or "ordinary mind." In this presentation, which is primarily from the perspective of the Dzogchen teachings, the ground luminosity is called the *luminosity of the alpha pure dharmakaya.* It is the state of *rigpa,* naked awareness, which has always been in the state of purity from beginningless time. The Vajrayana teachings point to this experience through a great variety of terms and symbols, including "the great bliss wisdom," "vajra heart," "vajra mind," "vajra nature" and "OM AH HUM." No matter what you call it, that is what we experience at the time of this bardo. It is a beautiful and blissful experience.

SEARCHING FOR HOME

While there are many imposing names that point to this reality, the basic experience of wisdom is always simple and it is always with us. It can be found in every moment of our present experience. The reason that we fail to recognize it is that we are looking for something that is extraordinary. That is our predicament. We may think we understand this—we may tell ourselves over and over, "the nature of anger is completely pure"—yet when we get angry, we look for something pure outside of that anger. We think of that anger as too ordinary and polluted. Then we are missing the point again. In order to meet with the experience we are looking for, we simply need to know where to look.

All of the most profound instructions tell us that we will find ordinary mind only by looking directly at what is right in front of us. It may be an unwelcome emotion or thought, but nevertheless, that is our world in that moment. Ordinary mind is something you find right where you live—in the streets, so to speak, of your hometown—and not by going to the Himalayan mountains. If you leave your home to search for ordinary mind in some exotic location or foreign land, then you will not find it there. The great yogi Milarepa stayed in Tibet, where he was born, and found ordinary mind in the mountains where he wandered. There is no record of him traveling to the West to seek his enlightenment, although you could check the history books.

Just as we find the lovely and pristine lotus flower growing in the waters of muddy ponds, we discover the primordially pure and blissful wisdom mind within the essence of the impure, polluted mind of samsara. If we can generate some experience of this absolute nature of mind now, then in the bardo of dharmata we will have no problem recognizing the motherlike luminosity and attaining some kind of realization. If, on the other hand, we become habituated to looking for ordinary mind outside of our own "home"—our being, our own minds—then that pattern will repeat itself at the time of death. We will fail to recognize our "mom," the mother luminosity appearing right in front of us, because we have never seen "her" before. However, if we grow up with her, seeing her face, hearing her voice, then it will be impossible not to recognize her and feel great joy at the moment of reunion.

AUSPICIOUS CAUSES AND CONDITIONS

When we connect with the lineage and its blessings and then recognize ordinary mind, the environment changes; it becomes sacred. Our recognition deepens and becomes more powerful. How can we create or participate in an environment of such sacredness? It is not created by simply arranging the external environment, by hanging religious paintings on the walls, placing rich, ornate brocades on the teacher's chair and table and then having somebody sit in that chair wearing curious-looking clothes. The causes and conditions that bring about the experience of sacred outlook and sacred world occur only when genuine devotion arises in our hearts. When we can place our heart of devotion in front of our guru and the lineage, then blessings are naturally present. They are the naturally present radiance of love and pure compassion that touches and transforms our hearts when they are open. We experience this in a heightened sense in the presence—actual or felt—of our guru and the lineage because they, too, are open. By the self-existing power of the wisdom they embody, we can be touched or provoked to go beyond the safety net of conceptual mind. Therefore, it should be understood that blessings are not gifts we receive for our accomplishments or good behavior, and they are not external to us.

GENERATING SAMADHI MIND

Through whatever auspicious conditions we can create and whatever skillful means we can accumulate, we should try to recognize the luminosity of emptiness that arises in the first phase of the bardo of dharmata. Because its duration can be measured only in samadhi days, nothing else counts. Thus, we have to be careful to familiarize ourselves with samadhi mind, the mind of meditation. When we possess that knowledge, and when we also have great determination, devotion, love and pure compassion as conditions, then that recognition will be absolutely natural for us. We say that it "comes naturally" rather than it "is guaranteed" because no one is in a position to guarantee you anything. You have to guarantee it yourself. Therefore, in order to recognize the ground luminosity in the bardo of dharmata, we apply ourselves to the practice of meditation during the bardo of this life.

The practices of shamatha and vipashyana, which were discussed previously, are the skillful means for producing insight into emptiness. Before we attain higher realizations, such as complete enlightenment, we must first find a way to enter the path of ultimate truth. We must go into the space of shunyata and come to recognize the egolessness of self and of phenomena. Two approaches to this are taught: *bringing oneself to the path of inference,* and *bringing oneself to the path of direct experience.*

The inferential approach is intellectual and conceptual. It is based on the use of valid cognition, or the science of reasonings, and the methods of logical analysis. We investigate the nature of phenomena by making inferences about them and then testing those conclusions with a process of precise reasoning. This is called analytical meditation, and it is a powerful tool for examining mind and uncovering how it works. The approach of direct experience is more intuitive than intellectual; its power comes from our experience of directly resting in mind's nature.

Path of Inference

When we first hear of these two approaches, we might think that directly resting sounds much better and much easier. However, to be practical, we have to examine ourselves closely to see if we are capable of remaining in a state of nondistraction, of not straying from present awareness. How long can we stay in the present moment before we are pulled away by our thoughts? If we do have trouble resting directly, then analytic meditation is necessary and helpful. If we have little or no trouble, then the analytical approach to meditation may not be necessary, or may be resorted to infrequently.

Either way, analytical meditation is essential when we study the dharma. It sharpens the intellect, cultivates mental precision and deepens our intuitive understanding. The greater our intellectual clarity, the more we will benefit from our studies. Therefore, in order to thoroughly penetrate the essence of the teachings, we need to work with the path of inference.

An example of this process is the meditation on emptiness, which examines whether or not the self exists by way of investigating the five skandhas. This is an appropriate meditation if we have heard of egolessness, but have not experienced it directly for ourselves. In brief, from the perspective of one who experiences having a self, we contemplate what "emptiness of self" means. We look at all possible components of that self, and determine whether or not its location can be found and its existence confirmed. In conjunction with this practice, we reflect on short verses of the Buddha's teachings, such as the lines from the *Heart Sutra*: "Form is emptiness, emptiness is form. Emptiness is no other than form, and form is no other than emptiness." This is an example of a logical reasoning called the "fourfold reasoning." We conclude by resting our mind. Another investigation is one that examines the "self of phenomena"; here, we focus our analysis on external phenomena to see if they possess true existence.

This approach includes many topics of study and skillful methods of analysis. It is a potent path of understanding that will lead to the realization of the nature of mind and phenomena, which is emptiness, or shunyata. We need to get to that point because that is the ground luminosity of the bardo of dharmata.

Path of Direct Experience

The second approach to realizing the emptiness nature of mind is the path of direct experience. Here we bring our immediate experience to the path of meditation. At this point, we do not look at or analyze external phenomena. We do not worry whether forms, sounds and so forth have true existence as external objects. We do not contemplate whether tables, houses, human beings or entire universes are really there in a substantial sense, or if they are empty, without a self, lacking ego. We do not start from there. Instead, we start by looking directly at mind itself—at the vivid experience of perceptions, thoughts and emotions.

When we see a form, that perception is an experience of mind. When we hear a sound, smell an aroma, taste a flavor, feel a sensation or discern a concept, these are all various mental events. Whether we are elated by happiness or dejected by sadness, we are experiencing mind. Whether we are stirred by feelings of compassion for those who are suffering, or by hatred toward our enemies, we are simply experiencing the display of mind.

If you rest directly within mind's reality, within its nature, then you penetrate all of these experiences at once. This is the approach of taking the experience of mind to the path. Even this approach involves a level of slight investigation. Here we take some time to look at the experience of mind more closely. What is this mind? We observe our experience to see what the nature of mind is. In what form does it arise? What is its shape, its color? How tangible is it? When we look deeply and try to pinpoint it, we reach a level of experience that is open, spacious and relaxed. If a thought arises during this process, we ask questions such as "Where is this thought located? Is it inside my body, outside my body or somewhere in between? How does it exist?" This is not actual analysis; rather it is resting in the nature of thought through slight analysis.

Most of the time, our experience is divided. There is the "apprehender" and the "apprehended." The apprehender is the aspect of mind that experiences and grasps on to its objects, and the apprehended is the aspect of mind that is objectified as solidly existing external phenomena. This process of division is continual and yet we never take the time to look at the mind that is going through all of this. Because we never look at it, it sounds as if we are talking about something substantial when we say "mind," something that exists in solid form, like the brain or the heart. However, if we really look at the experience of form, feeling or emotions, then we see that they have no genuine essence. There is nothing solid or real about them. Our ordinary concept of mind as a solid thing simply falls apart. That is when we begin to see what mind actually is.

In this way, our experience is brought to the path of meditation and becomes indistinguishable from the experience of shunyata, selflessness or freedom from ego. Then the experience of ordinary mind arises naturally.

Not Finding Mind

When we look at mind in this way, we begin to see its real essence. We see how the shape, color and form of mind truly are. We may originally hold the view that mind is solid and real, but when we penetrate our experience, we discover that we were mistaken: there is no true existence anywhere, whatsoever. With that discovery, we establish ourselves in the state of emptiness, the true reality, or suchness, of mind and phenomena. When we enter that realm—that space of openness—we experience the nature of mind known as "dharmata mind."

The reason we do not find any solid existence of mind is not because our search was not thorough or skillfully performed. We do not find anything tangible or perceptible because the nature of what we are looking at—mind—is empty. Emptiness, once again, does not mean nonexistence. Mind does exist, ultimately, in a way that is beyond the grasp of dualistic consciousness, which sees only its relative projections: self and other, apprehender and apprehended, and so forth. Although we cannot see this mind, or hear it, or anything like that, we can experience it directly. That is the whole purpose of our practice. Accordingly, when we look for mind and do not find it, that "not finding" itself is the discovery of the true nature of mind. That not finding is not a fault in our search, and it is not just another fabrication or projection of mind. It is the discovery of the ultimate truth, of the reality of mind's nature. When we reach that point, it is like a light going on in the darkness or a moment of revelation.

The actual practice is not difficult because what we are resting in, moment to moment, is simply conceptual mind, the thoughts and emotions that are already with us. We are not trying to rest in some pure realm that is currently invisible to us. If we were trying to do that, how would we see where to rest our mind? Since our object is plainly in view, we have no problem. On the one hand, the approach to meditation known as "bringing oneself to the path of direct experience" is very simple, yet it is perhaps the most important and powerful practice we can train in. It prepares us to realize the motherlike luminosity that arises in the first phase of the bardo of dharmata. If at that time we can recognize the luminosity of the alpha pure dharmakaya, then we will attain liberation and our journey through the bardos of death will end.

Sambhogakaya Luminosity: The Luminosity of Appearance

If we do not attain liberation at this point, then we must continue our journey. Having not recognized the ground luminosity, the TV flashes off. When it flashes on once more, we are in an entirely different state—

a different world. An array of dazzling sights and piercing sounds surround us. Because nothing in front of us is the way it used to be, or the way it is supposed to be, there may be a sense of alarm or even terror.

Spontaneously Arising Luminosity

As we enter the second phase of the bardo of dharmata, the clarity aspect of the dharmakaya luminosity begins to become more vivid. The luminosity that arises now from the ground nature of mind is the luminosity of appearance. It is called *spontaneously arising luminosity* or the *luminosity of spontaneous presence*. It is self-arising wisdom expressed in an elaborate variety of appearances. This occurs when *luminosity dissolves into unity.* Unity, here, refers to the unity of appearance and emptiness.

At this time, the wisdom of emptiness and the wisdom of appearance dissolve into one: the union of appearance-emptiness. This can also be described as the luminosity of emptiness and the luminosity of appearance dissolving into one, or as the union of mind's clarity aspect and its suchness, or dharmata quality. The key point is that union is actually taking place now and, with it, the sense of duality is dissolving.

Previously, we experienced luminosity in connection with appearance as the luminosity of example. Then we experienced luminosity in connection with emptiness as the luminosity of no appearance. Thus, up to this point, wisdom has been experienced as two separate things. The recognition of each of these helps us to recognize the state of union, when appearances arise from the dissolving of these two together. The natural unity of appearance-emptiness can be compared to a clear sunlit sky. The sky is not just clear; it is filled with light. When the light manifests, that is the signal that the appearances born of this union are coming.

The appearances that manifest at the time of the spontaneously arising luminosity are somewhat difficult to describe. Sometimes they arise as distinct forms; at other times they arise as bindus, as sharp and clear spheres or dots of light, similar to "pixels." These appearances may also simply arise as light or luminosity. We must understand that there are a variety of ways they can be experienced.

Even when they arise in particular forms, our experience of those forms is a personal one. We may think that we all see in the same way, but actually we do not. For example, when several people look at the same object at the same time, the way in which each person sees it is completely individual. Why? Our experience is unique to our makeup because everything is mind, and mind has no absolute existence; therefore it has no fixed way of appearing.

The Hundred Deities

The spontaneously arising luminosity manifests now in the appearance of the enlightened mandalas of the hundred peaceful and wrathful deities. The deities that appear now are the basic truth, or intrinsic nature, of our mind. They are the reflection in space of the enlightened qualities that are inseparable from the primordial wisdom that is the actual nature of our mind. This fundamental state of awareness, the ground nature of mind itself, is the origin of all appearances and is thus the source of the expression of the peaceful and wrathful deities.

That nature is symbolized as the primordial buddha Samantabhadra, also known as the dharmakaya buddha. In these teachings, he appears with his consort, the female buddha Samantabhadri. Their union shows the transcendence of all polarities and the indivisibility of space and awareness. Samantabhadra represents the peaceful manifestation of this wisdom. In his wrathful aspect, he is known as Mahottara, or the "supreme great Heruka,"[24] and he appears in union with the female buddha Krodheshvari. *Heruka* means "blood drinker," and in this context is the wrathful manifestation of wisdom that consumes the blood of ego-clinging, disturbing emotions and confusion. *Krodha* means "fierce" or "wrathful" and *ishvari* suggests "goddess;" so in this context Krodheshvari refers to the forceful positive energy of the feminine aspect of wisdom.

In the Dzogchen lineage, Samantabhadra has a special connection with the sambhogakaya buddha Vajrasattva, who is regarded as an embodiment of primordial purity and as the essence of all one hundred deities. It is traditionally taught that Samantabhadra transmitted the full cycle of the Dzogchen lineage to Vajrasattva, who transmitted it to the Indian mahasiddha Garab Dorje. The transmission then passed to Guru Padmasambhava, from whom our text originates. Thus Vajrasattva is regarded as the lord of the mandala of the hundred peaceful and wrathful deities. The hundred deities are classified as forty-two peaceful and fifty-eight wrathful deities.[25] They manifest in the form of the mandalas of the five buddha families. At the center of each of the mandalas are a male and a

female buddha in union. Each family is accompanied by a particular retinue and is associated with a specific color, element, direction and enlightened qualities.[26] The central figure in the mandalas of both is Buddha
Vairochana. In his peaceful form, he appears in union with his consort, the
female buddha Dhatvishvari, signifying the union of the two truths, the
union of method and wisdom, and the union of bliss-emptiness. In his
wrathful aspect, he transforms into Buddha Heruka and appears in union
with his consort Buddha Krodheshvari.

·   The forty-two peaceful manifestations include the primordial buddhas
Samantabhadra and Samantabhadri, the five male and five female buddhas
of the five buddha families, the eight male and eight female bodhisattvas,
the six buddhas of the six realms of existence, and the four male and four
female gatekeepers.

The fifty-eight wrathful deities include the five male herukas and their
consorts and forty-eight female figures, variously called yoginis and god-
desses: the eight *gauris*, the eight *tramens*, the four female gatekeepers,
and   the   twenty-eight   *ishvaris*.
When Mahottara Heruka and Krodheshvari, the wrathful aspects of the
primordial buddha, are counted, then there are sixty wrathful deities.

Symbol and Essence

From the point of view of our relative, conceptual meditation, we can
create visualized forms of the deities just as they are shown in thangka
paintings. However, this does not necessarily mean that we will see the
deities exactly as they are portrayed in such paintings. Those images are
all symbolic forms rather than literal representations. From the point of
view of essence, the particular forms of those images do not necessarily
mean anything. While it is necessary to visualize something that we can
relate to conceptually, experience goes beyond form. For example, the
squares and circles that form the traditional structure of a mandala as well
as the variety of colors used to indicate directions or qualities are solid
only from the point of view of a solid or basic duality. Here, we are talking about appearance-emptiness.

In addition, in traditional representations, there is always a certain
degree of imputed duality. For example, there are buddha images from
many different Asian cultures; Indian, Tibetan, Burmese, Thai, Chinese,
Japanese. And now we are seeing European and American buddhas. Yet

what in actuality is Buddha? Buddha will not appear in the way we impute or think. However, when we are familiar with the practice of the Vajrayana deity mandala and with the notions of vajra pride and sacred world, the symbolic forms of the deities become a potent means of communicating the aspects of buddha wisdom they embody. Therefore, it is helpful to refer to pictures of the hundred deities and to contemplate them (see Appendix VI). Although we may not be able to recognize each figure and each aspect of the deities' appearances, we can make a connection with their wisdom. In particular, it is important to familiarize ourselves to some degree with the iconography and practice of Vajrasattva. The sadhana of Vajrasattva includes the recitation of a one-hundred-syllable mantra. The syllables of the mantra are actually the heart syllables of all one hundred peaceful and wrathful deities. Thus, whenever we recite the Vajrasattva mantra, we are connecting with all the deities at once.

At the time of the appearance of the deities, we also experience forms that are perceived as sounds. It is said that these sounds are extremely intense and powerful, like the sound of a thousand thunderbolts simultaneously resounding through space. The Tibetan term for this translates as "dragon sound." Of course, since these are all symbolic teachings, the sounds you hear may not be exactly like that. However, at this time all perceptions are heightened and intensified. Sounds, too, may be so overwhelmingly sharp and clear that they inspire a sense of anxiety or dread.

What is occurring at this time is that the primordial wisdom of the ground expands and manifests in the form of these deities, sounds and lights. Sometimes it is taught that the wrathful deities will arise first, and at other times, it is taught that the peaceful deities will appear first. However, the order of the appearances does not matter, since they are not solid. In any case, the absolute deity that appears at this time is one's own nature of mind, brilliant, luminous and totally empty.

The Five Buddha Families

It is important to keep in mind that the five buddha families manifest from the ultimate nature of our mind. They are expressions of our own wisdom. Although wisdom itself is single—there is only one origin or basis of wisdom—it is from this ground that the principles of the five buddha families arise. In essence, the wisdom of each family is the same. There is really no difference. However, in terms of how they manifest, there are five wisdoms that connect with five different relative aspects of our enlightened potential.

When our mind is under the influence of confusion, we perceive the natural energy or expression of the five buddha families as the five poisons or kleshas: passion, aggression, ignorance, jealousy and pride. When we are free from confusion, the essence of the five poisons is realized as wisdom and we perceive the five buddha families. From the point of view of Tantra, the five poisons are referred to as vajra passion, vajra anger, vajra ignorance, vajra jealousy, and vajra pride. Their nature is the utterly pure, indestructible vajra nature.

The basic potential for awakening that abides within the minds of all sentient beings is connected to the principles of these five families. Moreover, our individual enlightened potential is sometimes said to be linked to our dominant klesha. When a certain klesha is stronger in our mind, we have a stronger opportunity, with or without intention, to have a profound connection with that particular type of wisdom. It is like a gate through which one can enter the mandala of complete enlightenment. It does not matter which gate you enter. It may look quite different from outside, but once you have entered, the families are all present in one sphere of buddha wisdom.

The buddhas of the five families, as represented in these teachings, are Vairochana, Vajrasattva, Ratnasambhava, Amitabha, and Amogasiddhi and the female buddhas that are their respective consorts.[27] Their peaceful and wrathful aspects are said to appear to us over a period of twelve days. However, as these days are samadhi days, they may appear as briefly as twelve moments. If the mandala of peaceful buddhas appears first, then Buddha Vairochana appears on the first day, Buddha Vajrasattva on the second, and so on. On the sixth day, all five buddhas appear simultaneously along with Buddha Samantabhadra. On the seventh day, we perceive the five awareness-holders, or *vidyadharas*, and their consorts.[28] On days eight through twelve, we perceive the wrathful manifestations of the five buddhas.

The peaceful and wrathful aspects manifest for different purposes. For example, in this life, we may be magnetized and awakened by pleasant circumstances and pleasing words and images. On the other hand, such peaceful expressions may simply put us to sleep or into a state of indifference. In that case, we may find that we are aroused into a state of awakening, of nonconceptual wisdom, by very unpleasant or shocking situations, such as coming face-to-face with impermanence. In the bardo of dharmata, the peaceful and wrathful aspects of the buddhas are nothing other than the wisdom energy of our own mind, doing the job of waking us up.

Mandala of the Five Buddhas

Vairochana resides in the center of the mandala. He is white in color, and his family is known as the "Buddha family." This family is associated with the element of space and with the poison of ignorance, bewilderment or dullness, which from the enlightened perspective is the wisdom of dharmadhatu.

Vajrasattva resides in the eastern quadrant of the mandala. He is blue in color and his family is known as the "Vajra family." This family is associated with the element of water and with the poison of aggression or anger, which from the enlightened perspective is mirrorlike wisdom.

Ratnasambhava resides in the southern quadrant of the mandala. He is yellow in color and his family is known as the "Ratna family." This family is associated with the element of earth and with the poison of pride, which from the enlightened perspective is the wisdom of equanimity.

Amitabha resides in the western quadrant of the mandala. He is red in color and his family is known as the "Padma family." This family is associated with the element of fire and with the poison of passion or desire, which from the enlightened perspective is discriminating awareness wisdom.

Amogasiddhi resides in the northern quadrant of the mandala. He is green in color and his family is known as the "Karma family." This family is associated with the element of wind and with the poison of jealousy, which from the enlightened perspective is the all-accomplishing wisdom. The bardo teachings go into further detail, describing the particular postures, mudras, implements, retinues, and so forth, of each deity. In order to become more familiar with these details, you can refer to the more exhaustive accounts that are available.[29] Again, all of these elements are symbolic. What is being presented here are the meanings of these symbolic teachings. As for our experience of these things, it is more important to simply look at the luminous appearances that arise as the play of unborn mind. They are the experience of *mahasukha,* the great bliss-emptiness.

FIVE BUDDHA FAMILIES

BUDDHA	LOCATION	COLOR	ELEMENT	POISON	WISDOM
Vairochana	Center	White	Space	Ignorance	Dharmadhatu
Vajrasattva	East	Blue	Water	Aggression	Mirrorlike
Ratnasambhava	South	Yellow	Earth	Pride	Equanimity
Amitabha	West	Red	Fire	Passion	Discriminating Awareness
Amogasiddhi	North	Green	Wind	Jealousy	All-accomplishing

Luminosity and Kleshas

In terms of practice, each buddha family has a distinct method and style of manifesting the enlightened qualities of the mandala that relate directly and purposefully to our kleshas. When we can fully connect with the wisdom energy of a family, that klesha is transmuted into its corresponding wisdom. For example, when we feel a strong emotion, in the language of our ordinary life, it is called a "klesha attack." Here, in the language of Vajrayana, it is called a "manifestation." It is seen as an enlightened buddha manifesting with a certain quality of clarity, luminosity, and primordial wisdom. Therefore, from this perspective, there is no need to alter that experience at all.

When the experience of klesha manifests, it can be so powerful that we feel overwhelmed. It is not only powerful, but it is also penetrating. It is so penetrating that it feels like a knockout punch. This is not a hidden experience; we go through such moments all the time. Such a manifestation can be stunning in its brilliance and overpowering in its intensity. It can appear so bright that we feel our senses cannot withstand it. Such vivid experiences bring a sense of non-thought. There is a feeling of dissolving right there. Dissolving does not have to occur only later, at death. It happens here and now, in the presence of such intense luminosity. It completely blinds the perception of duality. There are no sunglasses strong enough to filter the strength of this luminosity.

Usually, when we talk about things like luminosity, clarity, or clear light, it is very conceptual and abstract. In the end, we are still wondering what luminosity really means. However, it is nothing other than what we experience as these strong emotions. In the Vajrayana, dealing with kleshas is like riding a wave. When you ride a wave, if you try to change it, it is not going to work. But if you ride it naturally, if you go along with the wave and become one with it, then there is a sense of grace and beauty.

Threefold Purity

Whenever we experience the brilliance and intensity of our emotions, we are meeting these buddhas. If we learn to appreciate and be open to their energy now, then in the bardo of dharmata our experience will be no different. We will not be overwhelmed or feel powerless. We will recognize the buddhas as our own mind and the display of that mind as the source of our liberation.

Ordinarily, we experience our emotions through the filter of ego. However, our experience at this time is the experience of the *threefold purity:* subject, object and the interplay between them are completely pure, egoless. There is no separation because duality has already dissolved. The wisdom aspects of our own mind appear undiluted and undistorted by ego's limiting fixations. Therefore, when the appearances of the peaceful and wrathful deities arise, they arise with tremendous luminosity, great power, and without any true existence.

Right now, when we visualize the pure form of a deity in our practice, we are conceptually generating that form to the best of our ability and level of understanding. Although we may regard it as appearance-emptiness, it is still very conceptual. It still feels fabricated, manufactured by thought. However, the appearances of the deities, sounds and lights that arise before us in this bardo are not the result of anything we have been thinking; they are the spontaneously arising luminosity of our own mind, and when it appears, it is direct, naked experience: extremely sharp, clear, full of light and energy, and yet utterly groundless.

Sacred World
The Ground of Pure Appearance

When you do not recognize this vivid display as the expressive power of your own mind, you become fearful. If a form appears in front of you that does not seem to be solid and real, or if you feel that you, yourself, are standing there, but are not really present, then clearly there will be a strong sense of groundlessness and uncertainty. What is this groundlessness? The ground of samsara is not there. The ground of ego is not there. The ground of duality is not there. The same thing happens when you have a pure psychedelic experience. At first, it is nonconceptual, but then you conceptualize it and become fearful. Your experience is altered and you lose your balance. You feel that you are losing your grip on conventional reality.

On the other hand, if you are able to rest in the nonconceptual nature of your present experience, then that brings you back to the pure ground of mind itself. Dharmata is the ground and luminosity is the person—or the world—standing upon it. Emptiness is acting as the ground and whatever experience arises for us—form, sound, smell, taste or touch—is in union with that ground. At this time, your experience is transformed into the experience of sacred world—the genuine experience of mandala—and you are exactly where you want to be. If you have trained in taking appearances onto the path of enlightenment, then this is the experience you have been looking for. It is the goal you have sought to accomplish throughout your practice.

When we give rise to sacred outlook fully, that experience is without any concept and therefore without any fear. At that time, we are not thinking about whether the deities are appearing in Indian, Tibetan or Japanese forms. No such labeling takes place. In contrast, in our practice now, once we start to think about the deity or the "sacredness" of the sacred world, then the whole experience is gone. It loses the quality of sacredness. It loses the real meaning of what mandala is, and we disconnect from the vajra world. However, at the time of the arising of the spontaneous luminosity, conceptual thoughts cannot intrude. Our normal way of perceiving a solid reality is stopped.

If we are truly familiar with the creation and completion stages of practice, this is the moment when we realize the nature of mind; the unity of appearance-emptiness, the unity of sound-emptiness, and the unity of awareness-emptiness. We recognize all appearances as the luminous form of the deity, all sounds as the resonant speech of the deity, and all thoughts as the supreme wisdom mind of the deity. This is the direct perception of pure appearance and the genuine experience of vajra pride.

Aspiring to Sacred Outlook

This pure experience of the vajra world is the unfailing experience of all sentient beings who have passed through the stages of death and arrived at the bardo of dharmata. The experience is the same for every sentient being, whether its form is that of an ant, a donkey or a human. It is a choiceless experience in the sense that we cannot go back. It is as though we have already taken the psychedelic drug and now we cannot simply withdraw from the experience. It is too late to say, "I should not have taken this drug." There is no point in thinking that we should not have died. We *have* died and it is too late to change that. We have no alternative but to go through this bardo experience.

In some sense, it is similar to going on a roller coaster ride. Once we are sitting there, locked in, we may think, "Too late! No matter what, I have to go through with this!" That is like our experience of bardo. No matter what, we have to be on this ride until it stops. If we can relax and enjoy it, then it as though the ride is on our side. If we start off by thinking we are going to hate it, then we will go off full of fear and the experience will be terrible. We will not benefit from it. Therefore, we simply have to change our attitude toward this experience.

Normally, if someone were to tell you, "You have an attitude problem," you might become angry. However, instead, you could regard it as an opportunity to look at your mind and ask yourself, "What *is* my outlook on the world?" If you realize it is negative, distrustful or fearful, then you can say, "Yes, I do have an attitude problem. I want to change that attitude and view the world in a more positive light." When we aspire to the attitude of sacred outlook, our experience is transformed. Our world becomes a sacred world. Nobody can take it away from us because it is the sacred nature of our own mind that we are experiencing.

When we are enjoying the ride, no one can take it away from us. On the other hand, when we are not enjoying the ride, no one can make it enjoyable for us. No one can change our mind so as to make our experience sacred. That is the difficulty.

The Four Wisdom Lights

Our next experience of the luminosity of appearance occurs at the time of *unity dissolving into wisdom.* As the appearance of the deities dissolves, the pure essence of their wisdom manifests as luminous lights: white, blue, yellow and red. These four colors correspond to four of the five buddha family wisdoms. The fifth wisdom light, the green light that symbolizes all five buddha principles, appears later.

The luminous white light is the manifestation of the alpha pure dharmakaya nature of mind, or rigpa. It is the *dharmadhatu wisdom* of seeing the true nature of phenomena. That nature is unborn, and therefore it neither abides nor ceases. This means that no samsaric phenomena have ever truly existed. Confusion and pain, ego and ego-clinging, and the entire substantial world are utterly empty of true existence. When we misperceive the pure nature of the luminous white light of rigpa, we experience it as ignorance.

The luminous blue light reflects the changeless nature of primordial buddha wisdom, which is beyond ego-identification and untouched by confusion. It is the *mirror-like wisdom* that simultaneously reflects all phenomena of the three times clearly and precisely, in an instant, like images in a mirror. When a mirror reflects images, it reflects everything all at once. It does not reflect what is closer first, then what is farther away after that. When we misperceive the pure nature of the luminous blue light of rigpa, we experience it as aggression or anger.

The luminous yellow light expresses the richness and completeness of the state of pure wisdom. This means that mind's basic nature is naturally rich, naturally full of all enlightened qualities—nothing is missing. It is the *wisdom of equanimity* or *equality* that sees that all phenomena are equally selfless. The dualistic distinction between perceiver and perceived is no longer made. When we misperceive the pure nature of the luminous yellow light of rigpa, we experience it as pride.

The luminous red light is the manifestation of the magnetizing quality of primordial wisdom, which sees, attracts and draws all things in its direction—the direction of ultimate wisdom. It is the *wisdom of discriminating awareness* that discerns the distinctive features and qualities of individual, relative phenomena. It sees how things exist; that is, it distinguishes the impermanence of external objects, the emptiness of their nature, as well as levels of confusion. When we misperceive the pure nature of the luminous red light of rigpa, we experience it as passion or desire.

THE LIGHT OF BUDDHA ACTIVITY

If, at this time, we realize the ultimate truth of the nature of mind through our recognition of the first four wisdoms, then we will realize enlightenment. Once we come to this realization, we will then be capable of accomplishing all the activities of buddhahood. This is the essence of the wisdom of the final light to appear, the luminous green light. It manifests as the final light because we must become buddha before we can manifest buddha activity. This is the *all-accomplishing wisdom,* in which all of the wisdoms of buddha arise spontaneously and effortlessly to bring about the relative and ultimate benefit of beings. Such enlightened activity is the natural manifestation of unconditional compassion and love toward all beings. However, when we misperceive the pure nature of this light, we experience it as jealousy or envy.

The whole point of practice, of making this effort to recognize the nature of mind, is to benefit all sentient beings. When we say "all" sentient beings, our aspiration automatically encompasses our own welfare and spiritual journey. We do not need to worry about being left out or not attaining enlightenment. The aspiration to accomplish compassionate buddha activity helps us achieve enlightenment more rapidly. The power of compassion accelerates our realization and makes it more profound. Thus if you want to speed up your progress, push the accelerator of compassion, love and bodhichitta. If you want to slow down your discovery, put more focus on "self"—on self-liberation, individual salvation, or individual freedom.

Visions of Spontaneous Presence

The appearance of the luminous wisdom lights is followed by the final phase of the expansion of the spontaneously arising luminosity. When the wisdom lights dissolve, this is called *wisdom dissolving into spontaneous presence.* At this time, there is a tremendous experience of forms, sounds and lights—in brilliant sheets, rays and spheres—occurring all at once and extending throughout the universe. All previous sights, sounds and lights, along with visions of the pure and impure realms, amass as a single, spontaneous vision of sambhogakaya luminosity—the luminosity of appearance. At the same time, the dharmakaya luminosity of no appearance, of pure awareness-emptiness, dawns overhead like a clear sky.[30]

Of course, anything that we say about this experience is limited by words and concepts, which are not the actual experience. We may talk about "light" and its "brightness," or we can use words such as "emptiness" and "sacredness," but the actual experience is beyond anything we can grasp intellectually through listening to teachings or reading books. The actual experience can be known only when it is present in our hearts.

Padmasambhava says very clearly that all the appearances of the deities and mandalas, of the sounds and lights, arise from the basic nature of our own mind. Mind's basic nature manifests in the form of clarity-emptiness, sound-emptiness and awareness-emptiness. There is nothing external, nothing outside of us. In trying to talk about these experiences to others, or understand them ourselves, we might ask questions such as, "What size is a bindu? Are they flat or round like globes?" However, such questions are not relevant since we are talking only about the symbolic meanings of bindus and lights. To ask how bright the light is, or whether it is more like fluorescent light or sunlight, is extraneous to our point. We need to see that these are merely symbols. What we should be looking for is the actual experience.

Arriving at a deep and personal understanding of this light of wisdom is no different from coming to an understanding of shamatha. When we first receive instructions for shamatha practice, we are told about something called "mindfulness" that leads to a state of peace, clarity, and even to something called "nonthought." However, until we actually sit and apply the instructions to our mind, they do not mean anything. We have to taste the experience of peace to appreciate what it means. We have to see clarity emerge from confusion and be present at the cessation of a thought to understand what the language of shamatha is pointing to. Then we can say, "Ah, this is what the instructions mean." Up until that moment, our understanding is conceptual, lacking real depth.

In the same way, we arrive at a personal and meaningful understanding of luminosity—the radiance of wisdom that is our actual nature of mind, and our true homeland. When we meditate on the nature of mind, that luminosity is present, and we have access to a direct experience of it. When we can rest our mind in its natural state, we can feel the luminosity, we can feel the emptiness and egolessness; it is not an abstract experience. It is like an experience of taste—you know what something is when you have tasted it. There is no doubt. You know. It is that kind of knowing that we are talking about here as actual experience—even if it is only a glimpse. Therefore, while studying these teachings is important, it is by practicing the meditations that we come to fully understand them.

Taking the Bardo of Dharmata onto the Path

As preparation for our experience of this bardo, several methods for taking the bardo of dharmata onto the path of enlightenment are taught. These include practices for realizing both the ground luminosity of the first stage and the luminosity of appearance that arises in the succeeding stages. The methods traditionally taught include looking at the nature of mind, the visualization of the mandalas of the hundred deities, taking light as the path, taking sound as the path, taking pain and sickness as the path, taking delight and misery as the path, and taking emotions as the path.

LOOKING AT THE NATURE OF MIND

The primary method for taking the bardo of dharmata onto the path is the practice of looking at the nature of mind. This is taught to be the supreme method for recognizing the ground luminosity of the first stage. These methods have already been presented in detail. However, in brief, we look straight at whatever is arising in our mind and rest directly in that thought or that emotion. In this way, we penetrate our experience and come face to face with the essential nature of mind. This is the actual practice that enables us to transform this bardo. When we can rest in that experience, it is self-liberating. That self-liberation is an experience of enlightenment.

VISUALIZATION OF THE HUNDRED DEITIES

Although the hundred deities are not separate from the nature of our mind, when they manifest in this bardo they appear to be outside of us. In order to become familiar with these appearances and to recognize them as nothing other than the self-display of our own mind, we practice visualizing the hundred deities within our bodies. In this way, we make a personal connection with what otherwise might feel quite foreign.

In this method, we first visualize ourselves in the enlightened form of Vajrasattva, the essence of the hundred deities. At our heart center, we visualize the primordial buddha Samantabhadra in union with Samantabhadri, together with the mandala of the peaceful deities. The five male and five female buddhas are surrounded by the eight male and eight female bodhisattvas, and so on. The assembly is visualized in a radiant expanse of rainbow lights. Next, at our crown center, we visualize the mandala of the wrathful forms of the five buddha families, male and female, surrounded by the various gauris, tramens, gatekeepers, and ishvaris. They also are surrounded by a brilliant display of lights. Finally, at our throat center, we visualize the five male and female vidyadharas, or knowledge-holders, in semi-wrathful form, surrounded by gleaming rainbow lights.

When our visualization becomes clear and stable and we become accustomed to these vivid appearances, then we will not be terrified by them at the time of this bardo. Instead, we will recognize the hundred deities as nothing other than the spontaneous appearances of our own nature of mind. This practice is a means of taking the bardo as the path.

Taking Light as the Path

In addition to deity meditation, there are several methods taught for working directly with the experience of light. These include the Dzogchen practices of dark retreat and *thogal.* In Dzogchen, the *thogal* practices are regarded as transcendence practices. *Thogal* implies that we "leap over," or "cross beyond" at once from our mundane state of existence to a direct experience of the luminosity of spontaneous presence. There are thogal practices that work with different experiences and elements of light, such as sunlight, moonlight, basic daylight and candlelight. Thogal practices are also often called "sky-gazing," as gazing into space is one characteristic of thogal. When we are ready to practice one of these methods, the extensive explanation is given to us by our personal teacher.

Dark Retreats

The Dzogchen practice of dark retreat requires a retreat dwelling specifically constructed for this purpose, which consists of a series of rooms, each progressively darker. The first room admits some light, the second is dimmer, and the most interior room is pitch dark. In this practice, we enter a state of complete darkness gradually, somewhat as we do when we are falling asleep; when we remain in that darkness, it is like the state of deep sleep. When we bring awareness to these states in which clarity is normally absent, we experience the clear, luminous nature of mind.

In addition to the Dzogchen dark retreat, there are also forms of this practice taught in the traditions of the Kalachakra Tantra and the new tantra schools such as the Karma Kagyu.[31] In the Kalachakra tradition, the dark retreat is an aspect of the yogas known as the Six Applications. These are not the same as the Six Dharmas of Naropa, which are a separate practice. However, within the Six Dharmas of Naropa, the practice of luminosity yoga, which relates to the state of deep sleep, is a particularly helpful method for developing this awareness.

The Self-Light of Dharmata

There is one thogal method that can be practiced quite simply. The instructions say to sit up straight in the Seven Postures of Vairochana and to close your eyes as tightly as you can. Sometimes you may even cover your eyes with the palms of your hands. Once your eyes are shielded from any external source of light, you simply look into the darkness with a relaxed mind. At first, there is just darkness, but if you keep looking, then various light forms begin to manifest. You may see blue, white, yellow, red, green or even black bindus. The key is to remain relaxed and to watch straightforwardly whatever appears in the space before you.

When there are many bindus, practice by alternating your focus: at one time, place your mind on the whole field of lights, and at another time, on a single bindu. When you focus on only one, place your mind clearly on that bindu and simply rest your mind there. This is similar to shamatha meditation. Do not allow your gaze or concentration to waver. Look at this sphere of light in the same way that you would stare at an ordinary object when your eyes are open. As you continue to look, the light becomes more vivid, clear and sharp. Sometimes it changes its form, and sometimes it changes its size. It may become so radiant, so luminous, that the darkness is not dark anymore.

When you look at this experience, you can see that, yes, there are these lights. They are right before your eyes. However, you can also see that they do not in any way exist as solid objects outside of your mind. They arise from your own mind—from mind's very nature. If you find that the bindus are becoming solid and real, then you are fixating on them and conceptualizing too much. You should cut through that tendency with the wisdom of shunyata. Use the wisdom of emptiness to see the clarity-emptiness of these appearances, rather than making them into something solid like light bulbs.

When we look at light in this way, we are looking directly at the experience of dharmata—the experience of luminous emptiness that arises in this bardo. Therefore this is one of the practices that will help us bring the bardo of dharmata onto the path of enlightenment.

TAKING SOUND AS THE PATH

There are similar practices with sound that lead us to the experience of sound-emptiness. A simple method is given here for tuning in to the natural sound of dharmata, which is always present within our mind but is usually unobserved. The instruction, again, is to begin by assuming a correct posture. When you have settled your mind, you clench your jaws and close your ears to external sounds by plugging your ears with your fingers or pressing your hands against them. This will amplify the basic sound of dharmata and make it more perceptible. It is easiest to hear this sound when it is quiet, particularly at nighttime.

Once you have identified this sound, then you place your awareness on it without wavering. Resting your mind in the sound, you continue to listen, going further and further into the sound itself. The more precise and clear your focus is, the more vivid and sharp the sound becomes. Eventually, your experience of sound deepens to the point that you experience its emptiness, which here is known as the *self-sound of the emptiness of dharmata*. This is the same fundamental experience of sound, only in less intense form, which occurs in the bardo of dharmata. As mentioned earlier, because of the acuteness of our senses, sound is so sharp and penetrating at that time that it is compared to the sound of a thousand simultaneous thunderbolts.

It is easier for most of us to understand the emptiness of sound than the emptiness of form. This is because a visual object remains before our eyes for long periods of time, whereas a sound comes and goes. For example, when we read a book, the pages do not disappear as we read them. We can flip back through the book and read each page again. In contrast, when we hear a sound—a voice, a footstep or a whistle—it is gone in the very next moment. We cannot go back to the previous moment and hear it again. Therefore, when we listen to a sound closely, it is like listening to an echo. It conveys the same message of emptiness. That is the practice of the self-sound of the emptiness of dharmata, by which we transcend our mundane experience of sound and leap directly to the realization of sound-emptiness.

TAKING PAIN AND SICKNESS AS THE PATH

Another method of bringing the bardo of dharmata onto the path is the practice of bringing our individual instances of pain and sickness onto the path. In this context, we understand "sickness" to refer to physical illness and the pain associated with it. At the same time there, there is mental suffering, which is actually fear, that arises when we feel such pain. The purpose of this practice is to transform our experience of pain, and therefore to also transform the mental suffering that accompanies it.

It is very difficult to transform an experience of intense suffering if we have no basis for working with pain to begin with. Therefore it is initially necessary to work with minor pains and illness and discover how we can bring these to the path. Then, as more severe sicknesses come to us, we are able to bring those to the path as well. Eventually, we become capable of bringing even the most debilitating conditions to the path. We work with our mental suffering in the same way. We start by relating to situations in which we feel only a slight sense of discomfort or fear. When we can pacify our suffering in these instances, then we have a basis for facing greater and greater challenges and bringing them to the path.

Therefore, it is important to start small. For example, you might begin with a pain in your knee or with a backache or headache that develops while you are meditating. Whatever form the pain takes, you should simply look at it. Is the pain sharp or dull, hot or cool, constant or pulsating? The first time you look at it, it will be painful. The second time, it will also be painful. When you look for the third time, it will again be painful. Each time that you look at it, it will be painful. However, if you become accustomed to looking at the experience of pain—if that looking is genuine and you can rest your mind in the pure sensation—then you will see a difference in how you experience the pain.

The question we should ask ourselves about our experience of pain is not whether the pain is truly there. The question we should ask is, "What is this pain and how do I experience it?" We are not going to eradicate our pain right away simply by looking at it once, twice or three times. However, we can eradicate our concepts about pain, and therefore we can transform our perceptions of pain and our experience of it altogether.

When you can work directly with physical pain in this way, it means that you are present with your actual experience, just as it is. You are free of concepts about it. You are not labeling the pure energy that is arising. This can become a very interesting experience. At times the clarity you bring to such looking can be so penetrating that the pain itself becomes intoxicating. When pain intoxicates, it becomes less painful. At that point, you can see that the pain is working to liberate itself.

When we look at pain in any form, we employ the same method used when looking at the nature of mind. Pain is an experience, and all experiences are mind experiences, which arise directly from the nature of mind itself. Therefore, looking at that nature through the experience of pain becomes very important. When we continuously observe our pain with mindfulness and awareness, the way pain manifests begins to change. Its appearance transforms, and thus it is not difficult to transform our experience of it as well. For this reason, whenever pain arises, we need to look at it. We need to experience it, and then let go of it. We do not need to hold on to it. We do not need to look back at the last moment of pain or forward to the next moment of pain. We simply need to look straight at the present experience of the pain.

We begin this transformational process by immediately bringing to the path any small sickness or suffering that comes to us. In this way, we become habituated to looking at the most basic levels of pain and discomfort. However, we usually view anything small as unimportant and not really worth doing. For example, if we have only five minutes to meditate, we tell ourselves, "Oh, five minutes is nothing. It is not enough to change my life. I need to practice for at least an hour." It is the same when a small sickness comes along, perhaps a cold or flu; at that time, we do not feel like practicing. We tell ourselves that we will feel better sooner if we simply take drugs and rest.

That is a very convincing logic at the time. However, another kind of logic says, whenever you refuse to attend to a small suffering, it becomes a greater suffering. It does not go away on its own. If you take that five minutes to meditate or you use your cold as a basis for looking at your mind, then you are acclimating yourself to the practice of bringing mindfulness and awareness into ordinary moments in your life. Such moments are manageable; you can work with them. It is like running. You start by running around the block and then that becomes so easy that you find yourself running two blocks. Before long, you are able to run a long distance.

Of course we do not start out by saying, "I must be able to cope with the worst case scenario now." That is like starting a project that is too big. When we do that, the project becomes very difficult to handle. When we start small, however, there is always room to grow. And when we see such growth, we are happy. In the same way, when our practice grows from small to great, it is a blissful experience; but when our practice shrinks from great to small, it is a painful experience. We realize we are not really doing anything and no one is benefiting.

The point is that we are better off when we can join the mind of practice, of attentiveness, to the experiences of pain, sickness and suffering that run throughout our lives. Eventually, such mindfulness becomes easy, and when a greater sickness strikes us, we will not be hit by it in the same way. It will not be such a problem or a shock. We can face even the pain and suffering of dying with greater confidence because we are facing familiar territory instead of the unknown. When the actual moment of death arrives, we will be able to look at that pain and transform it.

Taking Delight and Misery as the Path

The practice of *bringing delight and misery to the path* is another method of preparing ourselves for the experiences we will meet in the bardo of dharmata. We engage in this practice by looking at any exceptionally strong experiences we may have of joy or suffering. We look at those experiences, and then we let go of any attachment or fixation that develops in relation to them. Normally, our tendency is to grasp or hang on to our experience, whether it is positive or negative. Therefore, the key point here is the practice of letting go. Furthermore, whenever such experiences arise in this life, we should bear in mind that we will also have such episodes when we die and in the bardos after death. Our habitual patterns inevitably repeat themselves. Thus, in order to transform these patterns, we bring them to the path of enlightenment through meditation.

When we feel a sense of euphoria or anguish begin to arise, we should remind ourselves that these are mind states as well, and that they arise directly from the nature of mind itself. The instruction here is very much the same as the instruction for looking at the nature of mind; only the objects are different. You look directly at the experience, whether it is delight or misery, as it arises and rest your mind in the feeling itself without becoming distracted. Working with these two states is particularly important and relevant to the experience of this bardo as they have great power to carry you away in an instant, sweeping aside all the mindfulness and awareness you have worked hard to develop. They can manifest with a tremendous manic or frenzied energy.

Nevertheless, it does not mean that you should renounce these particular experiences when they crop up. Instead, the instruction is to immediately join them with mindfulness. If it is joy that arises, then look at the very peak of that joy. Bring clarity to the experience by looking at it repeatedly and then let go of any attachment. In the same way, if it is misery that arises, then look at the peak of that experience and then let go, which is the key point of this practice.

It can be helpful to include some analytical meditation when you are doing this practice. For example, at the end of a formal meditation session, bring the feeling of intense joy to your mind. If you have difficulty in arousing such a heightened sense of joy, then think of some very happy moment that you experienced in the past—perhaps a long-awaited reunion or some unexpected demonstration of friendship, generosity or kindness. Bring that to your mind, look at it as it arises, and let go of any attachment. Whatever form it takes, simply look at the experience and try to see its luminous nature, its quality of inseparable awareness and emptiness. Make an effort to see that. In another session, recall an experience of great suffering—some moment of being tormented by doubt, fear or loss. Look at the empty-luminous nature of that mind, and let go as well.

In this way, we gradually bring our extreme states of mind to the path, and when we give rise to such peak experiences in the bardo of dharmata, we will recognize them as the luminous nature of our own mind. Their very vividness will help us attain this recognition. Instead of carrying us away into confusion, they will become vehicles for our enlightenment.

TAKING EMOTIONS AS THE PATH

The final method presented here is the practice of taking our emotions as a path. Working with our emotions is an aspect of all our practices in our journey through each bardo of life and death. Therefore, this is perhaps the most beneficial of all practices. As we have discussed the methods for working with our emotions previously, both in the context of analytical meditation and in the situation of looking directly at the nature of mind, there is no need to elaborate further here. However, it is essential to remember that the pure nature of our emotions is wisdom, and that we will find that wisdom nowhere else.

Knowing the Territory

THE TWO KAYAS OF THE BARDO OF DHARMATA

As mentioned earlier, the luminosity that manifests at the time of the bardo of dharmata arises in two phases. It is important for us to study this teaching and to understand these two aspects of luminosity. First, the ground luminosity manifests at the time of death. This is known as the "luminosity of the alpha pure dharmakaya." It is also known as the "luminosity of no appearance," which refers to the empty aspect of the nature of mind and to the level of absolute truth.

Second, the spontaneously arising luminosity develops from the ground luminosity. It is also known as the "sambhogakaya luminosity" and the "luminosity of appearance," which refer to the clarity aspect of the nature of mind and to the level of relative truth. We say "relative" truth in the sense that this is the first expression of appearance, or clarity, to arise from the ground of emptiness. Even though such appearances as the hundred deities are pure appearances, they do not exist permanently or inherently as solid forms.

These two kayas—dharmakaya and sambhogakaya—are the essence of our experience in this bardo. They are our first experiences of enlightenment after death. However, it is taught that mind possesses three levels of enlightened manifestation. Thus our mind is in the nature of the three-kaya buddhahood. The third, the nirmanakaya manifestation, arises later in the next bardo, the bardo of becoming.

OVER IN AN INSTANT

From the perspective of our study of these teachings, we might assume that the bardo of dharmata lasts a very long time. It takes quite some time to go through the detailed descriptions and symbolic meanings of the hundred deities alone. We tend to think, "Oh, this is going to go on for awhile. First there is the meeting of the mother and child, then the appearance of the hundred deities of the mandala, and then the wisdom lights…" and so forth. However, the actual experience of this bardo for ordinary sentient beings is said to last for only a very short moment. In that moment, all of these experiences transpire.

On the other hand, from within the experience itself, that brief moment might feel very, very long. The projector of the movie we are watching has slowed down and is showing the movie frame by frame. At this speed, the images seem to linger before us and all of their details stand out vividly. Nevertheless, however long it seems, it is only a few moments—the time that elapses between the moment you realize, "I am falling down the stairs," and the instant you hit the floor, or between the moment your realize your car has gone into a skid, and the instant it hits a tree. It happens very fast, but each moment is extremely clear and distinct. In the same way, the appearances of this bardo may seem to go on for some time, but for most of us the whole experience is over in an instant.

If we have not cultivated a sense of mindfulness and awareness, and if we have no understanding of emptiness, then we will not recognize these appearances or even realize that they have happened. In that case, our experience of this bardo is said to be like going unconscious. It is like "going under" when you have been given a general anaesthetic. Suddenly, you're gone—and the next thing you know, you are awake again in another realm. You are in the beginning of your next life and you have no memory of anything that happened while you were in that anaesthetized state.

Arriving at the Next Destination

When we depart from the bardo of dharmata for our next experience in the bardo of becoming, we are also departing from the pure state of nonconceptual awareness. Conceptual mind begins to stir and our habitual patterns come into play once again. When we wake up from our state of unconsciousness, just as when the television is turned on again, we perceive a new set of appearances. Those appearances are the lights and other manifestations that signal the approach of the six realms of samsaric existence—the six potential realms of our next rebirth, if enlightenment is not attained very soon.

At this point, we are drawing closer to what we call the next life. We are beginning to arrive at our next destination after one more leg of our travels. When does our arrival at a new destination begin? Does it begin when you get on the plane, or when your flight takes off? Or even before that, when your mind first turns toward the thought of travel, and you think, "Oh, I would love to go to India. I can see it now..." Our arrival at our destination actually begins whenever the appearance of that place starts to take a more dominant position in our minds, while the appearance of our homeland becomes more and more vague. Thoughts of the people there and the place itself are dimmer and arise less frequently. The actual point at which this occurs will depend on the individual traveler. For some people, it happens as soon as they hop on the plane. For others, it is a more difficult transition. Even after they have arrived at their destination, they are still clinging to their point of departure.

To Be or Not To Be
The Karmic Bardo of Becoming

7

WHEN WE AWAKEN from our anaesthetized state, we have a moment of clarity before confusion begins to cloud our mind. The TV that was switched off has clicked on again, and we are viewing a different set of images. We have no recollection of the luminous appearances of the bardo of dharmata. We are wondering what has happened to us and where we are. What has happened is that we have somehow failed to recognize the nature of mind in any of the previous bardo states, the intervals of this life, dream, meditation, dying and dharmata. If we had, then this sixth and final bardo experience would be unnecessary; it would be naturally transcended and transformed. However, since we are here, we are like a child who cannot find its mother. Once again the child has to take this lonely journey. One more time, we have to wander in samsara.

> E MA
> At this time, when the bardo of becoming appears to you,
> Hold the one-pointed mind of intention
> To continuously perform excellent activity.
> Closing the entrance to the womb, remember to reverse samsara
>   and nirvana.
> This is the time to be steadfast and to hold sacred outlook.
> Abandoning jealousy, meditate on the guru and consort in union.

The bardo of becoming begins when we regain consciousness after having fainted in the bardo of dharmata. It ends when we enter the womb of our future mother, thus beginning another cycle in samsaric existence. This bardo is known as the bardo of "becoming" or "existence" because at this time, there is a sense that anything is possible. It is taught that it is possible to take birth in any realm or state of existence. There is the possibility of taking birth in an utterly sane environment—of leaping into a buddha field—or of taking rebirth as a bodhisattva on the *bhumis*—one of the ten stages on the path to enlightenment. It is also possible to take birth as a human being or an animal, a god or a demon. Thus, this bardo is called the bardo of becoming since we can become anything—we can take birth in any form.

Nirmanakaya Luminosity

How is it that we can become anything? It is because this mind that is the basis for the appearances of both samsara and nirvana has an essence that is empty, a nature that is luminous, and an appearing aspect or manifestation that is unceasing. In the bardo of dharmata, we experience both the empty essence and the luminous nature as the dharmakaya and sambhogakaya luminosities. These two aspects of essence and nature are the ultimate truth aspects of this mind. Now, in the bardo of becoming, we experience mind's expressive power or aspect of unceasing manifestation, which is the nirmanakaya luminosity.[32]

From among the three, the aspect of unceasing manifestation is the mind's relative reality. What is being pointed out here is that all appearances we experience—whether these are pure or impure—are the expressive power of mind's empty, luminous nature, and this is the nirmanakaya luminosity. Does this aspect ever cease? No, it does not. The luminous-empty nature of mind is unceasing and can appear as anything. It appears in the variety of visible forms, sounds, smells, tastes and objects of touch that we experience, and it also appears as mental phenomena, as thoughts and emotions. In other words, our mind never remains blank. Another thought will always arise, another feeling will always surface, another perception will always present itself, until one is fully awakened.

The images that appear before us now, the pictures currently taking place on the TV screen, are the vivid play or self-display of the energy of mind. It does not matter what kind of pictures they are—good or bad—the experience of either is luminous from an ultimate perspective. The Mahamudra teachings say, for example, that thoughts are the self-display or the expressive power of mind's luminosity, and that what arises as the objects of those thoughts are their expressive power.[33]

It is important to understand the nature of appearances in this bardo because it is said that most beings will undergo experiences of some degree of fear at this time. To the extent that we do not recognize their actual nature, we will take the appearances we meet at this time to be real—to solidly exist as external phenomena. They will thus have the power to terrify, confuse or seduce us, depending on the form they take. What determines the form they take? It is our habitual patterns, the karmic tendencies we have developed in our life and indeed throughout our previous lifetimes. Since we have all accumulated many negative tendencies, as well as positive ones, our experience now will be mixed, and very unpredictable.

Unceasing Appearances

It is helpful to understand the way in which our consciousness serves as a basis for the unceasing manifestations of appearances that we now experience. If we have a clear view of this, then we will be more skillful in working with those appearances and more able to avoid states of extreme suffering. We will also have a greater opportunity to attain liberation.

As described previously, mind-itself, the fundamental nature of our mind—the state of suchness or dharmata—is the source or root of both pure and impure appearances. Because it is the ground of all appearances, it is also known as the *alaya,* which means "all-basis," or "basis of all." This all-basis mind has two aspects: the pure all-basis and the impure all-basis. In its pure state, it is called the *alaya-jnana,* the all-basis wisdom, which has the quality of luminosity, clarity and complete wakefulness. This mind is without beginning or end; it is beyond all time and it is the source or basis for all phenomena. It is synonymous with buddha nature and the dharmakaya. In its impure state, it is called the *alaya-vijnana,* the all-basis consciousness, the mind of duality, which is synonymous with the confused perception of ordinary beings. It is the mindstream that continues from moment to moment and is the holder of karmic seeds. In other words, when the all-basis, or the *alaya,* is impure, it is called "consciousness," but when seen in its pure aspect, it is called "wisdom."

The alaya-vijnana is a relative phenomenon which we do not generally perceive in a clear or distinct way because it is a neutral experience. It is neither positive nor negative; it is neither emotions nor thoughts nor perceptions. The actual experience of the alaya-vijnana is found simply in our sense of moment-to-moment continuity. For example, today we may visit a friend and sit in a room of his house, and tomorrow we may go somewhere that is totally new to us, but nevertheless, there is a sense of continuity to our experience. We feel we are the same person who is continuing from the past to the present and from the present to the future.

That continuity itself is relative. From the absolute point of view, there is no time, so there is no notion of continuity or of discontinuity. You would have to ask, "Continuing from what?" Absolute truth goes beyond the notion of continuity.

It is this moment-to-moment sense of continuity that becomes the basis for the imputation of a "self." As soon as we perceive this "self," we also perceive "other" and duality is complete. Whenever we fail to recognize the nature of mind, the alaya-vijnana continues. We do not have to try to recreate this experience—from one moment to another—over and over again. The power of our habitual patterns, the momentum and force of our karma, perpetuates this mind. However, its momentum is clearly interrupted from time to time; for example, when we enter the bardo of meditation, when we have an accident, or when consciousness dissolves at the time of death. Nevertheless, it comes back.

In addition to such perceptible instances, our mindstream continually ceases and rearises from moment to moment. In between each moment of thought, the pure nature of mind is there, but we fail to click into it or recognize it. So long as the alaya-vijnana is functioning, it will continue to project a steady flow and variety of appearances, and we will continue to label those appearances as good and bad, desirable and unpleasant and so on. In this way, we perpetuate the formation of karma and continue to experience states of happiness and suffering.

Therefore in this bardo, our experience is dominated by karma, by the unceasing manifestation of appearances that arise from the alaya-vijnana as a result of our habitual patterns. These projections of mind appear as thoughts, feelings, emotions and perceptions of an environment and beings. They may appear as blissful apparitions, as terrifying enemies or as menacing elements; they may inspire desire, panic or shock. Ultimately, they are all in the nature of the three kayas: empty in essence, luminous in nature, and unimpeded in their manifestation. They are the expressive power of mind, its self-display. Relatively, they are our confused thoughts.

REEMERGENCE OF CONFUSION

During the bardo of dying, the coarse and subtle elements of body and mind undergo a progressive and total dissolution. All aspects of dualistic consciousness dissolve into the state of dharmata. It is in this naked state of awareness that we experience the arising of the ground luminosity and the other ultimate phenomena of mind. Physical death has occurred, the connection between mind and body has been severed, and the white and red bindus at the heart center have collapsed, thus releasing the subtle consciousness—the indestructible wisdom bindu—which then naturally departs.

At this point, we wake up again and begin to regain consciousness. That is, the dualistic structure of mind begins to reassert itself. This is the reverse progression of appearance, increase and attainment, in which the consciousness that had dissolved into the wisdom of dharmakaya now re-arises from that wisdom, bringing with it the dualistic appearances of samsara. Why does this occur? From not having recognized the nature of mind, the subtle winds reappear, bringing back the eighty kinds of conceptuality, which correspond to the triad of the black, red and white appearances, now arising in reverse order: first, ignorance returns, then passion and then aggression. In other words, if we do not recognize the nature of our mind as all-basis wisdom, then this mind becomes the all-basis consciousness.

When we "wake up" and regain the sense of duality, we begin to have the thought that we have actually died and left our body. As we remember our death and come to this understanding, we are likely to feel intense confusion and anxiety. Fear arises because of our habitual tendencies to cling to this life and to this existence as solid and real. However, we have lost that ground. There is no solid basis for our existence. We still have the habit of clinging onto the self as "me," and we still appear to ourselves to be the same person. We appear to have the same body and mind. But at this point, our body is a mental body, or subtle body, which arises from the inner essential nature of mind. There is no solid physical form. Our perceptions are also mental perceptions.

It is also taught that one of our strongest habitual tendencies as sentient beings is that of moving, or being unstill. We do not have a very strong habitual tendency of stillness or resting. This is said to be the root of all confused habitual tendencies: not abiding or resting within the all-basis wisdom. The real meaning of the bardo of becoming is shown here in this fluidity of appearances. It is possible to arise in any form and to create any kind of world. When our mind lacks stability, however, our experience becomes very unpredictable and erratic. Due to the incessant movement of our thoughts, we are continually transported from one place to the next, from one environment to another. It is difficult to remain at rest for any length of time. Everything is vivid and clear in one moment, and in the next we have forgotten everything. We may even forget at times that we have died.

If we can connect with our path at this point, then the experience becomes profound. The groundlessness we are experiencing is not merely an intellectual understanding we have reached through study; it is not some conclusion we have arrived at through analysis; nor is it the result of visualizing emptiness. It is an actual experience of groundlessness, which transcends our normal modes of comprehension.

The Miraculous Power of Karmic Mind

At this point, the energy of karma manifests in the form of a kind of miraculous power. Whereas now, when we think about going from one room to another, we have to actually get up, walk across the room and pass through a door, in the bardo of becoming there is a miraculous power of karmic mind that allows us to travel anywhere in an instant. As soon as we think about New York City, we are in the city. If we think about Beijing, then we are there. There are no obstructions of any kind to our travels; for example, we do not have to think about going through doors—we can pass through walls or any solid object. Whatever comes to our mind, whether it is the thought of a person or the image of a place, appears before us at once. At the same time, we have the miraculous ability to read to a certain extent the thoughts of others, to know what they are thinking and feeling. This is not a state of omniscience, only a limited power of clairvoyance or heightened faculty of perceptiveness.

Throughout our lives, we have wondered about miracles—and here they are. We witness the astonishing power of our mind in the miraculous displays of our karma and manifestations of habitual tendencies. If our mind is habituated to negative thoughts, then our mind becomes filled with negative energy that manifests as unpleasant or seemingly hostile appearances. If our mind is habituated to positive thoughts, then, accordingly, we experience appearances that seem to us pleasant and welcoming. Furthermore, if we are habituated to the visualizations of deity yoga practice, then the mandala of the deity appears and we can rest in that sacred space and attain enlightenment. With the profound view of emptiness and sacred outlook, we can achieve ultimate realization now through the miraculous power of our mind.

CREATING AUSPICIOUS CONNECTIONS

In the first stage of this bardo, when we still see ourselves as who we are right now, the appearances of the life we have just left can arise for us quite vividly. At this time, we can see and hear all the people that we have known; our family and friends, as well as our teachers and members of our spiritual community. Since we possess a mental body, whenever we think about any one of them, we are there with that person. However, while we can see them and even know to some extent what they are thinking and feeling as a result of our death, they are unaware of our presence. They do not respond to us when we call out to them. We cannot directly comfort them or be comforted by them.

From the perspective of those who are left behind in the bardo of this life, it is important to understand that there is initially some possibility that the consciousness of the departed person may be drawn back into the presence of loved ones and familiar surroundings. Therefore, it is important for those of us remaining to have positive thoughts and to create a positive and stable environment, as this will assist the consciousness of that person and ease his or her passage through this bardo. If we are going through emotional turmoil, then our loved one may be distressed by our pain. If we are feeling angry or indifferent, then that may cause him or her to become angry or despairing, sensing a lack of love and support.

We should also be mindful of our thoughts regarding their possessions and of our actions in regard to the belongings they have left behind. We should handle them with care and respect. If we mishandle them, then the consciousness in the bardo may suffer, just as we would if we walked into a room and saw someone take something that we liked very much and destroy it. We would not be happy. Therefore we should remember that the departed person sees and reacts in the same way that we do; we are all vulnerable to states of confusion and suffering.

Because of the power of mind in the bardo, we have the possibility of helping anyone with whom we have a close connection during this stressful passage. By maintaining a clear, peaceful and positive mental state, we will help them to relax in that state as well. By relating to them with genuine love and compassion, and with the attitude of bodhichitta that wishes only for their happiness and liberation, then we will definitely help this person. That is the best practice we can do.

In the same way, we can also help those with whom we have more distant connections, as well as beings who are unknown to us. These days, we are in a situation where we hear reports from the media about people throughout the world who have died due to various causes: war, famine, disease, natural disasters and tragic accidents. When we read these reports or hear about them on TV and see the graphic images of these events, if we make a little prayer and generate positive thoughts, we will be making positive connections with the beings who are undergoing the experience of death. Based on making this connection, we can actually help those beings. We can help them attain enlightenment, and they can help us attain enlightenment, which is what we call a twofold benefit; benefiting oneself and benefiting others.

This is better than getting angry or simply feeling sad and depressed when we see such things happening in the world. It is preferable to becoming caught up in our beliefs about good and bad, right and wrong, and then generating thoughts of aggression and blame. Such negative thoughts do not ever help those who have died, and they are also harmful to our state of mind. Even though we may not be able to maintain completely pure thoughts from moment to moment, or throughout the period of forty-nine days, at least our first thought can be a positive one. When we can sincerely generate positive thoughts and prayers for the well being of friends and strangers alike, this is immediately beneficial and may even prove auspicious beyond our knowing for their spiritual journey as well as our own.

Traditional Tibetans, when hearing of someone's death, will immediately recite mantras, or short prayers, so to speak, which invoke blessings and connection with enlightened mind. Mantras are thus regarded as a form of mind protection. There are any number of mantras that can be recited, such as: OM MANI PADMA HUM, KARMAPA CHENO, or OM VAJRA GURU PADMA SIDDHI HUM. After reciting mantras, we make aspiration prayers and generate positive thoughts. We conclude by dedicating the merit of our positive thoughts and aspirations for the ultimate liberation of those beings.

It is said that the karmic connections we share with family members and friends endow the practices we engage in on their behalf with greater power. Reading the bardo instructions to a fellow sangha member while he or she is dying and after their consciousness has departed is one of the best ways we can help someone with whom we have a meaningful connection. We can read to them from *The Tibetan Book of the Dead,* or from the instructions of Padmasambhava that have been presented by the gurus of various lineages.

Of course, the dying person can read the instructions himself or herself; but it is also important for us to read to them during the dissolution process. That way, even if they fail to recognize the nature of mind initially, they will be reminded of what to do because they will be hearing the instructions again. If they are already familiar with these teachings, the instructions are even more potent. After death, during the potential confusion of the bardo of becoming, if they hear the bardo teachings again from their guru, a spiritual friend, or their dharma brothers and sisters, then they will be able to reconnect with this teaching and arouse the motivation to achieve some experience and realization of the nature of mind in that very moment.

Stages of the Bardo

It is said that the experience of this bardo lasts approximately seven weeks, or forty-nine days. However, there are some variations in how these weeks are described. Most accounts say that the first half of this bardo is more connected to the appearances and habitual tendencies of this life, while the second half is more connected to those of our next life. At some point, however, there is a shift in our experience and it begins to be colored by the qualities and attributes of the realm into which we will be reborn. Some teachings mark this turning point at three weeks, or twenty-one days. There is no hard and fast rule that it will be exactly one way or another. The timing depends on one's individual karmic makeup.

The bardo experiences that are presented here are for the average person—those who have some positive and some negative accumulation of karmic tendencies. However, there are two categories of exceptional beings that do not experience this bardo. Highly realized practitioners will achieve enlightenment during the bardo of dying or the bardo of dharmata. For them, this bardo does not exist. They are immediately liberated into the dharmakaya or sambhogakaya buddha realms. On the other hand, those who have accumulated a tremendous amount of negative karma also will not experience this bardo. The force of their negative karma is so powerful that it propels them immediately into another rebirth. They go straight into the continuation of that negativity, which leads them into further states of suffering. However, these two situations are rare. Most sentient beings will definitely experience the bardo of becoming.

Dawning of the Six Realms

About halfway through the bardo of becoming, we begin to witness the lights of the six realms, signaling the approach of our rebirth into one of the six states of samsaric existence. Since we have not yet been liberated, and we have wandered in an ever-changing and groundless state for what seems a long time, we may feel drawn to any opportunity to find another body and home. The "wind of karma," the momentum of our habitual tendencies, will push us toward a realm of rebirth that reflects our most dominant psychological tendencies. At this point, it is most important to be aware of our mental state and to apply the practices that will be most effective at this time. The lights that appear to us now are not purely "wisdom lights," like those that manifested in the bardo of dharmata. At this time, dualistic habits of mind have returned and so these lights, which emanate from our mind, are the lights of samsara. Their essence is emptiness, and their nature is luminous, but they are tinged with the colors and karmic traces of our habitual patterns. Even so, it is said that if our practice is exceptionally good, it is possible for the lights to appear as the five wisdom lights.

For most beings, the lights that appear now are pale in comparison to the vivid lights of the bardo of dharmata. When we see them, we will naturally feel drawn to one more than others. However, the instruction at this time is to refrain from allowing ourselves to be drawn into any one of these states. The white light that appears is associated with the realm of the gods, the red light with the realm of the jealous gods, the blue light with the human realm, the green light with the animal realm, the yellow light with the hungry ghost realm, and the dark, fog-like light with the hell realm.

In addition to the lights, we will see signs of the realm of our rebirth in the form of images of various landscapes. For example, if you follow the white light of the god realm, you may see a magnificent palace. If you follow the red light of the jealous god realm, you may see a ring of fire and feel that you are entering a battlefield. The green light of the animal realm may lead to appearances such as an empty dale, cave or hut. The yellow light of the hungry ghost realm may lead you to a pile of logs or a jungle. If you follow the dark foggy light of the hell realm, then you may see a dungeon or hole in the ground, or a metallic city. Descriptions of these images vary, and again these appearances will be a matter of individual experience.

If you are attracted by the blue light, it is said that your next birth will be in the human realm, which is made up of four distinct continents. Of these, three are places with many desirable qualities. The inhabitants of these continents enjoy wealth, various comforts, beautiful surroundings and long life, but they have no opportunity to practice the dharma. Only one continent affords that opportunity: the southern continent. It is said that if you see a lake with male and female swans, that indicates rebirth in the eastern continent. If you see a mountain lake with mares and stallions grazing around it, that indicates rebirth in the northern continent. If you see a lake with cows and bulls grazing nearby, that indicates rebirth in the western continent. If you seem to be entering a mist or you see a city with nice houses, that indicates rebirth in the southern continent. The mist is said to indicate simply a human rebirth, while a city with nice houses indicates a "precious human birth," one that will provide the opportunity to practice the dharma. Then you will see a man and woman engaged in sexual intercourse. If you continue to follow this course, you will enter the womb of the female and this couple will become your parents.

BECOMING: QUALITIES OF THE SIX REALMS

According to the Mahayana and Vajrayana views, the six realms are psychological states. They are not substantial physical locations to which we actually go. They are not like Seattle, Vancouver, New York or San Antonio. When we talk about these realms, we are speaking of mental states and the intensity of the various emotions that are experienced within those states. Thus each realm represents a psychological style that is dominated by a particular emotion, a particular type of fixation and a characteristic style of suffering, which is reflected in its basic genes or basic being.

Although we may conceptualize otherwise, the six realms are not created by any external agent or being. We are the creator of these states as well as the experiencer of these states. From the Buddhist perspective, they are the creation of our individual and group karma. They are projections of our mind manifesting in the experience of a specific realm. It is important to realize that the realm we inhabit right now is a projection of our mind as well. It is as unreal and insubstantial as the other five realms. Everything here is in flux and is nothing other than appearance-emptiness. Just as we project this realm, we can project another one. Furthermore, although we are currently in the human realm, within it, we go through the experiences of all six realms—physically, emotionally and mentally. It is possible to have agonizing hell realm experiences in this life as well as blissful god realm experiences.

From both the Mahayana and Vajrayana points of view, the six realms and all the suffering and causes of suffering associated with each exist only within our mind. Shantideva, the great Indian mahasiddha, said that this is what the Buddha taught when he said, "There is nothing dangerous in the three worlds, other than mind." That is, there is nothing more powerful than the mind in terms of its capacity to bring about both negative and positive states.

Traditionally, the six realms are categorized into three higher and three lower realms. The higher realms are the god realm, the jealous god realm and the human realm. The lower realms are the animal realm, the hungry ghost realm and the hell realm. Birth in the higher realms is said to be the result of the accumulation of positive karma, while birth in the lower realms is the result of less positive or negative karmic tendencies. Therefore, in the higher realms, there is less suffering, less obscuration of the nature of mind and consequently one enjoys more freedom. In the lower realms, there are progressively greater degrees of suffering and deeper states of mental obscurity. All six realms, however, are within cyclic existence and therefore all include some element of delusion and suffering.

The teachings tell us that we move towards the experiences of a particular realm based upon how great a connection we make with the lights that we see. At this point in our journey, we are in the process of "becoming" or taking birth in the experiences of one particular realm.

God Realm

If we follow the white light and take birth in the god realm, we will enjoy a state of being that seems to offer continual physical and mental bliss. God realm beings possess not only immeasurable material wealth, but also vast mental wealth in the form of the joy of perfect samadhi. Furthermore, the life span in this realm is exceedingly long by our standards. It is said that one day in the god realm is equivalent to one hundred human years. Therefore, one seems to be immortal.

However, for all its pleasures and lack of apparent suffering, the god realm is still an aspect of samsaric existence. Our experience here is dominated by the afflictive emotion of pride, which develops because we think we have achieved the very pinnacle of existence. We feel that nothing could surpass what we have accomplished. However, when our mind becomes inflated with such mundane pride, then we have an attitude problem. Because we think we have nothing more to learn, nothing further to achieve, our pride becomes destructive to our path. It is the end of our spiritual journey as well as the end of our development of mundane wisdom.

Furthermore, it is taught that, in this realm, we lose our faith in karma. This is because, sooner or later, the positive karma that produced this particular birth is exhausted. We eventually realize that we have not reached the state of ultimate liberation after all—our existence is still within the realm of samsara. We see that the god realm itself is impermanent and that we cannot remain in our blissful state forever. It finally dawns on us that we will have to undergo further sufferings in cyclic existence.

It is said that beings in the god realm can foresee their time of death one week in advance, which in human terms is seven hundred years. This realization brings about an experience of terrible suffering. It is said that when gods die, their particular suffering is so great that it is like falling from heaven into hell. Furthermore, one's imminent death is foreseen by the other inhabitants of that realm, who shun one's presence; thus during that "week," one is completely isolated.

The sudden alternation from pleasure to pain is a little like manic depression, a state of mind in which you can fall suddenly and drastically from euphoria into deep depression. In this context, when we are starting to fall down from the god realm mentality, we lose faith in all our achievements and in whatever has brought us joy. We lose faith in everything, even in ourselves. Therefore, in the god realm, there is no genuine path to liberation.

Jealous God Realm

If we are attracted to and follow after the pale red light, then we are born into the realm of jealous gods, who are also known as demi-gods, or *asuras*. In traditional Buddhist iconography, the jealous god realm is situated beneath the god realm. Although it is a higher realm birth with many positive advantages, its inhabitants enjoy less of a sense of richness, pleasure and power than the inhabitants of the god realm. The dominant emotion for beings in this realm is jealousy, which is closely related to envy and is also characterized by paranoia and competitiveness. Jealousy itself may appear to be relatively innocent, but it is actually destructive in nature.

The suffering in this realm is traditionally symbolized through the image of a beautiful wish-fulfilling tree that the jealous gods have planted in the middle of their world. They have worked diligently, tending and nurturing the tree, which has grown so high that its top branches extend upwards into the realm of the gods. The result is that now the gods have only to pick and enjoy the exquisite fruit, while the jealous gods below must continue to work and tend the tree. Therefore, the jealous gods wage a continual war upon the inhabitants of the god realm above, asserting their ownership of the tree and therefore all its fruit. The struggle is never-ending and always disastrous for the jealous gods, who never cease to envy the superior wealth and happiness of the gods.

What we learn from this illustration is that when we work on the seed level of any project, we are expending a great deal of labor in order to produce something that will be very fruitful and bring joy and prosperity in the future. However, if we become caught up in the psychological state of this realm, then we are willing to ruin the whole thing for everyone because we cannot bear to see others enjoying the fruit of our labors. We are jealous of their pleasure, their leisure and their happiness. When we are poisoned by such jealousy, we become willing to destroy others, and consequently all our efforts to create something beneficial will have been in vain. No matter how hard we work to bring our project to maturity, there will be no positive outcome. When we are invaded by the emotion of jealousy, there is no fruition.

Furthermore, jealousy brings with it tremendous paranoia. We tend to see others as competitors and rivals. We try to outdo them at every turn. If, for example, someone performs an act of generosity, we must perform an even more generous act. We are jealous not only of their wealth, but also of their merit. However, our gesture is not based on genuine altruism or compassion but on a wish to surpass or outshine our opponent. Jealousy is one of those emotions that can steal our mindfulness and awareness away. If we let such thoughts run wild, they can turn our whole world upside down. We might end up engaging in aggressive actions that escalate into anger and then into hatred and aversion—in this way our negative emotions can lead us to rebirth in a hell realm.

Human Realm

If we follow after the pale blue light, we will take birth in the human realm, which is dominated by the afflictive emotion of desire, or passion. Our experience in this realm is characterized by a sense of poverty mentality. No matter what our circumstances may be, we feel an underlying and pervasive sense of dissatisfaction. We might possess wealth, a good family, proper work, a healthy body and mind, and live in pleasurable surroundings. Still, we feel that something is missing in our life. We feel a sense of discontent and restlessness, which comes from passion that has no limit. Our desire is like a pot with a hole in it. No matter how much water we pour into the pot, it will never be full. It is always leaking.

The desire of the human realm is based on subtle craving that develops into coarser levels of attachments. These attachments are not always so easy to see. For example, you may feel that you are not attached to wealth. If you are poor and without many belongings, you can say, "See? I have no desire for material things." If you are wealthy and have plenty of possessions, you simply may not see the underlying attachment you have to those possessions.

The most prevalent and consistent form of suffering we experience in this realm is that which results from attachment. We often do not recognize this because we think that the worst suffering is a result of emotions like anger or hatred. Nevertheless, if we look at the full spectrum of suffering in this world, we will see that the suffering caused by attachment exceeds the suffering caused by any other source. This is so because desire arises in relation to many things; food, wealth, clothing, home, and loving friends and companions. It seems to be the essence of our moment-to-moment existence. Anger is devastating and injurious, of course, but it arises less frequently.

In the human realm, when we encounter beautiful forms, pleasant sounds, fragrant smells, delicious tastes and pleasurable tactile sensations, these are not neutral experiences; they incite mind's habitual craving and tendencies to grasp. These particular objects are known as the "five desirables," the five objects of the five sensory perceptions. Even when we do possess the object of our desire, our joy can only be momentary. Eventually, the beauty of the object fades, its appeal diminishes, or its true character is revealed; or perhaps it is lost, stolen or perishes naturally. It may even turn into its opposite—an object of revulsion. Thus, our satisfaction is always fleeting.

Shantideva reminds us that the pleasures we enjoy in samsara are like licking honey on a razor blade: When we lick the honey, it is very sweet and indescribably delicious—but we forget that the sharp edge of the razor is just underneath.

Animal Realm

If we follow after the pale green light, we will take birth in the animal realm, which is the first of the lower realms. This realm is dominated by the mental state of ignorance, which has the attribute of stupidity. Ignorance is regarded as one of the three root poisons, along with passion and aggression. However, it is not quite an emotion in the same sense. Rather, it is an afflicted state of mind that is destructive because it is the opposite of wakefulness and intelligence.

When we take birth in the animal realm, it is like wandering unprotected in a realm where our survival is constantly being threatened and where we are accordingly always full of fear. However, the animal realm mentality does not see things clearly or understand its true predicament. Mind's natural clarity is overcome by bewilderment. Consequently, we suffer from a mental state that is heavy, dark, and dull.

This does not mean that animals have no capacity to perceive or understand at all. It means that they do not know what it is crucial to know. They have no self-awareness and no capacity for self-reflection. They lack the prajna, or sharpness mind, which would lead them to transform their habitual tendencies and thus bring them into a state of greater wakefulness. For example, animals do know how to nourish themselves and take care of their young. However, they do not know how to avoid the negative actions, such as killing and fighting, which result in the perpetuation of negative karma and further obscuration of mind's natural clarity.

We can see by looking at our own mind that intelligence has two aspects. One is the kind of instinctive wisdom or natural understanding that allows us to know how to balance ourselves on two feet, or how to judge our own size in relation to the width of a doorway so that we can pass through it without hitting ourselves. The second kind of intelligence is intellectual knowledge that brings genuine wisdom. To gain that kind of knowledge is possible only when we have accumulated a certain amount of merit and are also willing to exert ourselves toward that end. No one is born a scholar or a sage. We must study and work hard. Even geniuses need to read books, if only once.

When we lack this second kind of intelligence, we are ruled by stupidity—a destructive mental state in which we repeat again and again patterns of behavior that lead us further into darkness and fear—all the while not really knowing what we are doing. This is not just true with animals, or the animal realm, of course. It is possible to experience the same nature of stupidity in our own realm.

Hungry Ghost Realm

If we follow after the pale yellow light, we will be born into the realm of hungry ghosts, or *pretas,* which is dominated by the disturbing emotion of greed. In this context, greed is an aspect of desire in general, which is expressed in the form of stinginess or miserliness. One clings to material possessions or resources of any kind, as well as to psychological states. The hungry ghost mentality suffers from having an insatiable appetite, while at the same time being unable to partake of any substances or enjoy any experiences. Therefore, such beings are pictured as tortured spirits.

Traditional Buddhist illustrations depict beings in the hungry ghost realm as having small mouths, needlelike necks and enormous stomachs. Although they are constantly hungry and filled with the desire to eat, drink and consume whatever they can, their tiny mouths and skinny necks make ingesting anything almost impossible.

In this realm, no matter how much food, wealth, or happiness we may have, it is still not enough. Because we feel incomplete and empty inside, we need to reach out and grasp on to something else. What we do possess we cannot let go of; we cannot give anything away or even share our possessions—material or immaterial—with others. We can give neither money nor happiness because we are too poor. We need everything we have and more.

This is an extreme experience of poverty mentality. In this psychological state, we develop the habit of clinging to such an extent that we cling to everything in our environment. In this way, we end up clinging to and cherishing not only what we perceive to be positive and valuable, but also to whatever we perceive to be "ours"—including our anger, our jealousy and all our negative habitual tendencies. Therefore, developing the habitual tendencies of greed and excessive attachment can lead to rebirth in the claustrophobic and painful realm of the hungry ghosts.

Hell Realm

If we follow after the dark, fog-like light, we will be born into the hell realm, which is dominated by the disturbing emotion of anger. Like all of the afflictive emotions, anger arises out of ego's fundamental fear—its insecurity about its existence. From that fear, the habit of aversion grows. When we inhabit this realm, aggression becomes the tool we use to defend ourselves against any perceived threat, whether that threat is realistic or not. There is a sense of ongoing friction in our relationships, which becomes entrenched and develops into violent mind. Our whole being—the very nature of our consciousness—becomes engulfed by anger. Out of that, verbal and physical violence take place. Body, speech and mind become consumed by hatred. In that situation, there is no space left for any openness or any other perception to enter our mind.

That complete state of hatred is the definition of hell. In Buddhist literature, this realm is described as an interminable state of suffering where beings are either burned and boiled, or subjected to bitter cold. While such depictions are not to be taken literally, they do graphically convey the psychological trauma endured by "hell beings." Shantideva says that the mind that is agitated by the poison of aggression is eternally burning; one cannot sleep at night, or work during the day, or practice meditation, because the angry mind is seething with hatred.

If we are habituated to anger, then everywhere we look, we will see an enemy. Instead of trying to destroy all these external enemies, the objects of our anger, Shantideva advises that we conquer the true enemy, the mind of aggression itself. If we fail to do this, then whatever virtue we have accumulated can be easily destroyed. For example, perhaps we have been working on a charitable project for many years, storing all our plans and data on our computer. Then a computer virus invades our system and, in a single moment, our hard drive is wiped clean. In the same way, it is said that one instant of anger can destroy eons of virtue. Therefore, while such a mental state is obviously harmful to others, it is clearly most destructive to oneself.

These are the six psychological realms into which we can be reborn. Of these, the human realm is said to be the most conducive for the practice of dharma. If we must take a samsaric rebirth, then we should concentrate on accomplishing a rebirth in the human realm.

Practices for Becoming

It is taught that as we draw very close to the time of taking rebirth, we will experience the arising of intense emotions, especially the emotions of passion and jealousy. This coincides with the experience of witnessing couples in union. When we see such appearances, we are perceiving a male and female who could become our parents, as well as seeing a potential place of rebirth. If our karma propels us in their direction and we blindly follow that path, then whatever samsaric realm the couple inhabits will be the realm of our rebirth. It could be an auspicious or an inauspicious situation. We could be seeing a loving couple who have a genuine spiritual practice, or we could be witnessing two dogs copulating. We will not necessarily know the difference if we are blinded by our desire. It is said that if we are to be reborn as a male, then we experience strong feelings of passion toward the mother and feelings of jealousy toward the father. The reverse is true if we are to be reborn as a female. In either case, passion and jealousy arise together.

What happens at this point is that the energy of the three root kleshas intensifies. As passion and aggression escalate, we fall further and further into a state of ignorance, until we do not know who or where we are. However, at this time, we can stop the momentum of rebirth through the different methods of practice in which we have trained. We can transform a samsaric experience into an experience of sacred world through the Vajrayana creation and completion stage practices, or we can rely on the Hinayana practices of renunciation. We can also apply the vipashyana methods of Mahamudra and Dzogchen. At the very least, we can slow the process and inject into it a degree of mindfulness and awareness that will allow us to examine the qualities of the parents and the location, and determine the potential to practice dharma that a particular birth will afford. If we train again and again according to these instructions, then at this crucial moment in the bardo of becoming, we will naturally manifest in a way that liberates us from samsara.

CREATION STAGE PRACTICES

In the Vajrayana, the most effective means for purifying our mindstream and bringing forth the qualities of enlightenment is the process of receiving empowerment, or *abhisheka*, from a qualified guru. There are four levels of empowerment, each of which relate to a different level of view and practice. They are known as the vase empowerment, secret empowerment, knowledge-wisdom, or *prajna-jnana* empowerment, and word empowerment. Here, the vase empowerment relates to the view of appearance-emptiness and practice of the creation stage. The second through the fourth empowerments are related to the completion stage practices. The secret empowerment relates to the view of clarity-emptiness and the practice of the Six Dharmas of Naropa. The knowledge-wisdom empowerment relates to the view of bliss-emptiness and the practices of inner heat, or *chandali*, and karmamudra. The word *abhisheka* relates to the view of awareness-emptiness and the practice of the ultimate nature of mind, in accordance with the instructions of Mahamudra and Dzogchen. Traditionally, these empowerments are bestowed consecutively. Once these transmissions have been received and practiced, the creation and completion stages become unified.

The creation stage practices of the Vajrayana path are the primary method taught for transforming the experiences of the bardo of becoming. They are particularly important at the stage where one begins to see the appearances of potential future parents and places of rebirth. The emotions of passion and jealousy that arise when one witnesses a couple in union present us with two possibilities: the intense energy of these emotions can either overwhelm our awareness, or rouse us into a state of greater wakefulness. If we are overwhelmed and do not recognize what is happening, then we will enter the womb of the female and continue our journey within cyclic existence. If, on the other hand, we recognize the moment, then we can transform the nature of the experience and change its outcome.

There are two approaches to interrupting the momentum toward birth, which are practiced through different methods. The first is called "blocking the person" who is about to enter the womb, and the second is called "closing the womb's door." We accomplish both through generating sacred outlook and transforming our perception of impure appearances into pure appearances. The first method consists of adopting vajra pride and arising in the form of one's chosen deity whenever we experience desire or witness the act of sexual union. The second consists of visualizing any couple we see engaged in sexual intercourse as the embodiment of our chosen deity or, alternately, as our principle guru. In both cases, our raw emotions are immediately transformed into enlightened wisdom. If we accomplish this through one of these methods, then we achieve the realization of the view and practice of the third abhisheka, the inseparability of bliss-emptiness. At the very least, delusive appearances based on fixation and clinging will dissolve. We will regain our sanity and be free to choose an auspicious rebirth.

Essentially, the entrance into another samsaric birth is stopped when we can connect with the true nature of mind and the empty, luminous nature of appearances. However, first it is necessary to train in these practices during the bardo of this life. By gaining some genuine experience of them now, we can manifest sacred outlook at the crucial time.

Transforming Desire
Visualizing the Yidam Deity

Training in the creation stage begins with generating a clear visualization of oneself in the form of a yidam, or fully awakened being. We habituate ourselves to arising in an enlightened form and to viewing others and the world around us with pure perception. Once we have trained for a while, our visualization becomes a clear appearance; it possesses the qualities of precision, vividness and transparency, like the reflection of the moon on water. When we can genuinely manifest such sacred outlook, then we possess the perfect antidote to the compelling yet delusive appearances of the bardo of becoming. We train in this practice in both our formal meditation sessions and the postmeditation state. In general, the instruction is to immediately remember your yidam and arise in that form whenever you have a conscious sense of clinging to ego—whenever the thought of "I" occurs in your mind. Furthermore, whenever any strong emotion arises, you transform that flash of energy into the yidam.

In your formal meditation sessions, you first assume the correct sitting posture and settle your mind. Then, with mindfulness and awareness, you observe the arising of any emotion and immediately visualize yourself as the deity as it comes up. By doing this again and again, you become habituated to this practice and, consequently, whenever an emotion arises in daily life, you naturally arise as the yidam. In addition to arising as the deity yourself, it is important to visualize the object of any emotion in the form of a yidam as well.

The yidam principle has both masculine and feminine aspects, which when unified, express the inseparability of form and emptiness. The masculine principle corresponds to the form aspect of this union and to the expression of compassion, or skillful means. The feminine principle corresponds to the emptiness aspect of this union, and to its essence of wisdom, or prajna. Thus, the yidam may be visualized in both its masculine and feminine aspects. On the ultimate level, however, these two are never separate; emptiness and compassion are always in the state of union. Conceptually, we can personify them as two as a skillful method to purify and transform the impure appearances of duality.

With this understanding, you practice visualizing the object of your emotion as the counterpart of your yidam, or in the form of a consort. For example, if you arise as Vajrasattva, as the embodiment of compassion, then you would visualize the object of any emotion as Vajratopa, the embodiment of emptiness and transcendental knowledge. In this way, the emotion or energy that arises and plays between the two automatically becomes the action of the mind of the deity—the movement of pure awareness. When you have this threefold situation, self as yidam, object as yidam, and emotion as yidam's action, then the result is that you give birth to the state of enlightenment.

In your practice, if you feel passion or lust toward another being, then in the same way, you arise as the yidam and visualize the object of your passion as your consort. The passion itself is visualized as an aspect of the fundamental energy of enlightened mind, the energy of wakefulness. Thus, instead of clouding your mind and intensifying habitual tendencies, your passion will wake you up. With practice, the arising of passion and the arising of the self-visualization of the yidam will occur simultaneously, so that, at the first flash of passion, you become the yidam, right on the spot. You do not have to stop or abandon the passion.

It is important to include all aspects of the afflictive emotions in this practice. It is necessary to transform aggression, pride, jealousy, greed and ignorance as well as passion—the emotions and mental states of all six realms of samsaric existence. When you experience anger, then the object of your anger becomes a yidam. When you experience envy, then the object of that envy becomes a yidam. Each time an emotion arises, its object becomes a yidam. In this way, the world becomes filled with yidams, and every object of a klesha becomes a sacred object. Therefore, the world becomes a sacred world.

In the final stage of the bardo of becoming, when you are about to take rebirth, then you can apply this practice. When you see a couple in union, you can arise in the form of the deity and visualize the objects of your passion and jealousy as deities. In that moment, with the strong aspiration to awaken, you flash a completely sacred world: self is yidam, objects are yidams and your emotions are the actions of the yidam. Through the power of this method, you may spontaneously realize the nature of your own mind as the union of bliss-emptiness, which is the recognition of the view and practice of the third empowerment.

In this way, you will achieve ultimate liberation, and the bardo of becoming—as well as cyclic existence—will come to an end. If you do take birth in that particular moment, then your birth will be a sacred birth. Even though you may not fully recognize the nature of mind, you will block the possibility of an impure birth. You may take birth in a pure land, or your birth will at least be positive because you have sacred outlook. With sacred outlook, whatever world you enter becomes a sacred world.

Visualizing the Guru

Another method of visualization for blocking an impure birth also involves transforming our ordinary perception into pure perception. In this case, we visualize the object of our attention—the couple in union—as the embodiment of our root guru. We may visualize the guru either alone or with consort. We may, alternately, visualize Guru Padmasambhava with his consort, Yeshe Tsogyal. At this time, we generate the pure heart of devotion and one-pointedly rest our mind in the essence of the guru's ultimate nature—the inseparability of bliss and emptiness. If throughout our path we have trained in devotion, then at this point, our heart connection with our lineage guru can awaken in us a genuine experience of the true nature of mind.

COMPLETION STAGE PRACTICES

Through the practices of the completion stage, we penetrate the experience of great bliss and arrive at a deep understanding of the true nature and goal of the spiritual path. In the Kagyu lineage, the completion stage practices consist of the Six Dharmas of Naropa. Within this set of practices, there are four root dharmas and two auxiliary or branch dharmas. The four root dharmas serve as antidotes to the "four situations" of life. Every type of conduct one can think of is included in these four situations, or four states. These are the state of waking, the state of deep sleep, the state of dream and the state of sexual union. The two branch dharmas relate to the experience of bardo and the transfer of consciousness.

Our experience of these four states is normally bound up with great confusion, and through the practice of these yogas that confusion is eradicated. Of the four root dharmas, we have previously discussed three: the yoga of illusory body, which is the antidote to the confusion of the waking state; the yoga of luminosity, which is the antidote to the confusion of the state of deep sleep; and dream yoga, which is the antidote to the confusion of the dream state.[34] The fourth root dharma includes the practices of inner heat and karmamudra, which are antidotes for the confusion of sexual intercourse. Both are methods for bringing about the direct realization of bliss-emptiness. In karmamudra practice, one accomplishes this by engaging in the practice of union with an actual physical consort. In inner heat, or chandali practice, the same realization is accomplished through relying on the skillful means of visualization instead of a physical consort.

In addition to deity yoga practice, we can rely on our training in these completion stage practices to transform our experience of the bardo of becoming and stop our entrance into an impure birth. We can, for example, recall the illusory nature of all appearances, which is the application of illusory body practice. In this case, we generate the strong intention to realize that whatever we see before us—whether it is a fearful object or the seeming refuge of a womb—is nothing other than appearance-emptiness. This will cause ordinary, impure appearances to cease, and from within the illusionlike samadhi, we will see the pure appearances of the sambhogakaya nature of mind. We can also rely on the practice of dream yoga. If we have gained some control over our dreams in this life, then we will be able to control our mind and mental body in this bardo. We will be able to travel to and take birth in a pure realm. It is also helpful at this time in the bardo to simply rely on the realization of emptiness—the empty nature of mind and appearances. This realization is enhanced through the practices of luminosity yoga and trekcho, the Dzogchen practice of directly "cutting through" all thoughts. In luminosity yoga, by bringing awareness to the state of deep sleep, we realize mind's essentially clear yet nonconceptual nature. In the practice of trekcho, we penetrate directly to mind's empty essence by cutting through all conceptual fabrications. Bringing our mind to the realization of emptiness will naturally cause delusive appearances to dissolve, thereby restoring our mindfulness and ability to direct the course of our rebirth.

Karmamudra is regarded as a particularly important method of transforming passion, aggression and ignorance altogether. It is taught in the Vajrayana teachings, especially in the highest teachings, such as the Anuttarayoga tantras. In order for this to become a genuinely transcendent practice, one that will transform our confused emotions now and in the bardo of becoming, it must be carried out within a proper environment. This means that there is a proper ground of practice as a foundation, and that one receives the details of the instructions directly from one's individual teacher. The transmission of the instructions is given personally, face-to-face. Without the support of this proper environment, then it becomes simply neurotic activity. When the proper ground is established, then the practice of karmamudra becomes very powerful and it can be engaged in without any problem.

As human beings and inhabitants of the desire realm, the primary ground for our world is desire, and all of our clinging is based on some kind of attachment or passion. From the Vajrayana perspective, it is important for us to work with the element of passion because it is regarded as the actual root of existence, or becoming. If we can work with the powerful energies of desire, then we are actually working with the fundamental ground of our being and transforming it. Of course, it is equally important to work with all the emotions; but working with passion is especially important because it is through transforming passion that we are able to transcend our clinging to this life, our attachment to existence, and to our next birth. For this reason, the Vajrayana teachings include extensive practices on this particular klesha.

These are the yogas of the completion stage. They are called the "profound yogas" and the "yogas without reference point." Through slowly moving through the stages of all of these, you will come to understand these practices. With the completion-stage instructions, we do not need to abandon the appearances of the present moment, but can practice within them and attain buddhahood.

Transforming Through Renunciation

If you practice strictly the Hinayana path, then the instruction given here is to concentrate on developing renunciation, which reverses the attachments that bind us to samsara. In this life, you can devote yourself to the contemplations on impermanence and on suffering and to the meditation on ugliness. If your aspiration and motivation are strong and clear, then these practices will transform your attachments to your physical body and to relative existence. Traditionally, you reflect on how your body and the bodies of others are impure or unclean to counteract the perception of our bodies as pure and wholesome. Altogether, you cultivate the view of the five skandhas as being "aggregates of filth." This meditation engenders a sense of disgust towards the body and strengthens one's sense of renunciation, of wishing to be free of samsara.

Then, in the bardo of becoming, whenever you feel that you are getting caught up in the temptations of desire, you can try to remove yourself from that situation through reinforcing your sense of detachment. If you have been practicing detachment for your whole life, then at this time these disciplines will be very powerful methods for closing the door to the womb until the appearance of signs indicating a fortunate human birth.

PLAN A AND PLAN B

These, then, are the main practices taught for transcending the bardo of becoming. The practices of Mahamudra and Dzogchen discussed earlier are, of course, also powerful methods that we can apply. However, since their transcendence is ultimate transcendence, they should be relied upon primarily as means of attaining liberation at once during the bardos of dying and dharmata. If we have reached the bardo of becoming, then we may need to rely on the practices described here. It is like having a back-up plan. Plan A relies on the direct realization of the nature of mind through the vipashyana practices of Mahamudra and Dzogchen. Plan B relies on Vajrayana methods, such as the creation and completion stage practices, or on the Hinayana methods prescribed in the monastic disciplines.

Although the experience of mind in the three bardos of death is said to be extremely vivid, and therefore easier to recognize than in the bardo of this life, we should not count on that as our salvation, as our means of liberation. We should concentrate fully on the practices we have now and appreciate our opportunity to train in them. It is actually much easier to work with our mind when we are free of pain, have a stable environment and possess the ground of a physical body. We should focus on achieving the realization of the nature of mind here and now.

At this time, we have a clear mind, and we can develop that further. However, as we have seen, during the bardo of dying we will undergo various experiences that are likely to cause confusion and arouse fear. We may also undergo difficult experiences of physical pain. Given your state of mind right now, how certain are you that you will be able to look directly at the nature of your mind while you are facing tremendous pain at the same time? That is a big question. If we can really look at the pain without moving, if we can manage it and transcend it—without freaking out, without looking for painkillers—then we can achieve great realization in that moment. Most often, whenever we are in pain, we look for a drugstore; if we have even a slight headache, we reach for the Tylenol.

Therefore, when we sit and meditate while we are relatively healthy and relatively free from pain, we are taking advantage of a great opportunity. We have a very good chance to connect with the experience of calmness and clarity and to habituate ourselves to that state, which is the mind that gives rise to transcendental insight. If we do not have that ground in place, then on what basis will realization arise? That is another big question.

Vajrayana View of Practice

In order to make use of the methods of deity yoga, it is essential to understand the profound view that underlies these practices and is the source of their transformative power. Without this understanding, such practices are either ineffective, or they lead us in the wrong direction altogether. Once we understand this view, we can focus the visualization practices in a way that can be applied directly to our experiences in the bardo of becoming. We know that we will be faced with certain challenges, and that we will be able to apply the methods of visualization to transform those experiences at once.

As in the earlier forms of shamatha and vipashyana, we are working in the deity yoga practice with two aspects of appearance—the impure, dualistic aspect that we perceive conventionally and the pure aspect that is the fundamental nature of those appearances. When we speak of impure and pure appearances, we are not speaking of two separate sets of objects. We are speaking of how phenomena are perceived. A mind that has recognized its own nature—its luminous emptiness—perceives the actual luminous, empty nature of appearances, while a mind that is obscured perceives a solid, dualistic self and world.

As discussed previously, deity yoga practice entails two phases known as the creation and completion stage practices. In the creation stage, we generate the visualization of a deity with whom we have a particular connection. First, we visualize ourselves in the form of that deity, then we visualize that deity as also being present in the space in front of us, and finally we visualize our whole environment as the sacred world, or mandala, of that deity. The creation stage practice is a skillful method of training that develops our intuitive wisdom or insight, our prajna, to the point that we are able to experience directly the vivid, pure nature of appearances.

At the end of our session, in the completion stage, we dissolve everything into emptiness and rest in that vivid, formless space. These two basic principles of creation and completion are something we have already cultivated in the Hinayana-Mahayana journey through shamatha-vipashyana meditation. In the Vajrayana, the shamatha, or calm abiding, aspect is the creation stage, and the vipashyana aspect is the completion stage.

Deity yoga is an aspect of the Vajrayana path, which is distinguished from other paths by three defining features. First, it possesses a rich variety of skillful means for working on the path of enlightenment. Second, the practitioners of Vajrayana possess sharp faculties; that is to say, their penetrating insight, or prajna, has become so sharp and precise that it cuts easily through any obstacle, obscuration or clinging that arises along the path. Third, it is a path without difficulties, meaning that the Vajrayana journey is short and it is fast. Why? It is a rapid path because it takes fruition, the goal, as its path. It sees the state of enlightenment, utter purity and complete awakening, as being fully present *right now,* and its methods are fearless expressions of confidence in the nature of mind. Furthermore, it introduces us to seeing and experiencing all emotions—all aspects of passion, aggression and ignorance—as the nature of great bliss. Consequently, from this perspective, there is no such thing in samsara as suffering, and there is nothing to be discarded. You can enter this path and fully practice the creation and completion stage practices when you have received the lineage transmission in the form of the empowerments and the pointing-out instructions from a qualified teacher.

VIEW OF CREATION STAGE

Creation stage practice, in which we generate a visualization of the body of a deity, is not a matter of newly creating something that does not exist already. We are not visualizing something that is purely imaginary. What we are doing at this stage is trying to get to the basic state of appearances, which we experience as subject, object, and the actions or interactions between these two—and see them as precisely, clearly and as sacredly as we can. When we see ourselves as a deity and the world around us as a sacred mandala, we are seeing the true nature of mind and appearances; we are seeing the lucidity of mind that is ever-present and continually manifesting as the variety of clear and vivid appearances.

If, when you visualize, you are imagining that you are somebody else other than who you truly are, and you are imagining that you are somewhere else other than where you truly are, then that is not beneficial. In that case, you are thinking that the world you see in front of you is not the world that you are visualizing—it is something else, something less sacred. That is not the view of Mahamudra or Dzogchen, and that is definitely not the Vajrayana view. That is also not the genuine creation stage. The view of the genuine creation stage is the union of appearance and emptiness; that is, everything that could possibly arise—ourselves, others, thoughts, emotions and concepts, as well as the totality of the physical universe—clearly appears while at the same time being empty of true existence.

Therefore, the creation stage is nothing but a skillful method that trains us how to experience this lucidity precisely, which is to say, in a manner that is free from concepts and therefore free from duality. Precision of seeing comes when there is no concept to obscure it. So long as you are viewing appearance through the filter of concepts, you are not seeing it accurately or precisely. For example, when you perceive a visual object, conceptual mind does not distinguish clearly between the actual object and the label that you place on top of it. As soon as you perceive something, you label it: red, blue, white, table, chair. Since these two—object and label—are not recognized as separate aspects of the perceptual process, then right from the beginning, they are mixed together. As soon as you label something and call it "red" or "chair," and so on, that label clouds, or distracts, the mind from what is actually an experience of vivid clarity.

In order to transcend our conceptual mind, the Vajrayana tradition uses many different methods. One of these is the *yoga involving signs,* which makes use of objects as reference points. Here, the signs or symbols we use are the body of the deity and the imagery of the mandala, or sacred world. When a practitioner visualizes a specific deity, that deity is associated with a particular lineage of gurus, particular buddhas and bodhi-

sattvas, as well as a particular retinue of other figures symbolizing principles of awakening and activity. Furthermore, the mandala, as the homeland or abode of the deity, is conceived of as a magnificent palace, which
becomes the visualized support for the deity and members of the enlightened assembly. Therefore the creation stage practice does involve a certain
element of conceptual fabrication; we are using concepts to transcend the
conceptual state. Like the practice of fighting fire with fire, or curing a poisonous snakebite with snake venom, the practice of visualizing these symbols brings us into a nonconceptual state. When we are free of concepts,
we can experience the vivid clarity of appearances fully and with great
precision.

Three Skillful Means

In the bardo of becoming, when we have a genuine experience of mind's
clarity, then we have sacred outlook: the mandala of the deity is right in
front of us. We are protected from fear and from developing any further
confusion. In order to achieve that experience, there are three things to
be purified, and in order to purify these three, we have three skillful
means, or *upayas*. Ordinary appearances are purified by visualizing the
deity mandala; ordinary clinging is purified by vajra pride; and taking
appearances to be truly existent is purified by the view of emptiness.

Clear Appearance

The intention of the first skillful means of the creation stage is to purify
ordinary appearances. Generally, we do not question appearances and take
them at face value. We believe that our body and the physical world both
exist in the ordinary way that we perceive them. When you hear teachings
that say everything is empty and you do not exist, it is difficult at first to
comprehend these concepts. Therefore, in order to counteract your habitual way of conceptualizing yourself as an ordinary, confused being, you
say, "Yes, I do exist, but not in this mundane, confused form. How I exist
truly is in the clear form of the deity, and my world is the pure, luminous
world of the mandala." Therefore, your clinging to ordinary appearances
is purified by generating a visualization of yourself as a deity and the world
around you as a mandala. To practice visualization in this way is a skillful
means of experiencing the clear nature of mind.

Vajra Pride

The intention of the second skillful means here is to purify our clinging to the mundane sense of self we experience as "I" or "me." While the first method relates to the outer, or external, level of appearances, here we are working on the level of concept. We are seeing how we hold on to a belief in the existence of a self that is in some sense independent of the body. In the Vajrayana, that concept of a mundane self is transformed through the skillful means of *vajra pride*, or the pride of the deity. As discussed, this is not ordinary, samsaric pride that we might feel in relation to ourselves, and it is not an attitude of superiority that we might feel in relation to others. Vajra pride refers to taking pride in our own basic buddha nature: we have full confidence that the nature of our mind is primordially, originally pure, awake and full of the qualities of enlightenment. We take pride in that nature, which exists fundamentally in the form of the ultimate deity, and we take that vajra pride as our path. It is said that without vajra pride our creation stage practice will not be very effective, nor will it be complete. No matter how clear your visualization may be, if there is no vajra pride, then it will not complete the transformation of mundane clinging.

View of Emptiness

The intention of the third skillful means is to purify our clinging to the true existence of appearances. We assume that the objects of our experience—sights, sounds, smells, tastes and tactile sensations—truly exist in some substantial way. As well, we believe that our thoughts and emotions truly exist as mental phenomena. The remedy for our clinging to this belief is the view of emptiness, which is the basis of any visualization practice.

It is taught that, when you create a visualization, it should appear to you like the reflection of the moon on water—appearing, yet empty; empty, yet appearing. The image of the moon is crystal clear in all its details, yet it is transparent and insubstantial at the same time. It is there, but not there. In the *Heart Sutra* it says, "Form is emptiness; emptiness also is form. Emptiness is no other than form; form is no other than emptiness." That should be the quality of our visualizations.

The same mark of emptiness applies to all elements of our experience.

In the creation stage in particular, the body of the deity is inseparable appearance and emptiness. Any mantras we recite are inseparable sound and emptiness. All movements of mind—our thoughts and emotions—are inseparable awareness and emptiness.

The key point here is to develop your visualization to the point that it is clear and vivid. Then, simply by focusing your mind on it, all kinds of clinging to mundane appearances, samsaric pride and dualistic thoughts will cease naturally. They all will be transformed through this very skillful and powerful practice.

In the beginning, the creation stage practice seems to be primarily a conceptual practice. However, once you become familiar with the process, then that reality will become natural to you. At some point, you will not have to think about the form of a deity or how to generate it. It will naturally arise within you, without the support of concepts. You will arise spontaneously in a sacred world. Your creation stage practice will be free of thoughts and beyond thought. When you get to that point, this is called the "unfabricated creation stage," and also called the "unfabricated yoga," which is getting close to the completion stage.

The two stages of creation and completion at some point become one, which means you are experiencing appearance and emptiness as inseparable. We must see the reality that the true experience of the creation stage goes beyond concept. The deity and mandala that we visualize are not just conceptually created; rather, they are vividly appearing expressions of mind's clarity, which has always existed within us right from the beginning. This capacity is not something new, and we are not visualizing something that we are not. We are at last actually experiencing the true nature of mind.

VIEW OF COMPLETION STAGE

The completion stage practice has two phases. The first stage consists of dissolving the visualization of the deity mandala into shunyata. We do this in order to free our mind from fixation on the luminous aspect of the union of appearance-emptiness. The dissolving is done either in stages, or all at once. Then we rest in that state as long as possible.

In the second phase of the completion stage, we engage in the actual awareness practices, which bring the experience known as "great bliss wisdom." These practices are connected to the process of invoking genuine blessing, which comes from within, and connecting with the principle of self-aware wisdom. The actual wisdom that one experiences at the highest level of completion stage practice is the wisdom of great bliss. This is the wisdom of union, which is self-arising and spontaneously existent. Until we experience the nature of union, the union of great bliss and emptiness, then we have not experienced the actual completion stage of Vajrayana tantra. The dissolving stage we practice in the first phase, resting in shunyata, is a way to begin to experience that. It is a process of moving toward the state of great bliss.

Postmeditation

In the postmeditation state, all appearances are visualizations, which is the aspect of creation stage, and when we look at these appearances and find no solid, true existence, that is the completion stage. The true practice of the creation stage in daily life consists of our efforts to maintain the view of sacred outlook and to experience the freshness and vividness of appearances as they arise before us. If you can experience the vividness and clarity of the true nature of reality that manifests and dances in front of your eyes and other senses, then that becomes a very pure experience of the deity-mandala. That is what it is, after all.

If you can touch upon that experience or reflect on it when you see the world, then that is the best creation stage practice for the postmeditation state. The illusory body practice, in which everything you see is regarded as illusionlike, dreamlike, is also very helpful. However, if you get into a situation where you have a very strong klesha take hold of you—you are having a klesha attack, as they say—or if you are generally having a very difficult time with someone, then you can apply the view of sacred outlook. You can visualize yourself and any others in the form of the deity, and recognize the pure nature of the emotion itself to be awareness-emptiness—the play of the deity's wisdom mind. Thus, everything in your environment becomes an aspect of the sacred world.

Mind Beyond Death

According to the Buddhist way of practicing, death is not something that we accept or reject. That is, we do not go toward death prematurely, nor do we try to hold it off indefinitely if its time has actually come. Buddhist practice consists of being who we are, which includes being where we are. Being who we are now is being in the bardo of this life. That is how and where we must be. If we try to be somewhere else, such as in the bardo of death, then that is not Buddhist practice. We are not being genuine. We are not being in a state of nowness. We are trying to be in the future.

In the same way, when the bardo of dying comes, if we try to be somewhere else, such as in the bardo of this life, then that is not Buddhist practice, either. We are not being who we are. We are trying to be in the past. When we are a dying person, we have to be that person, and we have to be there when death occurs. Woody Allen's joke—"I'm not afraid of death I just don't want to be there when it happens"—expresses our attitude toward death, and the prevailing message of our culture. The point here, however, is: do not be afraid of being who you are in any moment, or under any circumstance. That is the message of all the teachings of the buddhadharma, whether they are Hinayana, Mahayana or Vajrayana.

Whenever we talk about "our life," we are, in effect, talking about the present moment, which is where our life is truly lived. That is who and where we are most genuinely. Therefore, the practice of all three yanas is the practice of coming back to the present moment, over and over. Because the present is always within reach, we can always try to be there. Whatever our situation, whatever our surroundings may be, we can make the effort to be there without altering anything. If confusion is there, we can look nakedly at its essence. If joy is there, we can look directly at the peak of that experience.

Therefore, the most effective method for working with this experience of bardo is the practice of being in the present moment. This practice brings us to a recognition of the true nature of bardo, the absolute bardo, which is just this experience of nowness, of gap. That is why we bring our attention to our breath in shamatha practice. Breath is now. Breathing takes place now—we are neither in the past nor in the future. One moment dissolves, and there is an experience of pure openness, of groundlessness, in which nothing is truly solid. Yet, there is tremendous clarity and energy at the same time. That is the direct experience of the nature of mind, of naked awareness, which is the essence of bardo. When we recognize mind's nature, the appearances of samsaric confusion come to an end; when we do not recognize its nature, they continue on in the next moment.

Being in the present, in the state of nowness, is where we began our discussion of these teachings, and that is where it ends, too: not in any other place, but right here and now. When this bardo ends, we take birth either in samsara or in nirvana, in some form. From the Buddhist point of view, death is not the end because it is also a beginning. The end of this life's appearances is the beginning of the next life's appearances. It could be the end of samsara and the beginning of nirvana. It could also be the end of a precious human birth and the beginning of a painful samsaric experience. It is up to us—how we work with our journey through the bardos.

It is important for our spiritual journey that we connect with these teachings personally and review them periodically. These days, translations of the bardo teachings are available in a variety of languages. There are also many transcripts of oral teachings, many books and many charts. We may have more than we actually need to understand these teachings; however, it is necessary for us to utilize them. For example, it would be beneficial to set aside some time once a year to read the teachings and reflect on the instructions. We should stop what we are doing to remember impermanence and to prepare ourselves for death. When will our death come? It could be tomorrow. It could be today. The time that death will arrive is uncertain. Therefore, we have to be prepared for it. We have to be ready twenty-four hours a day.

Since I have simply repeated these instructions from Padmasambhava, there should be some benefit if you study them and some real effect if you practice them. All of the instructions and methods of practice that have been presented here come directly from the text. They are not the interpretations of any individual masters. These techniques have been used by many people. If you try them, then you will benefit by recognizing the bardo of this life as well as the bardos of death. Since the experiences of this life and the experiences of dying are common to all of us, it is clear that we will all go through the six bardo states in one way or another.

Therefore, these practices are relevant, even crucial, for all of us, until we transcend the journey itself. At some point, we make the discovery that, ultimately, mind transcends death. Who we are and where we are is mind. Mind endures because it is unborn and unceasing; it endures because it transcends our concepts of time and space; it is not fixed to one occurrence in time or to one place. It is mind that journeys as a guest in this physical body until we take full possession of the boundless wisdom and compassion that are innate to us, and realize the freedom and purity of our abiding nature.

Editors' Acknowledgments

THE EDITORS would like to acknowledge the many people who contributed to the creation of this book. Our first thanks are due to the Rigpe Dorje Center in San Antonio for their sponsorship of the 2002 Treasury of Knowledge Retreat, where Rinpoche presented these teachings, and to Jan Puckett and John Richardson, key figures there for many years. Special thanks to Gerry Wiener, who assisted Rinpoche with oral and written translations, and who continued to be a generous source of information during the development of this book. Thanks also to Pat Lee and Vajra Echoes for audio and video recording; to Bruce Roe for providing transcripts of the retreat talks; and to Helen Silman for creating an extensive outline and first edit of the manuscript.

We are especially grateful for the ongoing support of Nalandabodhi teachers and translators who were consistently available for advice, clarification of terms, and general assistance. In particular, we thank Acharya Tashi Wangchuk, Tenzin Namdak, Tyler Dewar, Karl Brunnhölzl and Tim Walton. Tyler, Karl and Tim also contributed significantly to the glossary. Tenzin Namdak provided the illustration of the visualized Tibetan syllables. Stephanie Johnston assisted with selection of artwork; she also read sections of the manuscript and offered helpful suggestions, as did Carole Fleming and Heather Chan. We would also like to thank Anna-Brown Griswold for her review of the text and insightful editing as the manuscript neared completion.

The editors benefited greatly from the advice of Dr. Andrew Holocek, a longtime practitioner-scholar, graduate of the three-year retreat, and teacher in the Shambhala Buddhist community. Dr. Holocek has been a dedicated student of these teachings for many years, and we are indebted to him for sharing the breadth of his knowledge with us, and for his generous commitment of time in reading the manuscript throughout its evolution.

We would like to thank Snow Lion Publications, especially Sidney Piburn, for support and encouragement in bringing this project to fruition. Our editors, Susan Kyser and Antonia Saxon, offered valuable editorial assistance and advice on the organization of the book. We also extend our appreciation to the Tsadra Foundation for permission to reprint artwork from Palpung Monastery, and to the Rubin Museum for permission to reprint artwork from the collectin of Shelley and Donald Rubin.

Most of all, we are grateful to The Dzogchen Ponlop Rinpoche, who holds the authentic lineage of these teachings and the transmission of Padmasambhava, for sharing these exceptional instructions in such a clear and accessible way. At every stage, Rinpoche made himself available to answer questions and elucidate difficult points, while continuing to emphasize the nontheistic nature of these teachings and the essential capacity of each individual to realize the brilliant nature of mind described herein. We are profoundly thankful to have been given this opportunity to work with these teachings under Rinpoche's wise and compassionate guidance. Whatever errors remain in the text are due entirely to the limitations of our understanding and our faults as editors. Nevertheless, may this effort reflect and serve Rinpoche's unwavering intention to accomplish the genuine and lasting benefit of beings.

Cindy Shelton and Marg Cooke
Nalandabodhi Editorial Committee

Appendix I:
The Sutra on Wisdom for the Time of Death

༄༅། །འདའ་ཀ་ཡེ་ཤེས་ཀྱི་མདོ་བཞུགས་སོ། །།

རྒྱ་གར་སྐད་དུ། ཨཱརྻ་ཨ་ཏྱ་ཛྙཱ་ན་མ་ཧཱ་ཡཱ་ན་སཱུ་ཏྲ།

བོད་སྐད་དུ། འཕགས་པ་འདའ་ཀ་ཡེ་ཤེས་ཞེས་བྱ་བ་ཐེག་པ་ཆེན་པོའི་མདོ།

སངས་རྒྱས་དང་བྱང་ཆུབ་སེམས་དཔའ་ཐམས་ཅད་ལ་ཕྱག་འཚལ་ལོ།

འདི་སྐད་བདག་གིས་ཐོས་པ་དུས་གཅིག་ན། བཅོམ་ལྡན་འདས་འོག་མིན་ལྷའི་རྒྱལ་
པོའི་ཁང་བཟང་ན་བཞུགས་ཏེ། འཁོར་ཐམས་ཅད་ལ་ཆོས་སྟོན་པ་དང་། བྱང་ཆུབ་སེམས་
དཔའ་ནམ་མཁའི་སྙིང་པོས་བཅོམ་ལྡན་འདས་ལ་ཕྱག་འཚལ་ནས། འདི་སྐད་ཅེས་གསོལ་
ཏོ། བཅོམ་ལྡན་འདས་བྱང་ཆུབ་སེམས་དཔས་ནམ་འཆི་ཀ་མའི་ཚེ་སེམས་ཇི་ལྟར་བལྟ་
བར་བགྱི། བཅོམ་ལྡན་འདས་ཀྱིས་བཀའ་སྩལ་པ། ནམ་མཁའི་སྙིང་པོ་བྱང་ཆུབ་སེམས་
དཔའ་ནམ་འཆི་ཀ་མའི་ཚེ། འདའ་ཀ་ཡེ་ཤེས་བསྒོམ་པར་བྱའོ། དེ་ལ་འདའ་ཀ་ཡེ་ཤེས་ནི།
ཆོས་ཐམས་ཅད་རང་བཞིན་གྱིས་རྣམ་པར་དག་པས་ན། དངོས་པོ་མེད་པའི་འདུ་ཤེས་
བསྒོམ་པར་བྱའོ། ཆོས་ཐམས་ཅད་བྱང་ཆུབ་ཀྱི་སེམས་སུ་འདུས་པས་ན་སྙིང་རྗེའི་འདུ་
ཤེས་རབ་ཏུ་བསྒོམ་པར་བྱའོ། རང་བཞིན་གྱིས་འོད་གསལ་བས་ན། མི་དམིགས་པའི་འདུ་

ཤེས་རབ་ཏུ་བསྒོམ་པར་བྱའོ། དངོས་པོ་ཐམས་ཅད་མི་རྟག་པ་ཡིན་པས་ན། ཅི་ལ་འང་མི་
ཆགས་པའི་འདུ་ཤེས་རབ་ཏུ་བསྒོམ་པར་བྱའོ། སེམས་རྟོགས་ན་ཡེ་ཤེས་ཡིན་པས་ན།
སངས་རྒྱས་གཞན་དུ་མི་བཙལ་བའི་འདུ་ཤེས་རབ་ཏུ་བསྒོམ་པར་བྱའོ།

བཅོམ་ལྡན་འདས་ཀྱིས་ཚིགས་སུ་བཅད་དེ་བཀའ་སྩལ་པ།

ཆོས་རྣམ་རང་བཞིན་རྣམ་དག་པས། །
དངོས་པོ་མེད་པའི་འདུ་ཤེས་བསྒོམ། །
བྱང་ཆུབ་སེམས་དང་རབ་ལྡན་པས། །
སྙིང་རྗེ་ཆེན་པོའི་འདུ་ཤེས་བསྒོམ། །

རང་བཞིན་མི་དམིགས་འོད་གསལ་བས། །
དངོས་པོ་ཅི་ལ་འང་མི་ཆགས་བསྒོམ། །
སེམས་ནི་ཡེ་ཤེས་འབྱུང་བའི་རྒྱུ། །
སངས་རྒྱས་གཞན་དུ་མ་ཚོལ་ཅིག །

བཅོམ་ལྡན་འདས་ཀྱིས་དེ་སྐད་ཅེས་བཀའ་སྩལ་པ་དང་། བྱང་ཆུབ་སེམས་དཔའ་
རྣམ་མཁའི་སྙིང་པོ་ལ་སོགས་པའི་འཁོར་ཐམས་ཅད་རབ་ཏུ་དགའ་ནས། བཅོམ་ལྡན་
འདས་ཀྱིས་གསུངས་པ་ལ་མངོན་པར་བསྟོད་དོ།

འཕགས་པ་འདའ་ཀ་ཡེ་ཤེས་ཞེས་བྱ་བ་ཐེག་པ་ཆེན་པོའི་མདོ་རྫོགས་སོ། །།

The Sūtra on Wisdom for the Time of Death

In the language of India: *Arya-atyaya-jnana-mahayana-sutra*
In the language of Tibet: *Pakpa da ka yeshe she jawa tekpa chenpö
do ('Phags pa 'da' ka ye shes zhes bya ba theg pa chen po'i mdo)*
In the English language: *The Noble Mahayana Sutra Called
Wisdom for the Time of Death*

Homage to all buddhas and bodhisattvas.

Thus have I heard. Once the Blessed One was dwelling in the palace of
the king of devas in Akanishtha and teaching the dharma to all assembled
there. At that time, the bodhisattva Akashagarbha paid homage to the
Blessed One and addressed him in this way: O Blessed One, when bodhisattvas are on the verge of dying, how should they look at their minds?

The Blessed One spoke: O Akashagarbha, when bodhisattvas are on the
verge of dying, they are to meditate on the wisdom for the time of death.
As to this wisdom for the time of death, since all dharmas are inherently
pure, meditate on the outlook of the lack of true existence. Since all dharmas are included in bodhichitta, meditate on the outlook of compassion.
Since they are naturally luminous, meditate on the outlook of nonrefer-
entiality. Since all things are impermanent, meditate on the outlook of
having no attachment to anything. Since, if one realizes mind, that is wisdom, meditate on the outlook that does not search for buddhahood elsewhere.

The Blessed One then spoke these verses:

Since all dharmas are inherently pure,
Meditate on the outlook of the lack of true existence.
Excellently possessing bodhichitta,
Meditate on the outlook of great compassion.

Since the true nature is nonreferential luminosity,
Meditate on the outlook of having no attachment to anything.
Mind is the cause for the arising of wisdom.
Do not search for buddhahood elsewhere.

When the Blessed One had said this, the bodhisattva Akashagarbha and the others, the entire assembly, became overwhelmed with joy and praised the words of the Blessed One.

Thus concludes the noble Mahayana sutra called Wisdom for the Time of Death.

Translated from the Tibetan under the guidance of The Dzogchen Ponlop Rinpoche by Tyler Dewar of the Nitartha Translation Network.

Appendix II:
Vajra Songs of Realization

ALL THESE FORMS

All these forms—appearance-emptiness
Like a rainbow with its shining glow
In the reaches of appearance-emptiness
Just let go and go where no mind goes

Every sound is sound and emptiness
Like the sound of an echo's roll
In the reaches of sound and emptiness
Just let go and go where no mind goes

Every feeling is bliss and emptiness
Way beyond what words can show
In the reaches of bliss and emptiness
Just let go and go where no mind goes

All awareness—awareness-emptiness
Way beyond what thoughts can know
In the reaches of awareness emptiness
Let awareness go—oh, where no mind goes

Composed by Khenpo Tsültrim Gyamtso Rinpoche in the Garden of Translation near the Great Stupa of Boudhanath in Nepal, 1998. © 2002 Marpa Translation Committee. Translated and arranged by Jim Scott.

The Eight Cases of
Basic Goodness Not To Be Shunned
A Vajra Song of Götsangpa

Namo Ratna Guru

I bow to the lord who grants the bliss that is utterly supreme
Which takes away the suffering of illness
For every being that's everywhere throughout the reaches of space
By administering the medicine of the three kayas

In the pure space of the sky that's the sky of essential mind itself
The clouds of negative actions thickly gather
But the mighty force of the powerful wind of the wisdom prana
Doesn't blow them away, but clears them up like this

The illness and its painfulness have neither base nor root
Relax into it, fresh and uncontrived
Revealing dharmakaya way beyond all speech and thought
Don't shun them, pain and illness are basically good

What confusion takes to be taking place is negative forces' work
But it's all your own mind, simple, unborn, unceasing
Without anxiety or even worrying at all
Don't shun them, demons and gods are basically good

When the agony of illness strikes your four-fold elements
Don't grasp at its stopping, don't get angry when it won't improve
Such adversities have the flavor of bliss that's free of contagion's blight
These kleshas are not to be shunned, they're basically good

All of our joys and the pain we go through, all of our highs and lows
When realized, have no ground, they are our friends
Don't try to stop pain, don't try to be happy, be free of all hope and fear
Samsara is not to be shunned, it's basically good

And though this human life is plagued by the torments of falling ill
Don't think that's bad, don't plan to get around it
Then it will be your badge, your proof of conduct of equal taste

Your suffering's not to be shunned, it's basically good
The mind that's sunk in dullness and torpor, when realized for what it is
Is pure being pure of every imperfection
So, free of thinking you should be wishing to clear this all away
Don't shun your dense state of mind, it's basically good

Habitual patterns' imprints printed throughout beginningless time
Are the myriad doors illusion comes marching through
If you do not take them as true, don't meditate on them as empty
Don't shun your thoughts, they're basically good in themselves

The state of coemergence has no birth and knows no death
Knows nothing of arising or ceasing or staying somewhere
It's infinity, it's the vast expanse of the unconditioned state
Don't shun your death, it's basically good in itself

All eight of these things that are not to be shunned since they're
    basically good in themselves
Need a meditation which turns them into equal taste
They are the thought that comes from the heart of the uncle and
    nephew lord
They are the hammer that hammers down the host of maras

They are the practice that's put into practice by beggars like you and me
These are the tools that keep us in natural retreat
They are the bliss supreme that performs the two forms of benefit
You've mastered this from the beginning, old father, but you'd better
    put it into practice

Composed by the Lord Götsangpa
© *2002 Marpa Translation Committee.*
Translated and arranged at Karme Choling, Vermont, August 1997.

GURU RINPOCHE PRAYER

A prayer that appearances be liberated as the deity, that sounds be liberated as mantra, that thoughts be liberated into pure being.

All these forms that appear to eyes that see,
All things on the outside and the inside,
The environment and its inhabitants
Appear, but let them rest where no self's found,
Perceiver and perceived when purified
Are the body of the deity, clear emptiness—
To the guru for whom desire frees itself,
To Orgyen Pema Jungnay I supplicate.

All these sounds that appear for ears that hear,
Taken as agreeable or not
Let them rest in the realm of sound and emptiness
Past all thought, beyond imagination
Sounds are empty, unarisen and unceasing,
These are what make up the Victor's teaching
To the teachings of the Victor, sound and emptiness,
To Orgyen Pema Jungnay I supplicate.

All these movements of mind towards its objects,
These thoughts that make five poisons and afflictions,
Leave thinking mind to rest without contrivances,
Do not review the past nor guess the future,
If you let such movement rest in its own place,
It liberates into the dharmakaya
To the guru for whom awareness frees itself
To Orgyen Pema Jungnay I supplicate

Grant your blessing that purifies appearance
Of objects perceived as being outside
Grant your blessing that liberates perceiving mind,
The mental operation seeming inside,
Grant your blessing that between the two of these

Clear light will come to recognize its own face,
In your compassion, sugatas of all three times,
Please bless me that a mind like mine be freed.

*Taught by Guru Rinpoche to Namkhai Nyingpo. Translated and arranged
by the Marpa Translation Committee in Denmark, September 28, 1997.
© 2002 Marpa Translation Committee.*

SEVEN DELIGHTS

Namo Ratna Guru

When thoughts that there is something perceived and a perceiver

Lure my mind away and distract,
I don't close my senses' gateways to meditate without them
But plunge straight into their essential point
They're like clouds in the sky, there's this shimmer where they fly,
Thoughts that rise, for me sheer delight!

When kleshas get me going and their heat has got me burning,
I try no antidote to set them right,
Like an alchemistic potion turning metal into gold,
What lies in kleshas' power to bestow
Is bliss without contagion, completely undefiled,
Kleshas coming up, sheer delight!

When I'm plagued by god-like forces or demonic interference,
I do not drive them out with rites and spells,
The thing to chase away is the egoistic thinking
Built up on the idea of a self
This will turn those ranks of maras into your own special forces,
When obstacles arise, sheer delight!

When samsara with its anguish has me writhing in its torments,
Instead of wallowing in misery,
I take the greater burden down the greater path to travel
And let compassion set me up
To take upon myself the sufferings of others,
When karmic consequences bloom, delight!

When my body has succumbed to attacks of painful illness,
I do not count on medical relief
But take that very illness as a path and by its power
Remove the obscurations blocking me,

And use it to encourage the qualities worthwhile,
When illness rears its head, sheer delight!

When it's time to leave this body, this illusionary tangle,
Don't cause yourself anxiety and grief;
The thing that you should train in and clear up for yourself
There's no such thing as dying to be done.
It's just clear light, the mother and child clear light uniting;
When mind forsakes the body, sheer delight!

When the whole thing's just not working, everything's lined up
    against you,
Don't try to find some way to change it all,
Here the point to make your practice is reverse the way you see it,
Don't try to make it stop or to improve
Adverse conditions happen, when they do it's so delightful
They make a little song of sheer delight!

Composed by the Lord Götsangpa. Translated by Jim Scott and Anne Buchardi, August 2, 1996, at Karme Choling, Barnet, Vermont. © 2002 Marpa Translation Committee.

DEDICATION

All you sentient beings I have a good or bad connection with
As soon as you have left this confused dimension
May you be born in the west in Sukhavati
And once you're born there, complete the bhumis and the paths.

Composed by Khenpo Tsültrim Gyamtso Rinpoche, August 29, 1999.
Translated and arranged by Jim Scott. ©Marpa Translation Committee.

The Six Bardos
by Rechungpa

From the later chapter of White Rock Vajra Fortress

I prostrate to the exalted gurus.

In the bardo between appearances and emptiness
There is no view of permanence or nihilism.
Made-up theories, I've none.
Instead I know what's unborn, what's beyond the intellect:
That's the view of this beggar-mendicant.
Among realized practitioners—
Now I won't feel ashamed.
Among realized practitioners—
Now I won't feel ashamed.

In the bardo between bliss and emptiness
There's no reference point for the practice of shamatha.
Instead of fighting my mind,
I rest in the innate state, not moving, undistracted:
That's the meditation of this beggar-mendicant.
Among experienced practitioners—
Now I won't feel ashamed.
Among experienced practitioners—
Now I won't feel ashamed.

In the bardo between passion and no passion
There is no trace, no place at all for defiled bliss.
I am no hypocrite; I have no use for wrong livelihood.
Now appearances arise as my aid:
That's the conduct of this beggar-mendicant.
Among yogin practitioners—
Now I won't feel ashamed.
Among yogin practitioners—
Now I won't feel ashamed.

In the bardo between being flawed and flawless
There is no purity, not at all, and nothing impure.
I am free of deceit; I am no impostor,
I take my mind as my witness:
That's the samaya of this beggar-mendicant.
Among disciplined practitioners—
Now I won't feel ashamed.
Among disciplined practitioners—
Now I won't feel ashamed.

In the bardo between samsara and nirvana,
Those sentient and those enlightened demonstrate no difference.
I look for no results that come from hopes or fears.
Now suffering rises up as bliss:
That's the result for this beggar-mendicant.
Among siddha practitioners—
Now I won't feel ashamed.
Among siddha practitioners—
Now I won't feel ashamed.

In the bardo between words and what they refer to,
There are no terms or conventions that scholars use.
Now my doubts are all gone:
All appearances are dharmakaya:
That's the realization of this beggar-mendicant.
Among learned practitioners—
Now I won't feel ashamed.
Among learned practitioners—
Now I won't feel ashamed.

Translated according to the explanations of Khenpo Tsültrim Gyamtso Rinpoche by Elizabeth Callahan with music by Patrick Reilly. New York, France, and Belgium, July 2002. © 2002 Marpa Translation Committee.

Appendix III:
Two Poems by Dzogchen Ponlop Rinpoche

A Reminder To Myself

Child of awareness
Is exhausted
Journey of mind is infinite
If only I could have accumulated the mileage
from this journey in samsaric realms
I would have two free tickets to nirvana by now.

This continuity of thoughts
If only I could be mindful
All the vivid experiences of kleshas
I would have gone home to my primordial rigpa by now.

Lucid beauty of six objects
So naked
Makes them utterly honest
If only I could just be present
I would have seen the buddha realm by now.

Enlightened beads threaded
Through the angel hair crown
Unique in rugged power
Genuinely shines in the hearts of samsara.

Hail, hail Karmapa!

Dzogchen Ponlop Rinpoche, Sunday, August 23, 1998, Gampo Abbey

HEAVEN

So blue is the ocean,
Infinite is the mind.
So bright are the heavens,
Luminous is the mind.

Expanse of heaven
Meets with deep blue ocean.
Union at horizon
Takes me beyond breath.

Heaven is bullshit.
And hell the religion of fear.
Man needs no God.
Freedom is innate.

Dzogchen Ponlop Rinpoche
July 13, 1997

Appendix IV:
Looking Back: The Purpose of Ngondro

IT IS IMPORTANT for practitioners of the Vajrayana to know something of the history of the four uncommon preliminary practices, or *ngondro,* as a way of coming to understand their fundamental purpose. These are the four foundational trainings one goes through before engaging in what we call the "main practice," whether that is Mahamudra, Dzogchen or the deity yoga practices of the tantric path. However, it is essential to realize that the preliminary practices are not only what "comes before" the main practice—they are what prepare us for the actual experience of the Vajrayana journey. That awareness is critical to our path.

My own teacher, Khenpo Tsültrim Gyamtso Rinpoche, often advises his students to look back at the history of the great Vajrayana masters: the Indian mahasiddhas, Saraha, Tilopa and Naropa, as well as the Tibetan masters, Marpa, Milarepa and Gampopa, who continued the lineage of these teachers in Tibet. What we find by reading their stories and historical accounts is that there was no fixed set of practices known as "preliminary practices" at that time.

The liturgy of the four uncommon preliminaries that are practiced today—refuge and prostrations, recitation of the Vajrasattva mantra, mandala offering, and guru yoga—was developed only after the time of the ninth Karmapa, Wangchuk Dorje (1560–1603). It is traditional these days to do 100,000 repetitions of each. Before the time of the ninth Karmapa, however, this aspect of the path did not exist in any set form.

Since there was no formal set of practices that required one hundred thousand recitations of this and one hundred thousand of that, what each of our lineage forefathers did as preparation for their actual practice was unique. What Saraha did as a preliminary practice was not repeated by Tilopa, Naropa, Marpa or Milarepa. Therefore, we should not regard the preliminary practices as only those rituals that conform to our existing cultural traditions. If we freeze them in this way, then we lose their very point. We lose contact with the actual, primary intention of such practices.

If we examine the lives and paths of such masters, we find that each had his own way of preparing the ground. We might even be grateful that all we have to do is one hundred thousand prostrations! The great Brahmin Saraha was an exceptional scholar and served many years as an abbot of Nalanda University in India. Later in his life, he abandoned his monk's robes and his respected position at Nalanda to become a less reputable tantric yogi and simple arrowmaker. Tilopa literally chained himself down for twelve years and practiced meditation in a cave. Later he earned his livelihood pounding sesame seeds during the day and working at a brothel at night. Tilopa's main student, Naropa, was also a renowned scholar. Naropa endured twelve years of major and minor trials with Tilopa; first searching for his guru, then faithfully serving him and following his instructions—such as jumping off a temple roof and stealing food from a wedding banquet (followed by beatings from angry guests). Naropa's main student, Marpa, was a famous and proud translator from Tibet. Marpa's preliminary practice was walking to India to search for his guru. Such travel was both difficult and risky. There was always the threat of attack by thieves and robbers, not to mention jealous translator companions! Marpa made this long journey three times. The stories of Marpa's student, Milarepa, and of Milarepa's student, Gampopa, also demonstrate very different and challenging periods of preparation.

When we look at the historical examples, we can see an environment of struggle in which a certain process took place. That process involved the ripening of karma, followed by its transcendence. Despite the very different forms each individual's preliminary practice took, common to each of them was the intensity of their experience.

THE VAJRAYANA ROLLER COASTER

You can see that environment of struggle and process of the ripening and transcending of karma in your own practice of ngondro. The form of your practice is different, but the intensity is the same. It is in this sense that tantric practices are different from those of the Hinayana-Mahayana path. In comparison, the Vajrayana journey is full of color and excitement that comes from working so directly with the vivid energies of our thoughts and emotions. It's like riding a roller coaster—there's no time to get bored. Once I was riding a roller coaster with the previous Jamgon Kongtrul Rinpoche. He talked me into it. I enjoyed the ride up—there was such a nice view. We could see the ocean and the beach. It was very beautiful for a moment. Then there was the sudden drop—it was quite shocking. That's the nature of this journey.

Vajrayana ngondro works in the same way as removing a splinter from your hand. If you soak your hand in warm salt water, the splinter is loosened and pokes out enough so you can pull it out easily. Likewise, Vajrayana ngondro is the process of working to loosen our negative karmic seeds, our ingrained habitual tendencies, and to bring them to the surface. Once they are exposed, we can deal with them and transcend them. Whether we are practicing prostrations, Vajrasattva mantra, mandala offering or guru yoga, we are creating the causes and conditions for our karmic seeds to ripen. That's what is happening. We shouldn't blame the Vajrayana preliminary practices for any of the discomfort we feel or the intensity we go through. That's what we are looking for; it's what makes transcendence possible. Otherwise, if we retreat from those experiences, if we don't take advantage of them and free ourselves from those patterns, it's like starting to pull a splinter out, but stopping halfway when it becomes painful. Instead of completing the job, we try to push it back in. We think, "I'll pull it out sometime later." Our aim here is to bring about the ripening of our negative karmic causes and conditions, and, when they are ripened, to transcend or overcome them.

Sometimes the ripening experiences can feel quite rough, but they can also feel quite wonderful—like when we are going up in a roller coaster. Naropa had some moments of joy with Tilopa, as well as hardships. So, whether we are stealing food from a wedding banquet at our guru's instruction or doing a hundred thousand prostrations, we are working with our mind and preparing for the next phase of our path.

Purpose of Ngondro

The purpose of the preliminary practices is to prepare us for what comes next. It is much like the way the storyline of a joke prepares us for the punch line. You have to get the storyline right first for the punch line to make sense. Everybody wants to hear the punch line, but if you tell it too soon, it doesn't serve its purpose. It won't have any impact. If you prepare the lead up to it well, however, then your listeners will really get the punch line and will laugh out loud. When you don't get the storyline right, then they will say the joke is just okay.

It is the same with the Vajrayana path. Ngondro is the storyline that prepares us to get the punch line—in this case, the pointing-out instructions that introduce us to the actual practice of the nature of mind. Therefore, the ngondro practices can be very precious, if done right. What makes them so is not just the number of recitations and repetitions that we do. It is the opportunity this process gives us to work with our mind. The process of counting our hundreds of thousands of prostrations, mantras and so forth brings up a lot of emotion, and at the same time brings many karmic seeds to the ripening stage. The whole purpose of ngondro practice is to work with our mind in that situation. If we miss this step and just focus on adding up our numbers until we're finished, then our practice turns into a game. In the end, it will be what we call "okay" ngondro. It's not bad; we did it. But that is not real preparation. Real preparation takes place when we work with our mind during that period.

When we hear the words "preliminary practice," we shouldn't automatically think about a list of four things that we have to complete. Instead, we should think about preparing for our actual practice. For example, if you are hosting a very important person like H.H. the Dalai Lama in your home, you will take a great deal of time to prepare for that visit. The actual visit may be just fifteen minutes, but you might spend months preparing for these fifteen minutes. That's ngondro, the preparation. Think, then, that ngondro is like preparation for an important event: the pointing-out instructions on the nature of mind, your actual practice. That's the most important visit we can have. The important visitor is our guru, and the important event is the pointing-out of the nature of mind.

Sometimes students ask me for a pointing-out instruction after I have already given it. The question of how we can "get" the pointing-out instruction is one that often lingers in our mind. We can only really get it if we have prepared well enough. The pointing-out doesn't take very long. Sometimes it can be just a few seconds, like in the story of Tilopa and Naropa. Naropa had received pointing-out instruction from Tilopa for many years, but he had not recognized those moments. Finally, Tilopa said to him, "You still do not get it, my son!" He took off his sandal and whacked Naropa on his forehead. That time, Naropa got it—the complete transmission—because he had prepared for twelve years. And that process of preparation is what we call ngondro.

The Four Tantra Ngondro Practices

Refuge

In our practice of each of the four preliminaries, we have an opportunity to connect with a profound point of the Vajrayana path. The first of the four—taking the sixfold refuge, arousing bodhichitta and offering prostrations—is our means of connecting with the lineage principal. We often talk about the lineage and our connection to it, but this is the time when we formally make our connection. When we offer prostrations, we are standing before a visualized image of a lineage tree, our family tree, which can be traced back to Vajradhara, the enlightened nature of mind itself. During our prostrations, we should focus all our effort on cultivating our devotion, on making a heart connection to the Vajrayana lineage that is right in front of us. In addition to the Three Jewels of Buddha, Dharma and Sangha, we discover our connection to the Three Roots: the lineage principle, embodied by our guru; the yidam deity principle; and the protector principle in general, represented by the dakas, dakinis and dharmapalas. Traditionally, it is said that the guru is the root of blessings; the yidam is the root of spiritual accomplishment; and the dharma protectors are the root of enlightened activity. This is a physical practice that works with our pride and other emotions. At the same time, however, this is the moment in our Vajrayana practice when we connect with our Vajrayana, Mahamudra and Dzogchen lineages on a deeper level—one that is more personal and less conceptual. At the conclusion of this practice, we give rise to bodhichitta.

Vajrasattva

The second preliminary, the recitation of the Vajrasattva mantra, is the means by which we purify the negative habitual tendencies or karmic seeds that obstruct our ability to see the true nature of mind, and prevent us from genuinely benefiting sentient beings. During this practice, we visualize the sambhogakaya buddha Vajrasattva, the embodiment of primordial purity, above our heads. Then, as the liturgy explains, we recite Vajrasattva's one-hundred syllable mantra while visualizing over and over again that our body, speech and mind are being cleansed of all impurities. In this way we become inseparable from Vajrasattva again and again. As Vajrayana practitioners, we must remember that the ultimate nature of mind is perfectly pure and has no stains right from the beginning. When we connect with Vajrasattva, we are connecting directly with our own buddha nature, our innate enlightened potential. However, in relative truth, we perceive our body and mind in a dualistic form with negativities, and that is what we are trying to purify. In the Vajrasattva practice, therefore, we are not only cleansing the relative karmic impurities, but we are also connecting with the basic heart of buddha nature. We are discovering that our mind is in the nature of Vajrasattva right from the beginning.

Mandala Offering

The third ngondro, the mandala offering, is the means by which we let go of all our attachments and clinging. Through the purification process of Vajrasattva practice, we have finally connected with the pure nature of mind and body, as well as the pure nature of the universe. Now we let go of even that pure reality. We first generate a visualization of the entire universe and imagine it is filled with a countless number of utterly pure and beautiful forms and other objects pleasing to the senses. We then offer this mandala to the six objects of refuge over and over again. In this way, we relinquish our attachment and clinging not only to impure objects and negative states of mind, but also to whatever is pure, delightful and desirable. We usually regard attachment to our negative habits, like anger or jealousy, as a mistake—something to overcome. However, we think that being attached to positive habits, like our craving for prajna, or pure objects, like the thought of buddha nature, is okay. We don't see that kind of attachment as an obstruction. In the mandala offering practice, however, we try to let go of the best of everything the world has to offer. We are not disposing of our garbage, giving away things we don't want. Rather, we are letting go of things we do really want, especially those of a pure nature.

Guru Yoga

The fourth preliminary, guru yoga, is the means by which we increase our devotion and connect with the blessings of the lineage. Having completed the first three practices, we have established some ground of confidence in our own buddha nature, our own vajra heart. We have some understanding of the profound nature of the teachings we have received. We have also developed a sense of appreciation and respect for our guru, and a longing to connect with him or her on a deeper level. In short, we have trust and confidence in ourselves, the teachings and the guru who holds the lineage. At this point, we are ready to open up fully and receive the blessings of the lineage.

AN IMPORTANT POINT

These days, we don't have to walk for a thousand miles across high mountains to find our guru. We may meet him or her in a mall in our neighborhood. Nevertheless, while our physical hardships may be less challenging, we often lack the opportunity for extended periods of close physical contact with our teacher. However, if done right, our ngondro practice, in whatever form it takes, brings the experience of the guru, of the teacher-student relationship, directly into our life. It brings us face to face with the vivid energy and color of our emotions and concepts in the same way as the literal presence of the guru. So there is nothing missing. Whatever age we live in, if we invite the guru and the lineage into our hearts, we have the same opportunity to recognize the nature of mind as Tilopa, Naropa and all the mahasiddhas of the past.

First, however, we need to understand what ngondro is, and what it is not, by knowing its history and purpose. It is not just a set of four things. It is a profound path of practice that prepares our body, speech and mind for the Vajrayana journey that will take us all the way to enlightenment. It could be five things, or six, or it could be an amount of time, like twelve years. It could also be just extensive study of the Buddhist philosophical views.

There's a saying in Tibetan that the preliminary practices are more profound than the actual practice. Why? Because without them we cannot experience the profundity of the actual practice. I once saw a sign in a bank that said: "Luck is when preparation meets opportunity." That's talking about ngondro: preparation is ngondro and opportunity is the actual practice. When these two meet it is an important point—a moment in which there could be a dramatic change in our experience of mind.

Appendix V:
The Stages of Dissolution

Bardo Of Dying: The Stages Of Death
1. The Coarse Dissolution of the Elements of the Physical Body

Element	Chakra	Skandha / Sense consciousness / Wisdom	Outer sign *(physical experience)*	Inner sign *(cognitive experience)*	Secret sign *(luminosity of example)*
EARTH →WATER	Navel	Form / Eye sense consciousness / Mirrorlike	Growing sense of heaviness followed by loss of physical strength and agility; diminishing of size or weight	Mind feels heavy and listless; visual perception dims	Miragelike appearance
WATER→FIRE	Heart	Feeling / Ear sense consciousness / Equanimity	Body begins to dry up; increasing thirst; leakage of bodily fluids	Progressive loss of mental clarity; mind may become more agitated and susceptible to confusion	Smokelike appearance
FIRE→WIND	Throat	Perception / Nose sense consciousness / Discriminating awareness	Loss of bodily heat beginning at extremities; one feels increasingly cold	Clarity of mind fluctuates between clear and unclear; increasing inability to recognize people or perceive objects distinctly	Appearance like fireflies
WIND→ CONSCIOUSNESS	Secret	Formations / Tongue and tactile sense consciousnesses / All-accomplishing	Breath becomes shortened; breathing becomes more difficult; gradually exhalations become longer than inhalations; cessation of outer respiration (medical point of death)	Mind becomes extremely confused and unstable; appearance of "hallucinations" or vivid thought states	Appearance like a brightly shining torch

II. THE SUBTLE DISSOLUTION OF CONSCIOUSNESS

Appearance *Mind of appearance dissolves into mind of increase*	HAM White bindu descends toward heart center	Masculine energy; compassion, or skillful means; the form aspect of the union of form and emptiness.	Luminous white appearance like moonlight shining in a cloudless sky	Thirty-three thoughts related to aggression cease
Increase *Mind of increase dissolves into mind of attainment*	ASHE Red bindu ascends toward heart center	Feminine energy; wisdom, or prajna; the emptiness aspect of the union of form and emptiness.	Luminous red appearance like sunlight shining in a cloudless sky	Forty thoughts related to passion cease
Attainment *Mind of attainment dissolves into space*	Two bindus meet at heart center and envelop intrinsic awareness	Inner respiration ceases; actual point of death	Luminous dark appearance like a cloudless sky without sunlight, moonlight or starlight	Seven thoughts related to ignorance cease; all conceptuality ceases
Full Attainment *Space dissolves into luminosity*	Consciousness is reabsorbed into the buddha wisdom or the all-basis wisdom at the heart center	Completes dissolution of skandha of consciousness and wisdom of dharmadhatu	Luminosity of no-appearance, or clear light of dharmakaya; pure (objectless) awareness vast and open like a clear sky	Dawning of the ultimate nature; one faints or attains liberation through recognition of mind's nature

Appendix VI:
The Hundred Peaceful and Wrathful Deities

THE HUNDRED PEACEFUL AND WRATHFUL DEITIES OF THE BARDO OF DHARMATA

42 PEACEFUL MANIFESTATIONS

DAY	APPEARING ASPECT	SYMBOLIZES
DHARMAKAYA LUMINOSITY		
Ever-present	Primordial Buddha Samantabhadra (dark blue) with Samantabhadri (white)	Ground luminosity Indivisibility of awareness and space
SAMBHOGAKAYA LUMINOSITY		
Day 1	Buddha Vairochana with female Buddha [Akasha]Dhatvishvari (white) Family: Buddha Wisdom: Dharmadhatu Realm: God and Animal	Natural purity of the skandha of consciousness (male buddha) and element of space (female buddha)
Day 2	Buddha Vajrasattva (-Akshobya) with female Buddha-Lochana (blue) Family: Vajra Wisdom: Mirrorlike Realm: Hell	Natural purity of the skandha of form (male buddha) and element of earth (female buddha)
	Male bodhisattvas Kshitigarbha and Maitreya Female bodhisattvas Lasya and Pushpa[1]	Pure nature of the eye and ear sense consciousnesses (male bodhisattvas); pure nature of the objects of visual consciousness and of past conceptual thoughts (female bodhisattvas)[2]

Day 3	Buddha Ratnasambhava with female Buddha Mamaki (yellow gold)	Natural purity of the skandha of feeling (male buddha) and element of water (female buddha)
	Family: Ratna Wisdom: Equanimity Realm: Hungry ghost	
	Male bodhisattvas Samantabhadra and Akashagarbha Female bodhisattvas Malya and Dhupa	Pure nature of the nose and tongue sense consciousnesses (male bodhisattvas); pure nature of the objects of the nose and mental sense consciousnesses (female bodhisattvas)
Day 4	Buddha Amitabhabha with female Buddha Pandaravasini (red)	Natural purity of the skandha of perception (male buddha) and element of fire (female buddha)
	Family: Padma Wisdom: Discriminating awareness Realm: Human	
	Male bodhisattvas Avalokiteshvara and Manjushri Female bodhisattvas Gita and Aloka	Pure nature of the tactile and mental sense consciousnesses (male bodhisattvas); pure nature of the objects of the ear sense consciousness and of future conceptual thoughts (female bodhisattvas)
Day 5	Buddha Amogasiddhi with female Buddha Samayatara (green)	Natural purity of the skandha of formation (male buddha) and element of wind (female buddha)
	Family: Karma Wisdom: All-accomplishing Realm: Jealous god	Pure nature of the all-basis consciousness and the afflicted consciousnesses (male bodhisattvas); pure nature of present conceptual thoughts and the objects of the tongue sense consciousnesses (female bodhisattvas)
	Male bodhisattvas [Sarva]Nivaranaviskambhin and Vajrapani Female bodhisattvas Ghandha and Naivedya	

Day 6	Appearance of full mandala of 42 Peaceful Deities. Above are Samantabhadra and Samantabhadri. The buddhas and bodhisattvas are gathered beneath them in their respective mandalas with their retinues. In addition, the assembly includes:	Natural purity of the afflicted emotions (6 buddhas); natural purity of wrong views (male gatekeepers); natural purity of the four kinds of birth (female gatekeepers)[3]
	6 Buddhas of the Six Realms 4 male gatekeepers 4 female gatekeepers	

Day 7	*The Five Vidyadharas, or Knowledge Holders, with their consorts Semi-wrathful *Not counted in the 100 Bardo Deities*

58 Wrathful Manifestations

DHARMAKAYA LUMINOSITY

Mahottara Heruka with Krodheshvari (dark brown to maroon)	Wrathful form of primordial buddha; transmutation of ignorance into pure awareness

SAMBHOGAKAYA LUMINOSITY

Day 8	Buddha Heruka with Buddha-Krodheshvari	Transmutation of energy of delusion into dharmadhatu wisdom[4] and overcoming conceptuality associated with visual objects
Day 9	Vajra Heruka with Vajra-Krodheshvari	Transmutation of energy of anger into mirrorlike wisdom and overcoming conceptuality associated with objects of sound
Day 10	Ratna Heruka with Ratna-Krodheshvari	Transmutation of energy of pride[5] into wisdom of equanimity and overcoming conceptuality associated with objects of smell

Day 11	Padma Heruka with Padma-Krodheshvari	Transmutation of energy of attachment into discriminating awareness wisdom and overcoming conceptuality associated with objects of taste
Day 12	Karma Heruka with Karma-Krodheshvari	Transmutation of energy of jealousy into all accomplishing wisdom and overcoming conceptuality associated with objects of touch

	Appearance of full mandala of 58 Wrathful Deities, plus the wrathful aspect of the primordial buddha, making 60. Above are Mahottara and Krodheshvari. Beneath them, the Herukas and consorts are gathered in their respective mandalas. In addition, the assembly includes 48 female figures, "yoginis" or "goddesses":
	    8 *gauris*
	    8 *tramen*
	    4 female gatekeepers
	    28 *ishvaris*
		Pure nature of the 8 consciousnesses and their objects (8 *gauris* and 8 *tramen*); protection from 4 kinds of samsaric birth and arousing of altruistic intentions (4 female gatekeepers); performance of the four kinds of activities: pacifying, enriching, magnetizing and destroying (28 *ishvaris*)[6]

1   There is some variation throughout in the names of the members of the retinues of the Buddhas.
2   Details on the symbolism of the retinues of the peaceful and wrathful buddhas—the bodhisattvas, gatekeepers, gauris, tramen and ishvaris—are drawn primarily from two sources: Francesca Fremantle, *Luminous Emptiness* (Shambhala, 2003), and *The Tibetan Book of the Dead,* trans. Gyurme Dorje (Viking, 2005).
3   Male gatekeepers in some texts are said to symbolize the four karmas and female gatekeepers, the four immeasurables. The four karmas are the actions of pacifying, enriching, magnetizing and destroying. The four immeasurables are the four limitless thoughts: loving kindness, compassion, sympathetic joy and equanimity.
4   In the system of the five buddha families, the Buddha family is associated with the transformation of ignorance into dharmadhatu wisdom. However, when the five buddha families are associated with the six realms of samsaric existence, then the Buddha family can be seen as having a connection with two realms: the realm of the gods, which is associated with pride, and the animal realm, which is associated with stupidity, both qualities rooted in fundamental ignorance.
5   See also note 2. The Ratna family, which is associated with the transformation of pride in the system of the five buddha families, may be linked to the hungry ghost realm and the affliction of greed, or extreme desire, in the system of the six realms.
6   Descriptions of these activities and protections vary.

Notes

1 The inherent nature of mind and all phenomena is called "suchness," or "thatness," or, in Sanskrit, *dharmata*. *Dharma* means "phenomena," and *ta* makes it "the nature" or "the essence." The bardo of dharmata is so called because it is at this time that the ultimate nature of mind—its true reality—manifests clearly and vividly.

2 There are said to be four types of birth: womb-birth, egg-birth, heat/moisture-birth, and instantaneous, or miraculous, birth. Womb birth is experienced by humans and mammals. Egg birth is experienced by animals, such as birds and reptiles. Birth through heat and moisture is explained in different ways—as a type of birth that gives rise to insects; or in modern times, it could refer to cloning, for example. Instantaneous birth refers to birth into a Pure Land, which is not dependent on gross elements. It also refers to the appearance in this world of a great being, such as Padmasambhava, who was born miraculously as an eight-year-old child seated upon a lotus flower.

3 The dates of Padmasambhava's activity in Tibet vary. Some sources give the time period as the ninth century.

4 Translation by The Dzogchen Ponlop Rinpoche and Gerry Wiener. © 2002, The Dzogchen Ponlop Rinpoche and Gerry Wiener.

5 "The term prajña —knowledge or understanding—in Buddhism . . . does not refer to some kind of passive knowledge or to merely knowing some facts. Rather, it stands for the vast range of actively knowing and investigating the appearances and the true nature of all phenomena from form up to omniscience . . .Thus, the definition of 'knowledge' in Buddhism is 'that which fully and exhaustively discriminates the general and specific characteristics of phenomena' . . . [T]here is a very close connection between knowledge (*prajña*) and wisdom (*jñana*). Often, these terms are used simply as synonyms, or it is said that wisdom is nothing but the culmination or perfection of knowledge, prajñaparamita. In general, however, knowledge stands more for the analytical and discriminating aspect of superior insight and realization (both conceptual and nonconceptual) while wisdom mainly emphasizes the nonconceptual, immediate, and panoramic aspects of realization." Karl Brunnhölzl, *Center of the Sunlit Sky: Madhyamaka in the Kagyu Tradition* (Ithaca, New York: Snow Lion Publications, 2004), pp. 143-146.

6 The Sevenfold Posture of Vairochana is the meditation posture in which the meditator sits with (1) the legs in a cross-legged position, (2) the spine straight, (3) the shoulders even and relaxed, (4) the neck slightly bent, (5) the hands in the gesture of equanimity (one hand placed palm upright upon the other, resting four fingers below the navel), (6) the tip of tongue touching the palate and the lips slightly open, and (7) the eyes half-open with the gaze directed along the direction of the nose.

7   Further details on the deity yoga practices are presented in chapter 7, "The Bardo of Becoming."

8   The six realms are six states of samsaric existence into which beings can be reborn at the end of the sixth bardo, the bardo of becoming. From the Mahayana perspective, they are regarded as psychological rather than physical realities, with each realm representing a mental state that is dominated by a particular emotion and a characteristic style of suffering. The six realms are categorized into three higher and three lower realms. The higher realms are: the god realm, the jealous god realm, and the human realm. The lower realms are: the animal realm, the hungry ghost realm, and the hell realm.

9   According to the Buddhist view, the process of perception, or of mental and sensory experience altogether, involves three components: (1) the six consciousnesses of eye, ear, nose, tongue, body and the mind; (2) the sense faculty that perceives these six; and (3) the objects experienced by them—form, sound, smell, taste, physical sensation and mental phenomena; i.e., thoughts, concepts and so forth.

10 The training for dream yoga, such as the illusory body and lucid dreaming practices outlined here, is similar to some of the methods developed by Western scholars and researchers such as Stephen LaBerge of Stanford University. Both the Western exercises and the methods given here can be used, since they are essentially the same thing.

11 "Wild Horses," written by Mick Jagger & Keith Richards. Published by ABKCO Music, Inc. © 1970 ABKCO Music, Inc., www.abkco.com.

12 An excellent book by Khenpo Tsültrim Gyamtso Rinpoche that presents the complete teachings on these stages is *The Progressive Stages of Meditation on Emptiness* (Prajna Editions, 2001). It is a concise and exceptionally clear presentation of the teachings of many great masters that helps to clarify the view of emptiness as well as the practice of vipashyana. See also, by the same author, *The Sun of Wisdom: Teachings on the Noble Nagarjuna's Fundamental Wisdom of the Middle Way* (Shambhala, 2003). Additionally, instruction on the progressive stages of the view and meditation are available in the Nalandabodhi Study Curriculum; see the Mahayana View sourcebook, *Not Even a Middle* (www.nalandabodhi.org).

13 There are further details about the correlation of the eye consciousness with the pranas and nadis of the subtle body that are studied later with one's individual teacher.

14 Garab Dorje was a renowned Indian mahasiddha, often regarded as a nirmanakaya buddha, or perfectly enlightened being. It is said that he received the full teachings of the Dzogchen lineage not from a human teacher, but directly from the sambhogakaya buddha Vajrasattva. Thus, he is regarded as the first human teacher of this lineage. From Garab Dorje, the lineage passed to his primary disciple, Manjushrimitra.

15 The process of the development of the human body is described in more detail in both the sutras and tantras. There are detailed descriptions of the coming together of the channels and winds at the stage of embryonic existence and how these affect the progressive development of the body. A text composed by the Third Gyalwang Karmapa, Rangjung Dorje, *The Profound Inner Reality*, provides very clear teachings on the chakras and on channels, winds and essences. Studying this text with a qualified teacher is the best method for gaining a clearer understanding of the subtle body. Currently, only portions of this text are translated into English, and these are not yet published. A commentary on this text, *Illuminating the Profound Reality: A Commentary on the Profound Inner Reality* (Tib. *zab mo nang don gyi 'grel pa zab don snang byed*)

by Jamgön Kongtrül Lodrö Thaye, is available in Tibetan through the Nitartha International Document Input Center. See www.nitartha.org. A partial translation of the commentary by Elizabeth Callahan was taught at Nitartha Institute 2003. See www.nitarthainstitute.org.

16 There is an entire collection of teachings in the tantras known as the *lung-sem-nyi-me*, or "inseparable prana and mind." In particular, there is an extensive instruction by the Eighth Gyalwa Karmapa, Mikyo Dorje, called *The Inseparability of Prana and Mind* (Tib. *rlung sems dbyer med kyi khrid yig chen mo*). It contains excellent instructions on completion stage practice, which are most important for the dissolution stages and the time when death occurs. Published in Tibetan. (Delhi: Delhi Karmapae Chodhey, Gyalwae Sungrab Partun Khang, 1980.) See Tibetan Buddhist Resource Center: www.tbrc.org.

17 There are six realms within the desire realm; the god realm, the realm of the jealous gods, the human realm, the animal realm, the realm of the hungry ghosts and the hell realm. The form and formless realms also have various divisions but are generally regarded as god realms. All are within the realm of samsara.

18 For clarification, it should be noted that the instruction to focus one's mind upward is specific to this practice of phowa. The earlier instruction to focus one's mind at the various chakras where the dissolutions are taking place is specific to the practice of using devotion as a path. Therefore, there is no conflict in these instructions and one does not try to combine the instructions on focus indicated in the two methods.

19 The Six Dharmas of Naropa are the yogic practices of inner heat, illusory body, dream yoga, luminosity yoga, bardo, and phowa. See chapter 7 for brief commentary on these yogas.

20 See endnote 6 above for a description of this posture.

21 The cleansing of the stale breath is a simple breathing exercise practiced at the beginning of a meditation session, in which one inhales deeply and then slowly expels all air from the lungs. It is said to refresh or purify the stale air or karmic winds within the channels of the subtle body.

22 See chapter 7, pp. 205–207, for further details on creating a supportive environment.

23 Dharmakaya is often described as a cloudless blue sky. Here, however, it is depicted without color or any source of light other than the natural brilliance of awareness itself.

24 In Tibetan, Mahottara is Chemchok Heruka (*che mchog he ru ka*).

25 While it is traditional to count one hundred deities—forty-two peaceful and fifty-eight wrathful—the Dzogchen tantras count sixty wrathful deities, resulting in a total of one hundred and two.

26 See appendix VI on page 267 for chart listing details of peaceful and wrathful deities.

27 The arrangement and even the composition of the Buddha mandala can change according to the particular lineage of teachings it represents. Here, Vairochana appears in the center and Vajrasattva resides in the eastern quadrant; however, at times those positions are reversed. Also, when Vajrasattva appears in the eastern quadrant, he is sometimes linked with Akshobya and called "Vajrasattva-Akshobya."

28 The awareness holders that appear at this time are manifestations of our own primordial awareness. They are symbolic of the levels of attainment or stages in the path to the realization of complete buddhahood. They represent the Vajrayana, or tantric, expression of these stages, which correspond to the higher stages of the five bodhisattva

paths of the Mahayana. The five awareness-holders and their dakini consorts are not technically counted as members of the assembly of the hundred deities.

29 A list of suggested readings is provided on p. 297. Several of these authors provide detailed descriptions of the deities' appearance and symbolism.

30 More detailed descriptions of the visions of the bardo of dharmata and in particular of the visions of spontaneous presence can be found in books by both Tibetan teachers and Western practitioner-scholars. See list of suggested readings on p. 297.

31 In the classification of old and new tantra schools, the former refers to the Nyingma (or Dzogchen) system of counting six tantras, or yogas, and the latter to the system of counting four tantras followed by the Kagyu, Sakya and Gelug, and so on.

32 The Tibetan word for nirmanakaya, *tupa* (Tib. *sprul pa,* Skt. *nirmana*), can be translated as "emanation." It forms the root of the word *tulku* (Tib. *sprul sku,* Skt. *nirmanakaya*), which is "emanation body."

33 The Tibetan term is *tsal* (Tib. *rtsal*), and is translated as "expressive power," "display," "energy," or "expression."

34 In this context, when the term "yoga" is used, it refers to the practice of one of the six root dharmas of the Six Dharmas of Naropa.

Glossary

Note: Where the Tibetan language equivalent of terms is provided, the Wylie transliteration of the term appears to the left of the slash, and the phonetic pronunciation appears to the right.

absolute truth (Skt. *paramārthasatya*; Tib. *don dam bden pa /töndam denpa*): The "truth" that is seen by enlightened beings. This is usually described either as emptiness, mind's luminous nature or buddha nature. See also **two truths.**

adhisththana (*byin rlabs /jinlab*): Blessings conferred by one's teachers, realized masters or through one's own meditation practice and supplications.

afflictive obscurations (Skt. *kleśāvaraña*; Tib. *nyon mongs pa'i sgrib pa*): also, "klesha obscurations": Obscurations to liberation from samsara. They are of the nature of any of the five root kleshas of aggression, pride, passion, ignorance and jealousy, and their related mental states. They are the coarser of the two types of **obscurations.**

alaya-jnana (Tib. *kun gzhi ye shes /künshi yeshe*). This refers to mind's pure wisdom nature, or buddha nature, primordially undefiled by any adventitious stains, recognizing itself. See also **alaya-vijnana.**

alaya-vijnana (Tib. *kun gzhi rnam shes / künshi namshe*): According to the Chittamatra philosophical system, this is the eighth consciousness and is the storehouse for all of one's karmic imprints and patterns. It is equivalent to ignorance, or the sum total of adventitious stains. See also **all-basis.**

all-basis (Skt. *ālaya*; Tib. *kun gzhi /künshi*): In general, the term alaya is used for both *dharmata*, or mind's true nature, and the *alaya-vijnana*. When mind's nature is not recognized, it is called "all-basis consciousness," or *alaya-vijnana*. When it is recognized, it is called "all-basis wisdom," or *alaya-jnana*. See also **alaya-vijnana** and **alaya-jnana**.

alpha pure (Tib. *ka dag /kadak*): In general, this is a term for the primordial purity and equality of all phenomena of samsara and nirvana; in particular, it is the fundamental view of the Dzogchen practice of **trekcho**. See also **primordial wisdom**.

anuttarayogatantra (Tib. *rnal 'byor bla med rgyud /naljor lame gyü*): This is the highest of the four tantra classes according to the system of the later translation period in Tibetan Buddhism.

appearances (Tib. *snang ba /nangwa*): The objects of the six senses. Also translated as "experiences" or "perceptions." See also **impure appearances** and **pure appearances**.

appearance, increase and attainment (Tib. *snang ba mched pa thob pa /nangwa chepa thobpa*): These terms refer to the gradual dissolution of consciousness in the process of dying, culminating in the experience of mind's basic luminosity. They are also found in corresponding ways in various Vajrayana practices.

Avalokiteshvara (Tib. *spyan ras gzigs /Chenrezi*): Bodhisattva of compassion.

awakening (Skt. *bodhi*; Tib. *byang chub /changchub*): The state of a buddha. Also translated as "enlightenment." All obscurations of mind are overcome or purified and wisdom is perfectly realized.

bardo (Skt. *antarābhava*; Tib. *bar do /bardo*; "intermediate state"): Translated as "intermediate," "interval" or "in-between" state. In one sense, it refers to the experience of the present moment; in another, it refers to an experience of certain duration of time, marked by a clear beginning, a sense of continuity and distinct end. In the latter sense, six bardos are taught: the **natural bardo of this life**, the **bardo of dream**, the **bardo of meditation**, the **painful bardo of dying**, the **luminous bardo of dharmata**, and the **karmic bardo of becoming**. See also respective entries.

bardo of dream (Tib. *rmi lam gyi bar do /milam gi bardo*): The interval between falling asleep and re-awakening, in which one experiences the arising of dream appearances.

bardo of meditation (Tib. *bsam gtan gyi bar do /samten gi bardo*): The interval in which one's mind is resting in a state of meditative absorption, or *samadhi*.

bhumi (Tib. *sa /sa*; "grounds"): The ten stages or levels traversed by bodhisattvas. Attainment of the first bhumi signifies one's first full realization of emptiness. As one progresses through the bhumis, one's realization becomes increasingly profound. There are an additional four paramitas that correspond to and are perfected on the journey of the ten bhumis. To the six paramitas are added: method, aspiration, power and wisdom.

bindu: See nadis, pranas and bindus.

bliss-emptiness (Tib. *bde stong /detong*): This means the experience of nonconceptual all-pervasive bliss that is completely free of any attachment and reference points.

bodhichitta (Tib. *byang chub kyi sems /changchub kyi sem*; "awakened mind"): Generally, the term is used to mean the intention to attain complete buddhahood in order to benefit all beings. Specifically, it is classified as ultimate and relative bodhichitta; the latter being divided into aspirational and application bodhichitta.

bodhisattva (Tib. *byang chub sems dpa' /changchub sempa*; "awake courageous one"): An aspirant on the path of Mahayana who has vowed to attain complete awakening in order to liberate all beings from samsara. The term may refer to either an ordinary being practicing the trainings of **bodhichitta** (called "a beginner bodhisattva"), or to someone who has attained the realizations of any of the ten bodhisattva **bhumis** (called a "bodhisattva mahasattva").

Buddha (Tib. *sangs rgyas / sangye*): This can refer to the historical founder of Buddhism, Buddha Shakyamuni (also known as Siddhartha, or Gautama), or more generally to one who has attained the state of enlightenment or complete awakening. This is achieved when one has overcome "the two veils," the afflictive and knowledge obscurations, and realized the two wisdoms: the wisdom that knows the ultimate nature of mind and phenomena, and the wisdom that knows the multiplicity of these phenomena. It can also be descriptive of the enlightened qualities of mind itself, i.e., buddha nature, or buddha wisdom.

Buddhadharma (Tib. *nang pa sangs rgyas pa'i chos /nangpa sangye pe chö*): Teachings of the Buddha.

buddha nature (Skt. *tathāgatagarbha;* Tib. *de bzhin gshegs pa'i snying po /deshin shek pe nyingpo*): The potential to attain complete spiritual awakening that exists in the mindstream of every sentient being.

chakra (Tib. *'khor lo /korlo*): A point along the central channel of the **subtle body** where the three primary **nadis** intersect to form a specific configuration, or "dharma wheel." There are four main chakras: at the head, throat, heart, and navel. Meditations involving the chakras are utilized in **completion stage** practices.

Chandrakirti (Tib. *Zla ba grags pa /da wa drak pa*): A seventh-century Indian master, scholar and abbot of Nalanda University. As founder of the Prasangika Madhyamaka School, he became the intellectual and spiritual heir of the great Madhyamaka master Nagarjuna.

Chittamatra (Tib. *sems tsam /sem tsam*; "mind-only"): The Mahayana school of Buddhism that teaches that there are no things that exist as something other than mind, and asserts mind — mere clear and aware consciousness — to be truly existent.

completion stage (Skt. *sampannakrama*; Tib. *rdzogs rim /dzokrim*): This is the second of the two major types of meditation in the Vajrayana (the first being the **creation stage**), which consists of gradually refining **nadi**, **prana**, and **bindu**, and culminates in the increasingly nonreferential meditations of Mahamudra and Dzogchen. Through such practices, one becomes familiar with and realizes the union of clarity and emptiness, bliss and emptiness, and awareness and emptiness. See also **creation stage**.

connate wisdom (Skt. *sahajajnana*; Tib. *lhan cig skyes pa'i ye shes /lhenchik kye pe yeshe*): The primordial **dharmakaya** nature of mind.

creation stage (Skt. *utpattikrama*; Tib. *bskyed rim /kyerim*): This is the first of the two major types of meditation in the Vajrayana (the second being the **completion stage**), which focuses on the visualization of meditational deities in order to become familiar with and realize the union of appearance and emptiness. See also **completion stage**.

deity (Skt. *deva*; Tib. *lha /hla*): Various **sambhogakaya** forms, which can appear in peaceful or wrathful attire, symbolizing the union of appearance and emptiness; used in **deity yoga** visualizations (**utpattikrama**). See also **yidam**.

deity yoga (Tib. *lha'i rnal 'byor /hla yi naljor*): Meditation practice involving the visualization of deities; a skillful method for connecting with the wisdoms embodied by deities. (Equivalent to **utpattikrama**.)

defilements (Tib. *glo bur gyi dri ma /lobur gi drima*): Those defilements or impurities that are not indigenous to **buddha nature**, the nature of mind, but which nonetheless obscure one's perception of it, like the clouds blocking the rays of the sun. Also, "incidental" or "adventitious" stains. See also **two obscurations**.

dharmadhatu (Tib. *chos dbyings /chöying*; "expanse /space of phenomena"): The ultimate, primordial expanse of the phenomena of samsara and nirvana, which is nonarising and unceasing, unconditioned and unchanging.

dharmakaya (Tib. *chos kyi sku /chökyi ku*; "phenomenal /truth body"): The dharmakaya is the realization of the essence of **vipashyana**, or the result of perfecting the nature of nonconceptuality. It is the fruition achieved for one's own benefit. In regard to the nature of mind, dharmakaya is mind's empty essence, beyond all speech, thought and expression. It is also said that it is the nonarising of the mind-itself and is free from all conceptual elaborations. From the triad of body, speech and mind, it is taught as the *mind* quality of buddhahood.

dharmata (Tib. *chos nyid /chönyi*; "reality"): The ultimate nature or reality of mind and phenomena. Synonymous with emptiness, suchness, nature of mind and **buddha nature**.

display (Tib. *rtsal /tsal*): The manifesting quality of mind. Also translated as "manifestation" or "expressive power."

doha (Tib. *mgur /gur*): A type of spontaneous song of spiritual realization, sung historically by masters such as Milarepa.

Dzogchen (Tib. *rdzogs chen*): "The Great Perfection"; The tradition of meditation emphasizing the mind's primordial purity and the methods for realizing it. This meditation is the pinnacle practice within the Nyingma lineage. It is taught to be the most advanced of all forms of meditation practice. In Tibet, these teachings were widely spread by Padmasambhava, and they encompass the present instructions on dying and the cycle of the six bardos.

ego-clinging (Skt. *atmagraha*; Tib. *bdag 'dzin /dak dzin*): The confused tendency of the mind to apprehend a truly existent "me" or "I" within the continuum of body and mind.

egolessness (Skt. *nairātmya*; Tib. *bdag med /dak me*): Similar in meaning to shunyata. Also translated as "selflessness" and "identitylessness," it is the absence of something singular, permanent or independent that could be called an ego, self, soul or identity, or "I." There are two main types of egolessness: that of persons (Skt. *pudgala-nairātmya*; Tib. *gang zag gi bdag* *med /kangzak gi dakme*) and that of phenomena (Skt. *dharma-nairātmya*; Tib. *chos kyi bdag med /chö kyi dakme*).

elaborations, conceptual (Skt. *prapañca*; Tib. *sprod pa /tröpa*): The conceptual constructs that are falsely imputed to phenomena. Generally, there are four elaborations, which are the four extremes: existence, nonexistence, both, or neither.

emptiness (Skt. *śūnyatā*; Tib. *stong pa nyid /tongpa nyi*): A term that refers to the lack of true existence of a self of person or outer phenomena on the absolute level, while not refuting such relative appearances of self. In effect, the natural state of "emptiness" means that all phenomena are beyond the extremes of existence or nonexistence in any permanent or solid sense. See also **shunyata**.

five sense pleasures (Tib. *'dod yon lnga /döyön nga*): Beautiful forms, pleasant sounds, fragrant scents, delicious tastes and soft tangible objects.

five skandhas (Tib. *phung po lnga/pungpo nga*, "five aggregates"): The term "skandha" literally means "group," "heap," or "aggregate." The five skandhas are: forms (Tib. *gzugs /zuk*), feelings (Tib. *tshor ba /tsorwa*), discriminations (Tib. *'du shes /dushe*), formations (Tib. *'du byed /duje*) and consciousnesses (Tib. *rnam shes /namshe*). These five comprise all possible aspects of our experience and are said to be the basis of our clinging to a "self," as well as the basis for the examination of the "nonexistence of a self."

Four Great Modes of Liberation (Tib. *grol lugs chen po bzhi*): These are primordial liberation, self liberation, naked liberation and complete liberation, all referring to mind's conflicting emotions and thoughts being nothing but the unobstructed creative display of mind's nature and the recognition of this.

Four Noble Truths (Skt. *caturāryasatya*; Tib. *'phags pa'i bden pa bzhi /pak pe denpa shi*): Buddha's teaching in the first turning of the wheel of dharma. The first two truths—the truth of suffering and the truth of the origin of suffering—present the cause and result of samsara; the second two truths—the truth of the cessation of suffering and the truth of the path leading to the cessation of suffering—present the cause and result of nirvana.

Gampopa (Tib. *sGam po pa*)(1079–1153): Also known as Dakpo Rinpoche (Tib. *Dvags po rin po che*). Foremost student of Milarepa, he also studied with Kadampa teachers. He was the founder of the monastic order of the Kagyu School and the lineage of his direct successors is known as the Dakpo Kagyu (also known as Karma Kagyu from the First Karmapa onward). His main disciples included the First Karmapa, Düsum Khyenpa and Pakmo Drupa.

ganachakra (Tib. *tshogs kyi 'khor lo /tsok gi kor lo*): A unique group practice of Vajrayana Buddhism in which participants restore samaya and gather the two accumulations of merit and wisdom extremely quickly.

great emptiness (Skt. *mahāśūnyatā*; Tib. *stong pa chen po /tongpa chenpo*): The inseparability of appearances and emptiness, or the inseparability of clarity and emptiness.

guru mandala: The environment of wisdom invoked through the presence and blessing of the spiritual master, as well as through the devotion and receptivity of his or her students.

Guru Rinpoche: The Indian master of tantric Buddhism who, through various styles of conventional and unconventional conduct, was primarily responsible for transplanting the teachings of Vajrayana Buddhism to Tibet. He was invited to Tibet by the Indian abbot Shantarakshita and the Tibetan King Trisong Deutsen in the eighth century. In addition to being the primary holder and transmitter of the cycle of bardo teachings, he concealed innumerable dharma teachings, known as hidden treasures, throughout Tibet, Nepal and Bhutan to be revealed by destined disciples in the centuries to come. He is sometimes called the "second Buddha" and is also known by the names Padmakara, or "the lotus-born," and Padmasambhava.

habitual tendencies (Skt. *vāsanā*, Tib. *bag chags /bakchak*): The propensities created by the mind's habituations, which are stored in a latent form in the all-basis consciousness. Habitual tendencies are always neutral in character, though their ripening can elicit physical, verbal and mental actions that are positive, negative or neutral.

Hinayana (Tib. *theg pa dman pa /thekpa menpa*, "lesser vehicle"): Includes the first two yanas, or stages of the general Buddhist path, the Shravakayana and Pratyekabuddhayana, whose fruition is individual liberation.

illusory body (Tib. *sgyu lus/gyulü*): The practice of impure illusory body (Tib. *ma dag pa'i sgyu lus/ma dak pe gyu lü*) means to familiarize oneself with and realize the illusory nature of all phenomena as being appearance and emptiness inseparable. The practice of pure illusory body (Tib. *dag pa'i sgyu lus/dakpe gyulü*) is related to **completion stage** practices. See also **impure appearance** and **pure appearance**.

impermanence (Tib. *mi rtag pa /mitakpa*): An impermanent phenomenon is that which arises, abides and ceases. Gross impermanence refers to changes that can be directly observed with the passage of time by undeveloped minds. Subtle impermanence refers to momentary changes, which generally cannot be directly observed.

impure appearance (Tib. *ma dag pa'i snang ba /madak pe nangwa*): The dualistic and afflictive appearances and experiences of ordinary beings in samsara.

interdependent origination (Tib. *rten cing 'brel bar 'byung ba /tenching drelwar jungwa*): The interconnectedness of all things; the fact that phenomena arise only in dependence upon the meeting of their causes and conditions, and therefore are understood to not exist inherently or ultimately.

jnana (Tib. *ye shes /yeshe*): The non-dual wisdom of enlightened ones.

karmic bardo of becoming (Tib. *srid pa'i bar do /si pe bardo*): The interval that begins after the **luminous bardo of dharmata** and ends when we enter the womb of our future parents.

klesha (Tib. *nyon mongs /nyönmong*; mental afflictions): The negative, deluded states of mind that afflict sentient beings. Also known as afflictive emotions. The six root afflictions are ignorance (*ma rig pa*), desire (*'dod chags*), anger (*khong 'khro*), pride (*nga rgyal*), doubt (*the tshom*), and wrong views (*lta ba*).

knowledge obscurations (Tib. *shes bya'i sgrib pa*): Obscurations that block or hinder one's attainment of omniscient buddhahood, which mainly consist in the ignorance of the true nature of phenomena, i.e., **shunyata**. This is taught to be the more subtle of the two obscurations, the other being the **afflictive obscurations**.

liberation (Tib. *thar pa /tarpa* or Tib. *grol ba /drolwa*): Two different Tibetan terms are translated by the English word "liberation." *Tarpa* refers primarily to the state of freedom from suffering attained in the Shravaka and Pratyekabuddha yanas, as opposed to the full awakening of a buddha attained through the Mahayana. *Drolwa* has a vaster connotation, and often refers to the spontaneously available, innate liberation that one connects with through the practices of Mahamudra and Dzogchen, such as in the term "self-liberation" (Tib. *rang grol /rangdrol*).

luminosity (Skt. *prabhāsvara*; Tib. *'od gsal /ösel*): A main topic of the third cycle of the Buddha's teachings, it is the natural quality of clarity and radiance that is inseparable from the shunyata nature of phenomena.

luminous bardo of dharmata (Tib. *chos nyid kyi bar do /chönyi gi bardo*): The interval that begins immediately following the moment of death and ends when we enter the **bardo of becoming**.

Madhyamaka (Tib. *dbu ma pa /umapa*; "proponents of the Middle Way"): The Mahayana school of Buddhism founded by the master Nagarjuna that propounds the absence of true existence of all phenomena. Since the Madhyamikas teach the union of the relative and ultimate truths in a way that is beyond the two extremes of permanence and nihilism, they are called "[Proponents] of the Middle." The etymology of the Tibetan *uma* lends insight into Madhyamaka philosophy: *u* means "center" or "middle," whereas the *ma* syllable can be understood both as a nominal suffix and a negating particle. Thus, the latter would make the term literally mean "not the middle." This illustrates that this school does not even propound a "middle" that would truly or ultimately exist as a remainder after the two extremes had been transcended.

Mahamudra (Tib. *phyag rgya chen po /chakgya chenpo;* "Great Seal"): A tradition of profound methods of meditation based on direct realization of the mind's true nature. This is the highest meditation practice within the Kagyu, Sakya, and Geluk lineages of Tibetan Buddhism.

mahasiddha (Tib. *grub chen /drubchen;* "one of great accomplishment"): A name used to refer to practitioners of Vajrayana Buddhism who have through their practice attained extremely sophisticated states of awareness and spiritual capability.

Mahayana (Tib. *theg pa chen po /thekpa chenpo;* "Great Vehicle"): Also called the Bodhisattvayana, it is the teachings and practice of the second and third turnings of the wheel of dharma taught by Buddha Shakyamuni. It is characterized by its dual emphasis on compassion, which desires the liberation from suffering of all beings, and wisdom, which perceives the true nature of phenomena. Through entering and riding this vehicle, one brings all sentient beings to the state of complete enlightenment.

Maitreya (Tib. *Byams pa /jam pa*): The bodhisattva now residing in the Tushita god realm who will be the fifth buddha of this eon.

mala (Tib. *'phreng ba /trengwa*): Similar to a rosary, it is a string of beads or stones used to count mantra recitations, prayers, and so on.

manifestations (Tib. *'char sgo /chargo*): The manifestations or experiences of mind: thoughts and appearances.

mantra (Tib. *sngags /ngak*): Sacred sounds that represent the essence of individual deities and are said to purify one's speech.

Mantrayana. See **Vajrayana.**

Marpa (Tib. *mar pa*)(1012-1097): One of the foremost students of the Indian mahasiddhas Naropa and Maitripa, and founding father of the Kagyu lineage in Tibet. His principle student was the great yogi Milarepa. He traveled to India several times, bringing back oral transmissions and texts, which he translated into Tibetan.

Milarepa (Tib. *mi la ras pa*)(1040–1123): One of the foremost students of Marpa Lotsawa and teacher of Gampopa. Renowned as the greatest yogi of Tibet, Milarepa is an example of the ability to purify all of one's karma and obscurations in a single lifetime. His songs of realization, or **dohas**, are testaments of his realization, and are sung by many.

mandala (Tib. *dkyil 'khor /kyilkhor*): The Tibetan term for mandala literally means "the center and its surroundings." In Vajrayana Buddhism, a mandala is the abode of the **yidam,** or meditational deity; it is an environment composed of utterly pure appearances that communicate the essence of the wisdom of enlightenment.

Maitripa (1012-1097): Indian mahasiddha; one of the principal Mahamudra masters of Marpa Lotsawa.

nadis, pranas, and **bindus** (Tib. *rtsa rlung thig le /tsa lung thigle*): The channels or pathways (**nadis**) of the subtle body through which the winds or subtle energies (**pranas**) of the body circulate, carrying the essences of the physical body (**bindus**).

Nagarjuna (c. 2nd century CE) (Tib. *klu sgrub /lu drub*): Renowned Indian scholar who was an abbot of Nalanda University. His writings, such as the *Fundamental Verses on the Middle Way (Mūlamadhyamakakārikā)*, were extremely influential and became the basis of the Madhyamaka School of the Mahayana. Also, a great tantric master, one of the eighty-four mahasiddhas. See also **Madhyamaka.**

Naropa (1016-1100) (Tib. *na ro pa*): One of the foremost Indian mahasiddhas and masters of Mahamudra and Tantra. Before meeting his guru, Tilopa, he was a famous scholar at Nalanda University in northern India. He received the Mahamudra and Tantra lineage teachings from Tilopa and transmitted them to his own principle disciple, Marpa, the Great Translator of Tibet.

natural bardo of this life (Tib. *skye gnas kyi bar do /kye ne gi bar do*): the interval between our birth and the moment we meet with the condition that will cause our death.

nature of mind (Tib. *sems kyi gnas lugs /sem kyi ne luk*): A term for the intrinsic state (*gnyug ma*) or true nature of mind; the uncontrived, natural state, also known as "ordinary mind," or the wisdom of self-arisen awareness. Synonymous with "the way things are" (*gnas tshul*). Also translated as "natural state," "abiding nature" or "abiding mode."

nirmanakaya (Tib. *sprul pa'i sku /trul pe ku*; "manifestation body," "emanation body"): The form kaya (body) of a buddha that can appear to both ordinary (impure) and noble (pure) beings. It is the fruition that is achieved for the benefit of other sentient beings. Therefore, this kaya is closely associated with compassion. It is also said that the mind, though free from arising and ceasing, manifests in various ways, or that it is the unceasing appearances of the expressive power of mind. From the triad of body, speech and mind, it is taught as the *body* quality of buddhahood. According to history that is held in common, the most recent nirmanakaya buddha was Buddha Shakyamuni. However, in the Tibetan tradition, **Guru Rinpoche** is also considered a nirmanakaya buddha.

nirvana (Tib. *mya ngan las 'das pa /nya ngen le depa;* "pass beyond suffering"): Can mean either the liberation (*thar pa*) from suffering achieved through the Shravakayana or the Pratyekabuddhayana, or the state of omniscience (Tib. *thams cad mkhyen pa /thamche khyenpa*), complete awakening, achieved through the Mahayana.

ordinary mind (Tib. *tha mal gyi shes pa /thamal gyi shepa*): A Mahamudra term that signifies the basic, unfabricated, awake nature of mind. The term "ordinary" is used to indicate that all beings possess this, whether they recognize it or not. In the Mahamudra tradition, it is taught that this aspect of mind must be pointed out by a realized master to a qualified student in order for its realization to occur. See also **nature of mind.**

Padampa Sangye (Tib. *phadam pa sangs rgyas*): Indian siddha who introduced the Shi-je ("Pacification of Suffering") system of meditation in Tibet. He was the teacher of Machik Labdrön (1055-1153), the founder of the Chö lineage.

Padmasambhava: See **Guru Rinpoche.**

painful bardo of dying (Tib. *'chi kha'i bar do/chi ke bar do*): Interval between the moment one meets with the condition that will cause one's death and the actual moment of one's death.

paramitas (Tib. *pha rol tu phyin pa/paröl tu chinpa*): Literally, "gone to the other shore." These practices consist of generosity, discipline, patience, joyful exertion, meditative concentration and discriminating awareness, or transcendental knowledge.

prana: see **nadis, pranas** and **bindus.**

prajna *(*Tib. *shes rab/sherap)*: Wisdom or transcendental knowledge relating to insight into emptiness; also, the naturally sharp discriminating quality of awareness. While prajna functions in one's mundane activities, on the highest level, it is the awareness that "sees" impermanence, selflessness, egolessness and shunyata.

Prajnaparamita (Tib. *shes rab kyi pha rol tu phyin pa/sherap kyi parol tu chinpa*): The name given to both the teachings on and the reality of the perfection of supreme knowledge, the realization of emptiness. Also called the "Great Mother" Prajnaparamita (Tib. *yum chen mo/yum chenmo*).

precious human birth (Tib. *mi lus rin po che/milü rinpoche*): A human birth that is endowed with the favorable conditions required to practice the dharma. It is taught that in order for a human birth to become precious, one must be endowed with the three qualities of confidence or faith, diligence, and wisdom, or supreme knowledge — *prajna.*

primordial purity (Tib. *ka dag/kadak*): The basic nature of the mind of sentient beings, which is originally or primordially pure. It has never been stained by any defilements and is beyond either confusion or liberation. Also, one of the two main aspects of Dzogchen teaching, the other being "spontaneous presence." Dzogchen has two main sections: **trekcho,** or "Cutting Through," and **thogal,** or "Direct Leaping." The former emphasizes primordial purity and the latter, spontaneous presence (Tib. *lhun grub*).

pure appearance (*Tib. dag pa'i snang ba /dakpe nangwa*): The nondualistic appearances and experiences of those who have realized mind's primordially pure nature, manifesting as freedom from afflictions, and the appearance of deity mandalas and pure Buddha realms and so on.

renunciation (Skt. *niḥsarana;* Tib. *nges 'byung/nge jung,* "definite emergence"): A mind that, motivated by a "feeling of disgust with…neuroses…[and] ego-clinging," wishes to be completely free from the prison of samsara.

relative truth (Tib. *kun rdzob bden pa /kündzop denpa*): Synonymous with "conventional" truth; one's ordinary experience of reality, in which phenomena are perceived as truly existing and separate from mind. Also called "deceptive truth," as it conceals the true nature of phenomena—emptiness. This term is defined and understood differently across the various Hinayana-Mahayana Buddhist philosophical schools. See also **two truths.**

rigpa (Skt. *vidyā;* Tib. *rig pa*): Naked awareness; the primordially pure state of mind that is realized through Dzogchen meditation.

sadhana (Tib. *sgrub thabs/drup tap*): These are Vajrayana practices that require a ritual empowerment in order to practice them.

samadhi (Tib. *ting nge 'dzin /ting nge dzin*): A state of undistracted meditative absorption or meditative concentration. The definition of samadhi is "a one-pointed mind concerning objects to be examined."

samaya (Tib. *dam tshig/damtsik*): Commitments of the Vajrayana path. Samayas essentially consist of, outwardly, maintaining harmonious relationship with the vajra master and one's Dharma friends and, inwardly, not straying from the continuity of the practice.

sambhogakaya (Tib. *longs spyod rdzogs pa'i sku/longchö dzokpe ku;* "body of perfect [or complete] enjoyment"): In an outer sense, this kaya refers to the manifestations of buddhas as they appear in celestial "pure realms," giving teachings only to the assembly of noble bodhisattvas by way of light-bodies, rather than physical ones. The buddhas of the five buddha families taught in Vajrayana Buddhism are sambhogakaya buddhas. However, sambhogakaya in a special sense also refers to the luminous nature of mind, mind's unimpeded, radiant and blissful energy. From the triad of body, speech, and mind, it is taught as the *speech* quality of buddhahood.

sampannakrama: See **completion stage.**

samsara (Tib. *'khor ba/khorwa;* "cyclic existence"): The state of existence experienced by sentient beings due to their ignorance, in which suffering is the predominant characteristic.

self-aware wisdom (Tib. *rang rig pa'i ye shes/rang rik pe yeshe*): Refers to mind's intrinsic nature of enlightened wisdom realizing itself.

shamatha (Tib. *zhi gnas/shi ne)*: Tranquility meditation. Its aspects are mindfulness (recollection of the object of meditation) and alertness (continuity of mindfulness). *Shama* means "calm," and *tha* is "abiding": so *shamatha* means "calm abiding." It is thus called since distraction towards objects such as form and so on has been calmed, and the mind abides one-pointedly in whichever samadhi one is practicing.

Shantideva (Tib. *zhi ba lha/shiwa hla*): An eighth-century Indian Buddhist scholar at Nalanda University, one of the eighty-four mahasiddhas; he is renowned as the author of the long poem, *Guide to the Bodhisattva's Way of Life*, or the *Bodhicharyavatara,* a poetic and inspirational treatise on the path to enlightenment.

shastra (Tib. *bstan bcos/ten chö*): Philosophical treatises, commentaries of panditas, learned masters of India and Tibet on the words of the Buddha.

shravakas (Tib. *nyan thos/nyenthö*; "hearers"): Hinayana practitioners who attain nirvana through practicing the first turning of the dharma wheel, the teachings on the four noble truths.

shunyata (Tib. *stong pa nyid/tongpa nyi*; "emptiness"): The true nature or suchness of all phenomena that is devoid of true, inherent and independent existence and is beyond all levels of conceptual elaboration. See also **emptiness**.

six realms: The six realms are six states of samsaric existence into which beings can be reborn at the end of the sixth bardo, the bardo of becoming. From the Mahayana perspective, they are regarded as psychological rather than physical realities, with each realm representing a mental state that is dominated by a particular emotion and a characteristic style of suffering. The six realms are categorized into three higher and three lower realms. The higher realms are the god realm, the jealous god realm, and the human realm. The lower realms are the animal realm, the hungry ghost realm, and the hell realm.

skandha: See **five skandhas**.

subtle body: The elaborate network of **nadis**, **pranas**, and **bindus** within the physical body. Also called the "vajra body."

suchness (Skt. *tathātā*; Tib. *de kho na nyid/dekona nyi*): Synonym for emptiness or **dharmata**, the ultimate nature.

sugata (Tib. *bde bar gshegs pa/dewar shekpa*; "those gone to bliss"): An epithet for the Buddha or buddhas.

sutras (Tib. *mdo/do*; "discourses"): Refers to either (1) the Hinayana and Mahayana teachings given by the Buddha, as opposed to the tantras of the Vajrayana, or (2) the scriptures of the sutra pitaka within the tripitaka, which are concerned with the training in samadhi (*ting nge 'dzin gyi bslab pa*).

tantra (Tib. *rgyud /gyü*): The Vajrayana teachings given by the Buddha in his sambhogakaya form. The real sense of tantra is "continuity," the innate buddha nature, which is known as the "tantra of the expressed meaning." The general sense of tantra is the extraordinary tantric scriptures also known as the "tantra of the expressing words." Can also refer to all the resultant teachings of Vajrayana as a whole.

tathagatagarba (Tib. *de bzhin gshegs pa'i snying po /deshin shek pe nyingpo*): The seed or essence of the tathagatas, or buddhas; usually translated as "buddha nature" or "buddha essence." It is the innate potential possessed by all sentient beings to attain the state of buddhahood, or complete awakening. Another name is *sugatagarbha*.

terma (Tib. *gter ma*): Texts, often called "treasure texts," hidden by Padmasambhava to be revealed and propagated at a later, more appropriate time by a destined disciple.

terton (Tib. *gter ston*): One who discovers texts that were hidden by Padmasambhava.

thamal gyi shepa (Tib. *tha mal gyi shes pa*): See **ordinary mind**.

thogal (Tib. *thöd rgal*): The second of the two phases of Dzogchen Atiyoga practice, usually translated as "leap over" or "direct crossing," which emphasizes the view of the spontaneous presence of mind's unimpeded display. See **trekcho**.

Three Jewels (Tib. *dkon mchog gsum /könchok sum*): Buddha (Tib. *sang rgyas /sangye*), dharma (Tib. *chos /chö*), and sangha (Tib. *dge 'dun /gendün*).

Three Kayas (Skt. *trikāya*; Tib. *sku gsum /ku sum*; "three bodies"): Three inseparable aspects of the enlightened nature of mind; three levels of enlightened manifestation: dharmakaya, sambhogakaya, and nirmanakaya. See respective entries.

Three Prajnas (Tib. *shes rab gsum /she rap sum*): The three prajnas are the prajna of hearing, the prajna of contemplating, and the prajna of meditation.

Three Yanas (Tib. *theg pa gsum /thekpa sum*; "three vehicles"): Shravakayana (Tib. *nyan thos kyi theg pa /nyenthö kyi thekpa*); Pratyek-abuddhayana (Tib. *rang rgyal gyi theg pa /rang gyal gi thekpa*); Bodhi-sattvayana and Mahayana (Tib. *theg pa chen po /thekpa chenpo*). See also respective entries. See also **yana**.

threefold purity (Tib. *'khor gsum rnam par dag pa /khorsum nampar dakpa*): The term that refers to the criterion that must be present in order for paramita practice to become genuine. This is the insight into the emptiness of, and the absence of attachment to, the three spheres or aspects of an action: 1) the object of the action, 2) the action itself and 3) the agent or performer of the action. For example, in the context of generosity, this would mean 1) the person or group toward which the generosity is directed, 2) the "generosity" itself, which includes the gift given and 3) the person engaged in giving.

Tilopa (989-1069) (Tib. *ti lo pa*): One of the eighty-four mahasiddhas of India, Tilopa received teachings and transmissions, especially the "Four Special Transmission Lineages," from great tantric masters of India. It is also said that, from ultimate point of view, Tilopa had no human teachers, but received the full Mahamudra and Vajrayana transmissions directly from Buddha Vajradhara. He was the guru of Naropa.

trikaya (Tib. *sku gsum*): See **three kayas**.

trekcho (Tib. *khregs chöd*): The first of the two phases of Dzogchen Atiyoga practice, directly "cutting through" all coarse and subtle thoughts by emphasizing the view of alpha-purity. See also **thogal**.

two accumulations (Skt. *sambhāra-dvaya*; Tib. *tshogs gnyis /tsok nyi*): The accumulation of merit (Skt. *puṇya-sambhāra*; Tib. *bsod nams kyi tshogs /sönam gi tsok*) and the accumulation of wisdom (Skt. *jñāna-sambhāra*; Tib. *ye shes kyi tshogs /yeshe gi tsok*). The two basic classes of that which is to be gathered or accumulated on the path to enlightenment; the perfection of both of these is synonymous with enlightenment itself. The accumulation of merit corresponds to the aspect of skillful means (Skt. *upaya*) and involves conceptual reference points, while the accumulation of wisdom corresponds to prajna and is increasingly free of reference points.

two benefits (Tib. *don gnyis /dön nyi*): Benefit for oneself (Tib. *rang don /rang dön*) and benefit for others (*gzhan don /shen dön*).

two obscurations (Tib. *sgrib gnyis /drib nyi*): The two classifications of everything that prevents or blocks one from realizing enlightenment: the afflictive obscurations and knowledge obscurations. The afflictive obscurations obstruct the attainment of liberation from samsara; the cognitive obscurations obstruct the attainment of omniscience. Only perfect buddhas have relinquished both obscurations. See also **afflictive obscurations** and **knowledge obscurations.**

two truths (Skt. *dvisatya;* Tib. *bden pa gnyis /denpa nyi*): Two levels of truth—absolute and relative, or genuine and seeming. See **absolute truth** and **relative truth.**

unborn (Tib. *skye ba med pa /kyewa mepa*): A synonym for emptiness. It means that, ultimately, nothing has any true arising or birth, although on a relative level there appears to be arising or birth. Also translated as "nonarising."

utpattikrama: See **creation stage.**

vajra (Tib. *rdo rje /dorje*): "Diamond," "king of stones." As an adjective it means indestructible, invincible, firm, adamantine, diamond-like. The ultimate vajra is emptiness; the conventional vajra is the ritual implement of material substance.

Vajradhara (Tib. *rdo rje 'chang /dorje chang*): Literally "vajra holder." The name of the dharmakaya buddha. Many of the teachings of the Kagyu lineage come from Vajradhara. Often appended to the name of the root guru.

Vajrayana (Tib. *rdo rje theg pa /dorje tekpa*): The tantric teachings of the Mahayana. It is the short path (*nye lam*) that utilizes a variety of methods that take the results of awakening as the path. Also called Secret Mantra or the resultant vehicle (Tib. *'bras bu'i theg pa /drebü thekpa*).

vipashyana (Tib. *lhag mthong /lhaktong*): Meditation which develops insight into the nature of reality. Vipashyana is practiced on the basis of shamatha meditation. In the word *vi(shesha)pashyanā*, *vishesha* means "special" or "superior," and *pashyanā* means "seeing" or "observing": so *vi(shesha)pashyanā* means "superior seeing." It is thus called since one sees "the superior"—i.e., the nature of phenomena—with the eye of wisdom.

wisdom (San. *jñāna*; Tib. *ye shes /yeshe*): Also translated as "primordial wisdom," or "basic wakefulness." It refers to the nondual, nonconceptual insight of both bodhisattvas in meditative equipoise and Buddhas.

yana (Tib. *theg pa /tekpa*): Literally means "that which carries," "vehicle." A set of teachings that can convey one to rebirth in the higher realms, liberation from samsara or complete buddhahood. There are different classifications of yanas, such as triple division of Hinayana, Mahayana, and Vajrayana; triple division of Shravakayana, Pratyekabuddhayana and Bodhisattvayana; or nine gradual vehicles of Shravaka, Pratyekabuddha, Bodhisattva, Kriya, Upa, Yoga, Mahayoga, Anuyoga, and Atiyoga.

yidam (Skt. *devatā*): Meditational deities that represent the enlightened qualities of mind. They are called "the root of siddhis" (*dngos grub kyi rtsa ba*).

Suggested Reading

TRADITIONAL TEXTS

Dorje, Gyurme, trans. *The Tibetan Book of the Dead.* Ed. by Graham Coleman with Thupten Jinpa. New York: Viking, 2005.

Gyatrul Rinpoche. *Natural Liberation: Padmasambhava's Teachings on the Six Bardos.* Trans. by B. Alan Wallace. Boston: Wisdom Publications, 1998.

Rangdrol, Tsele Natsok. *Mirror of Mindfulness.* Trans. by Erik Pema Kunsang. Boston: Shambhala Publications, 1989.

Thurman, Robert, trans. *The Tibetan Book of the Dead.* New York: Bantam Books, 1994.

Trungpa, Chogyam and Francesca Fremantle. *The Tibetan Book of the Dead.* Boston: Shambhala Publications, 2003.

CONTEMPORARY COMMENTARIES

Bokar Rinpoche. *Death and the Art of Dying in Tibetan Buddhism.* English trans. by Christiane Buchet. (Original trans. from Tib. into French by François Jacquemart.) San Francisco: Clear Point Press, 1993.

Fremantle, Francesca. *Luminous Emptiness: Understanding the Tibetan Book of the Dead.* Boston: Shambhala Publications, 2001.

Gyatso, Tenzin, H.H. the Fourteenth Dalai Lama. *Advice on Dying and Living a Better Life.* Trans. and ed. by Jeffrey Hopkins. New York: Atria Books, 2002.

Gyatso, Tenzin, H.H. the Fourteenth Dalai Lama. *Sleeping, Dreaming, and Dying: an Exploration of Consciousness.* Trans. by B. Alan Wallace and Thupten Jinpa. Boston: Wisdom Publications, 1997.

Hanh, Thich Nhat. *No Death, No Fear.* New York: Riverhead Books, 2002.

Lati Rinpoche and Jeffrey Hopkins. *Death, Intermediate State, and Rebirth in Tibetan Buddhism.* Ithaca, New York: Snow Lion Publications, 1979.

Lodö, Lama. *Bardo Teaching.* Ithaca: Snow Lion Publications, 1987.

Smith, Rodney. *Lessons from the Dying.* Boston: Wisdom Publications, 1998.

Sogyal Rinpoche. *The Tibetan Book of Living and Dying.* San Francisco: Harper Collins, 1992.

Tenga Rinpoche, *Transition and Liberation.* English trans. Alex Wilding. (Original German trans. by Susanne Schefczyk.) Osterby: Khampa Buchverlag, 1996.

Thondup, Tulku. *Peaceful Death, Joyful Rebirth.* Ed. by Harold Talbott. Boston: Shambhala, 2005.

Thrangu Rinpoche. *Journey of the Mind.* Trans. by Lama Yeshe Gyamtso. Vancouver: Karme Thekchen Choling, 1997.

Trungpa, Chogyam. *Transcending Madness: The Experience of the Six Bardos.* Boston: Shambhala Publications, 1992.

AUDIO AND VIDEO TAPES

Karthar, Khenpo. *Death, Dying and the Bardo.* May 1982. DVD/audiotape.

Ponlop, Dzogchen. *Bardo Teachings.* March 2002. DVD/audiotape.

Tai Situ Rinpoche. *Overcoming the Fear of Dying.* June 1997. DVD/audiotape.

Nalandabodhi Centers

NALANDABODHI USA
www.nalandabodhi.org
General inquiries:
info@nalandabodhi.org

NALANDA WEST
3902 Woodland Park Ave. N.
Seattle, WA 98103 USA
www.nalandawest.org

Nalanda West Programs
Email: programs@nalandawest.org

Nalandabodhi Boulder
Boulder, CO USA
Email: info@nbboulder.org
www.nbboulder.org

Nalandabodhi Connecticut
Simsbury, CT USA
Email: connecticut@nalandabodhi.org
www.nbconnecticut.org

Nalandabodhi Seattle
3902 Woodland Park Ave. N.
Seattle, WA 98103 USA
Email: seattle@nalandabodhi.org
www.nbseattle.org

Nalandabodhi SF Bay Area
Mt. View, CA USA
Email: sfbayarea@nalandabodhi.org
www.nbsfbayarea.org

Nalandabodhi Texas
Corpus Christi, TX USA
Email: texas@nalandabodhi.org
www.nalandabodhi.org/texas

STUDY GROUPS: USA

New York City NB Study Group
New York, NY USA
Email: nbnyc@nalandabodhi.org
www.nbnewyork.org

Louisville NB Study Group
Louisville, Kentucky USA
Email: programs@nblouisville.org
www.nblouisville.org

Philadelphia NB Study Group
Philadelphia, PA USA
Email: philadelphia@nalandabodhi.org

Rhode Island NB Study Group
Email: rhode_island@nalanda
bodhi.org

NALANDABODHI CANADA

www.nalandabodhi.org

Nalandabodhi Foundation, Canada
4610 Earles St.
Vancouver, BC V5R 3R2 Canada
Email: canada@nalandabodhi.org

Nalandabodhi Vancouver
4610 Earles St.
Vancouver, BC V5R 3R2 Canada
Email: vancouver@nalandabodhi.org
www.nbvancouver.org

STUDY GROUPS: CANADA

Halifax NB Study Group
Halifax, Nova Scotia CANADA
Email: halifax@nalandabodhi.org
www.nbhalifax.org

Montreal NB English Study Group
Email: montre-al.english@nalandabodhi.org
www.nbmontreal.org/index-an.html

Montreal NB French Study Group
Laval, Quebec CANADA
Email: montre-al.francais@nalandabodhi.org
www.nbmontreal.org

Toronto NB Study Group
Email: toronto@nalandabodhi.org
www.nbtoronto.org

STUDY GROUPS: MEXICO

Mexico NB Study Group
Email: mexico@nalandabodhi.org

NALANDABODHI EUROPE

Nalandabodhi Vienna
Herklotzgasse 20
A-1150 Vienna AUSTRIA
Email: vienna@nalandabodhi.org
www.nbvienna.org

Hamburg NB Study Group
Hamburg GERMANY
Email: hamburg@nalandabodhi.org

Berlin NB Study Group
Berlin, GERMANY
Email: berlin@nalandabodhi.org

CENTERS UNDER THE DIRECTION OF THE DZOGCHEN PONLOP RINPOCHE

Kamalashila Institute
Kloster Langenfeld, Kirchstrasse 22a
D-56729 Langenfeld GERMANY
Email: kamalashila@t-online.de
www.kamalashila.de

Theksum Tashi Choling
Harkortsteig 4
D-22765 Hamburg GERMANY
Email: germany@nalandabodhi.org
www.ttc-hamburg.de

Nitartha International

www.nitartha.org

Nitartha International
3902 Woodland Park Ave. N.
Seattle, WA 98103 USA
Email: lcmarvet@nitartha.org
Or: mmarvet@nitartha.org

Nitartha International Document Input Center (NIDIC)
GPO – 8974, CPC – 150
Kathmandu, NEPAL
Email: nidic@nitartha.org

Nitartha Institute
Email: info@nitarthainstitute.org
www.nitarthainstitute.org

Bodhi Magazine

Managing Editor
Email: bodhi@nalandabodhi.org
www.bodhionline.org

Illustration Credits

Image of thangka painting of Guru Padmasambhava, plate 1, central figure from "The Eight Manifestations of Guru Rinpoche" by R. D. Salga. © 1999 by Nalandabodhi and The Dzogchen Ponlop Rinpoche. Used with permission.

Reclining Buddha: The Sleeping Lion Posture, page 78, courtesy of Nalandabodhi. Used with permission.

Diagram of Channels and Chakras of the Subtle Body, page 127, © 2006 Nitartha International and Nalandabodhi.

Syllables HĀM and ASHE, page 138, designed by Tenzin Namdak. Nitartha-Sambhota fonts © Nitartha International.

Image of thangka painting of Samantabhadra and Samantabhadri: Peaceful Manifestation of the Primordial Buddha, plate 2, courtesy of Shelley and Donald Rubin. http://www.himalayanart.org.

Image of thangka painting of Mahottara Heruka and Krodheshvari: Wrathful Manifestation of the Primordial Buddha, plate 3, from Palpung Monastery. © Tsadra Foundation. Used with permission.

Image of Shitro Thangka: Peaceful and Wrathful Deities, plate 4, from Palpung Monastery. © Tsadra Foundation. Used with permission.

Index